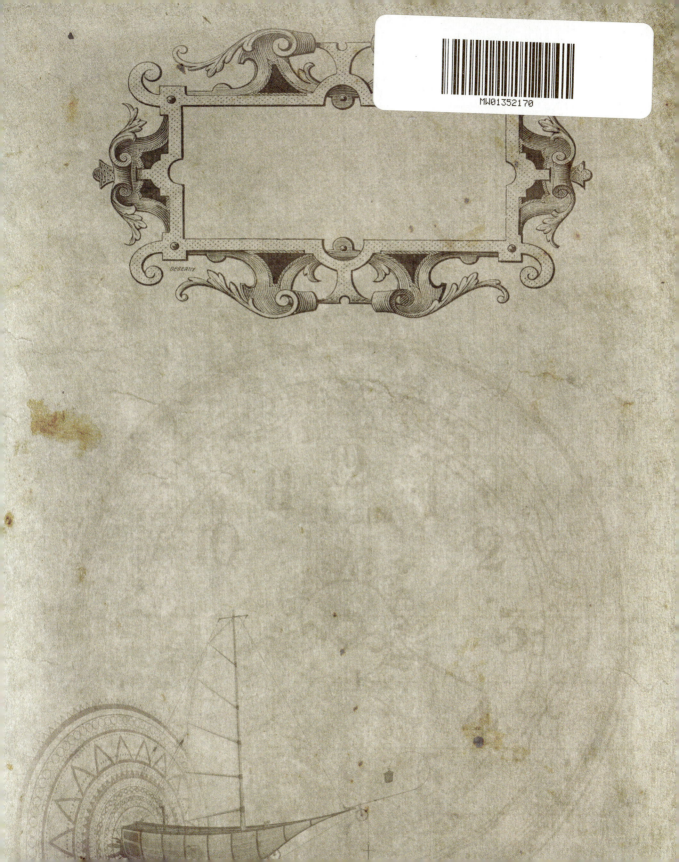

What "They" Are Saying About
Analogue Network Security

"It is all about the Architecture. *Analogue Network Security* presents a wide variety of first principles, models, and frameworks that security architects, software engineers, and programmers should pay attention to. *Analogue Network Security* is a treasure trove of tools for improving the security of every system you encounter."

Dennis Groves, Co-Founder of OWASP

"Winn's ANS framework will really make you wonder why the rest of the security world hasn't *already* structured itself around time-based security, feedback loops, and taking a probabilistic view of everything. Do yourself a favor and study it now."

Clarence Ciao, Neuroscientist and Co-Author of *Machine Learning & Security*

"You don't have to take my word for it, but if you do, you won't be disappointed: This book will melt your brain and reset your visions back to base. It is so hard, yet so terrifyingly simple. Yes, it can be a tough ride, but if you get it, you'll feel reborn. So study this, visualise this, and map it to all you thought you knew, and prepare to be utterly surprised!"

Edwin van Andel aka @yafsec, Grumpy Old Hacker and CEO @Zerocopter

"Another Winner! Winn again addresses fundamental misimpressions the cyber-security community has by contributing to the future of the field in unexpected ways."

Dr. Fred Cohen

"As Winn is quick to point out, we've had 50+ years to work out the kinks in the digital world that surrounds us, however, we've managed to do nothing more than tie ourselves in ever-increasingly complex knots from which we know no escape. I put it to you that this book is the Holy Hand Grenade of Antioch that our industry needs. The chapters DO need to be approached carefully as there's a wealth of knowledge and experience that takes time to absorb. I'd keep a pencil and paper close as well as your favorite Whiskey to help ease the WTF moments that you will surely go through. Winn has masterfully managed to take a series of complex ideas and boil them into something we can ALL use. Enjoy."

Chris Roberts, Co-Founder, HillbillyHitSquad.com

"This book will make you rethink your security strategy, make you ask fundamental questions, and force you to re-evaluate your beliefs. You can always disagree with Winn's conclusions, but the book will improve your results." (ALT-QUOTE: "Read the f****** book, and form your own opinion. I did.")

Spencer Wilcox, Executive Director Technology and Security, PNM Resources, Inc.

"Binary is just dumbed down analogue. Winn explains, and you learn."

Gregory Carpenter, Ret. Military Officer & Chief of Security Testing, Titania Solutions Group

"Winn continues to challenge the security industry. If you're looking for a new perspective on security, read this book! It's provocative - you're going to rethink some of your preconceived notions about security."

Tim McCreight, President/Owner, Risk Rebels

"*Analogue Network Security* is a refreshing look at how we begin to measure dynamic cyber technical debt and the negative externalities injected by standards groups, product companies, and decisions of managing computing devices in a connected world composed of people and nations with evil designs on your data."

Joe Klein, CISSP, Lead Computer Scientist at [REDACTED]

"This is a new book by Winn Schwartau - the first in I don't know how many years - with each of his previous ones being decades ahead of their time. I mean, why on earth wouldn't you want to buy it and read it?"

Eric Green, Security Strategist, CyberadAPT

"A few decades ago I came across a thin paperback with the intriguing title Time-Based Security. It contained some ideas that the IT security world was not ready for at the time, but are now implemented from monitoring systems to SOCs and more. Now Winn is back with an even more concise description and I can only wonder when our industry will be ready to implement those ideas as well."

Hans "Quux" Van de Looy — Unicorn Security

"Winn Schwartau once again challenges the status quo in his latest book, *Analogue Network Security*. This book explores the fundamentals of network security, from its inception to current day implementation, which is clearly ineffective and needs to be rethought from the ground up. Schwartau argues that analogue methods can deliver meaningful metrics leading to stronger and better managed security controls, which ultimately raises the economic cost to adversaries and reduces cybersecurity risk in an increasingly connected world."

Dr. John D. Johnson, CEO/Founder, Aligned Security

AND LAST, BUT NOT LEAST…

"This is truly a book. I believe that Winn has put a lot of words into this book. He has also put in punctuation marks. I couldn't put it down. That may be because my copy had glue on it. Exercise caution — he is a prankster."

Professor Eugene H. Spafford, Purdue University CERIAS

ANALOGUE NETWORK SECURITY

Time, Broken Stuff, Engineering, Systems, My Audio Career, and Other Musings on Six Decades of Thinking About it All

by Winn Schwartau

Design by Kayley Melton

Written by Winn Schwartau.
Designed by Kayley Melton, with the mathematical expertise of Mark Carney, artistic assistance of Alissa Phillips, services of Brenda McClearen from McClearen Design, and editing skills of Erica Rodgers. Oh, Yeah! My bride and partner of 40 years, Sherra, has been at the core of keeping me on track with this insanely complex project. And, boy, can she edit!

1. Computer Security. 2. Information Security. 3. Network Security. 4. Internet Security. 5. Application Security. 6. Network Management. 7. Information Warfare. 8. Critical Infrastructures. 9. National Security. 10. Deep Learning. 11. Neural Networks. 12. SCADA. 13. ICS. 14. Analogue Systems. 15. AI. 16. Machine Learning. 17. Social Engineering. 18. Phishing. 19. Feedback. 20. OODA Loops. 21. Hackers. 22. Denial of Service. 23. Defense in Depth. 24. Network Defense. 25. Data Protection. 26. Phishing.

ISBN: 978-0-9964019-0-6

© 2018 Winn Schwartau, LLC. All rights reserved.

No portion of this book may be reproduced in any form without written permission from the publisher, except: Some portions of *Analogue Network Security* can be found at http://www.winnschwartau.com/analoguenetworksecurity/ and may be freely copied and distributed in both electronic and hard copy form as long as no content changes of any form are made, and full credit is given. For all other reproductions, reprinting, translations, and uses, prior written permission from the publisher is required. Fees may apply. Private labeled, company branded, and customized versions of this book are also available. Portions of the content of this book describe inventions that are currently patent pending. Contact us at Rights@WinnSchwartau.Com for details.

Published by: SCHWARTAU HAUS

Quick Disclaimer, Dedication, & Errata

Analogue Network Security is a suite of ideas, not solutions. It's just a different way of looking at the cyber world we have created.

By any academic standards, I fail at pointing to every single reference, source, and citation. I chose this approach to make the topic more accessible, encourage new thinking versus pure regurgative-EDU, and besides, links do expire. I give credit where I am aware of it; any such omissions are my fault and not intentional.

I also did not attempt to define every term or acronym. I assume a basic level of technical awareness and the ability to learn on the fly. Wiki is an easy go-to starting place. *(Please remember to contribute $.)*

Regarding my ideas, call me out if you want, please! But do so with constructive feedback on the ANS thesis, not on academic minutiae I have avoided by choice or error. There WILL be errata. Please let us know – gently – where we messed up.

And yes, I do hope to invoke analogue nostalgia. Plus, some of my stories might trigger you to delve deeper into 'ancient engineering'. Not everything new is always better. Just sayin'.

Analogue Network Security is first dedicated to my wife, Sherra. F**k Cancer. She is my rock and a survivor. She has tolerated me working on this project for the last 17 years. She has worked relentlessly with me as editor and critic, inserting clarity as necessary, and this book is now far better than the first 100 drafts.

Finally, I dedicate this book to the Hacking and Security Communities of which I am proud to be a part. You all have been incessantly, constructively critical in calling out my bullshit when needed, contributing and adding where appropriate, and tolerating how long this process has taken. You are equally friends, colleagues, and family.

With deep respect,

Winn

You will notice, occasionally, some "Gear Boxes" like this one, with seemingly random comments which may appear to have no reference to any associated text. Please consider them as side thoughts, points of interest, facts, etc. I akin them to Bright Blue Shiny Objects floating by, which just cannot be ignored. So I wrote them down.

Contents

0 Why Analogue Security?

Read It Your Way... But, HARK! ii
Analogue Network Security is a Bear iv
The Analogue Genesis v

1 50 Years of Security

Walled Cities and Other Battles Lost 2
   Deterrence 5
The Yardstick 6
   The Guarantee 8
A Brief History of Security Models 9
Symmetric Security 13
Profile of a Security Model 17
Synergy 20
Lessons Learned 21

2 The Basics of Time-Based Security

Time-Based Security Genesis 24
The Pawn Shop 25
   It's a War Out There 28
Jesse James 31
The Vault 33

It's About Time 37
Analyzing the Time-Based Security Formula 40
    IS Time Analogue? 40
There is No Protection 43
E(t) Phone Home: Exposure 45
    An Extremely Extreme, Yet Unwise Case 47
Reactions 48
    Physical Time-Based Security Metaphors 52
Divide by Time 54
    Padding 55
Compressors & Limiters 56

3 WTF, ANALOGUE?

The Brain 60
Analogue 101 61
Square Waves are Analogue 63
Digital is Not Binary 65
    Is It Analogue? 67
    The Ladies' Room 69
    The Fastest Computer 70
Granularity in Digital Audio 72
    You Can Add Them Easily 74
Smoothing Functions 75
The Power of Perception 77
    Flatland 79
    Trending 80
Fractals 81
Static vs. Dynamic 84
Electronics 101 88
Analogue Computers in History 91
The Inequality of it All 94
    On the Quantum Nature of I.T. 96

4 LET'S KILL ROOT

The Buck Stops with Root 98
I Have Trust Issues 102
    The Case of the Sole Admin 109
    The Case of Multiple Admins 111
The 2-Man Rule 101 113
The 2-Man Rule 201 116

5 FEEDBACK

Feedback 120
    Feedback in Nature 124
SCADA & ICS 126
    Dutch Dikes 128
Time & Clocks 129
Flip-Flops 132
    Step in Time: Boolean Relays 133
Memristors 134
The Basic Building Block of ANS: The Time-Based Flip-Flop 138
    My Wife's Car 143
When Bob is No Alice 153
    Degrading Trust 157
Trust Factor Feedback 159
    Top 10 of Analogue Network Feedback 161

6 OODA, TCP/IP, & OOB

Getting Loopy 164
Green Furry Things 166
    OODA Everywhere 169
The Trust Engine From an OODA View 171
Squeezing the Loop 174
    Sub-OODA Loop 176

OODA in Security	178
TCP/IP & OOB: Putting the Pieces Together	180
TCP/IP: The Best & the Worst of Times	181
Out of Band (Not a Rock 'n Roll Term...)	182
Negative Time	186
My Bank	187
OOB & Negative Time	190

7 Detection in Depth

Carbon Units Before Silicon	192
Defense in Depth	195
Detection in Depth Factoids	197
Defense in Depth: The Time-Based Security Way	198
Graceful Degradation	205
Pen-Testing Analogue Style	207
The Vanishing Chip	208
Detection Limits	209
Behavioral Algorithms	213

8 ANS Applications

Ping, McFly!	216
Measure Your Security	217
The Horror of It All (Time-Wise)	227
A Short Form	228
Damn! Stop It!	230
Social Media, Bikini-Grams, and NSFW	236
Anti-Phishing	240
Fake News is Bullshit	242
DDoS	243
Stopping Spam & Saving Granny	264
Detection/Reaction Protocol	267
Time-Based Security and I & A	268
Miscellaneous Application Thoughts	271

Encryption 274
Time-Based Deception 277
    The Many Facets of Deception 280
Honey 282
Privacy 283
Metamorphic Networking 284
Offensive Time-Based Security 285
    Offensive Time-Based OODA 287
    Inside the Attacker's Loop 289
Security Awareness 290
ANS, OWASP, & Software Programming 293

Analogue Epilogues

The Analogue Epilogues' Prologue 296
Real Math Behind ANS and Detection in Depth *by Mark "Math Bitch" Carney* 298
Infinity Begets Chaos 316
What Does Security Look Like? 319
Security Management Porn 322
    Visualizing Security 326
Policy Makers: Your Turn 328
    Speed of Signal 329
    Wall Street Bitches at Me 330
Errrorrz 332
Six Sigma in Networking 334
3 Domains of ANS Interaction 338
AI & ANS 340
    Predicting the Future 344
Hiring the Unhireable 345
Prison in the Cloud: My Outrage 346
How Much is that Data in the Window? 348
ANS Design Tools Cheat Sheet 353
This is the End 362
Bibliography 362

0
Why Analogue Security?

READ IT YOUR WAY...
BUT HARK!!

Please, do not try to sit down and just read this book. It won't work. At least it didn't for me.

Some of my thoughts may not initially seem to have a relevance to security. Please bear with me. We are going to cover a lot of topics.

First, as a foundation, a little history. It will be brief. After all, we are talking about security models, so a little context would be useful. Some medieval network security thinking, ancient models that fail us, and a high level view of how we got into this mess.

Next, I will re-introduce the traditional basics of the TBS (Time-Based Security) model, from the 1998 book of the same name (*http://amzn.to/1MAv8Qz*). I'll position it with additional metaphors and add a bit more to complete some current thinking about it, with a dose of analogue terms thrown in to get your analogue neurons stirring.

Since I propose that "digital is not binary" as a core tenet necessary for revised network security thinking, a brief look at "WTF, Analogue?" (Chapter 3) will provide some engineering (and a hint of quantum) context for the way the world worked (indeed, works!) This is also where I get to have some fun, recalling my first career as a sound and recording-engineer/producer during the rock'n'roll heyday.

For those of you who grew up thinking "digital is God", I will attempt to show you the error of your ways. Or at least, show you another way of looking at networks. The idea of **binary vs. analogue spectrum** has hurt our field, as well as real-politiks globally. I will stick to the tech aspects, I promise.

Then, we travel to the early 19th Century and re-meet George Boole for a refresher on Logic 101. You will learn that Boolean algebra is powerful, but time-static. I will attempt to solve that limitation with a new way of viewing Boolean logic using min-max and TBS-conditioning.

The Two-Man Rule (aka Four Eyes) – and this escapes me entirely – has been almost completely ignored in security. I don't get it. Maybe you can help me understand how we messed up, and created one of the foulest four-letter words in the English language: ROOT.

Trust is, unfortunately, often viewed as a binary function. I want to examine how an analogue view of trust will give us a more accurate approach to trust in an ever-connected world. Yes, I mean the IoT or whatever current term is popular.

Then, some really cool stuff, as I begin to tie some of these thoughts together. Feedback is a decidedly analogue concept that I will approach in all three security domains and from differing fields of expertise. It permeates engineering, yet is not actively used in network security. Led Zeppelin taught me a lot about feedback. I will pass-on those lessons as they relate to network security, as well as why the Netherlands is still a country - only because of feedback.

With the discussions of feedback we will explore how to launch nukes, address some of women's equality issues, and drastically increase the efficacy of network security. Instead of doing the same things over and over and expecting different results, Analogue Network Security will give you the strategic concepts and some tactical tools to get a provable improvement in any network or data security effort.

I do hope that some of my proposed ideas around Detection in Depth will supplant gut reaction traditionalism.

The OODA Loop has been relegated, unfortunately, to military thinking. Since **Information Warfare** (*http://amzn.to/1LTZeL*), we have been at war, but we behave like everyone else is playing fair. In fact, one popular network security view is that we have to assume our networks have already been completely compromised. Ergo, we continue to lose. But perhaps, the OODA loop offers some direction.

In audio engineering, we mostly used Out-of-Band (OOB) methods for control and communications. In network security, we have another example of a *failure to adapt a model which already works* - TCP/IP. It is the best of protocols; it is also the worst.

I will finally glue those ideas together, into one massively reimagined architecture to be used as the basis for networks, applications, and all things security. By combining many of these concepts, I believe we find new approaches to solve DOS, DDoS, spam, and a significant percentage of 'internet noise' - read, security. I believe we can mitigate risk by granularizing Root. I believe that by looking at security controls with an analogue eye and mindset, we can develop far better network security tools and solutions than those with which we are still tinkering.

Much of what you will read may seem *obvious* once you have read it. I hope that is true, because then it will be easier for you to first accept, then apply these concepts into products, operations, processes, controls, and of course, security.

I hope you can read a section and think about it for a while before plunging ahead.

I do not claim to have solved anything. Rather, I am proposing a new way of thinking about networks and security. I probably have lots of things wrong... so, no hating; only constructive synergistic critique, please.

Our industry needs a massive rethink. So, let me attempt to explain Analogue Network Security.

Winn Schwartau

(I first started this project on a beach on the Indian Ocean. I finish it at the top of ski mountain.)

Analogue Network Security
IS A BEAR

Two men are walking through a forest. Suddenly, they see a bear in the distance, running towards them. They turn and start running away. But then the first of the men stops, takes some fancy running shoes from his bag, and starts putting them on.

"What are you doing?" asks the second man. "Do you think you will run faster than the bear with those?"

"I don't have to run faster than the bear," he says. "I just have to run faster than you."

The Bear Formula, measured in speed:

> Man 1 > Bear > Man 2

The first key to survival and autonomy is the ability to adapt to change.

The second key to survival is the ability to accurately predict the future.

THIS IS THE BASIS OF ANALOGUE NETWORK SECURITY.

The Analogue Genesis

Along I came, and I was fixing TVs by age five. Don't be so impressed. In those days, it meant removing all of the vacuum tubes from the back of the set, trundling down to the drug store, and testing them one by one until the faulty one failed. Hell, it was a paying job!

Yeah, we had the 60s equivalent of a portable recording facility.

My parents were both analogue engineers.

Dad worked on radar development in WWII. My mother was a voice actress, then trained as an audio engineer at NBC's 30 Rock while men were off fighting the war.

Weekends with my dad were chock-full of engineering. I'd help him wire up the audio in Greenwich Village speak-easy-like clubs by hauling wires and crawling through the ceilings. We'd build model engines. Then we built an analogue computer – yeah, more about that later. All the while, I received a non-optional, comprehensive education in analogue electronics by age 11.

My mom had a small recording studio at home, and I was paid 50¢ per afternoon to cut and splice 1/4" magnetic tapes by the tens of thousands from 1st to 6th grade or so. When I was 12, we spent 4 months in Europe recording sound effects for my mom's clients. That same year, the New York World's Fair opened and it was absolutely necessary for me, obviously, to build a scale model of it, add audio, and *roughly* synchronize a barely adequate light show.

I learned how to solder and build radios alongside a fellow nerd and it wasn't until 2010 or so, that I realized, that same childhood neighbor, Dickie, grew up to be Richard Stallman of GNU fame.

At 16, I went to work for MiraSound Recording Studios. (Yes, all analogue.) Bob Goldman took me under his wing and taught me vinyl mastering *(analogue electronic and mechanical audio)* and systems design philosophy *(his, anyway)*, and at 17 I was the lead engineer to build Studio-C .

My first digital audio experience was at the Nashville factory for Harrison Systems *(where I met my future bride, Sherra)*, and its disastrous audio automation system called Auto-Set. Neve Electronics *(don't worry, you never heard of them)* introduced its automated audio system by attaching DC-motors to the faders *(volume controls on a mixing desk)* and Nashville's Valley People introduced VCAs *(Voltage Controlled Amplifiers)* as the audio industry attempted to early-adapt the fusion of analogue and digital audio.

A few years prior, I had ventured into building an automated assembly system for U.S. Army training material. The design was fine. The problem was I wired all of the boards. And, being color blind, I used Green instead of Orange as my exponent in the color coded pull-up resistors. My wiring career ended abruptly.

I resisted. I fought the first generation digital audio systems on both aural and engineering grounds. I abhorred the total lack of discipline that this new audio engineering technology seemed to bring along with it. That's why I left professional audio in 1981.

2012 was a conceptual watershed year for me in security. Disparate, seemingly unconnected ideas were falling into their proper places with clarity. I became absorbed in systems, processes, quantum consciousness, memory, chaos, unpredictability, and predictive modeling. I discovered I was re-establishing many of my analogue roots and felt the first waves of an inchoate synergetic calmness.

This book is the result of some of that thinking.

It doesn't matter whether you agree with these ideas or not. **All I ask is that you think about them.** Add your own flavor or twist to them. Or, discard them.

And please, let me know your thoughts. As long as they're analogue, of course.

1.
50 Years of Security

Back in "the day," as a broke audio-kid, I used to get utility bills with a punch card, a corresponding paper bill, and a pre-stamped return envelope. I discovered several blank (null) spaces (punch card fields) to the left of the amount I owed and asked myself, "What if I punch a minus sign in that vacant field?" I got monthly refunds for the amount of services I used for almost two years. (Statute of limitations is up.)

Walled Cities & OTHER BATTLES LOST

Let's just admit it. Information, Computer, and Network Security is abysmal.

Nation-states, NGOs, and organized crime are kicking our butts.

When business and government must operate on the assumption that their networks are P0wn3d, common sense says we've been doing something very wrong for decades. When entire populations can suffer for security failures beyond their control, we know we have failed to build-in balanced protection and remediation mechanisms. When we deploy billions of mobile devices designed for function over security and privacy, one must question and consider the motivations.

P0wn3d : you have been compromised by hostile forces who have established an electronic beachhead.

Let's step back to the 1970s to consider the original thinking behind computer security.

The Trojans defended their walled acropolis for years by closing the gates to the city. The Mycenaean invaders were forced to wait outside on the wide plain, in the slim hopes of starving out the defenders. So, as Homer tells us, they found another way.

The Chinese attempted to protect their empire with a physical firewall 1,500 miles long.

The Athenian Acropolis.

Wall Street in New York protected the European immigrants from the native "savages" of Northern Manhattan Island.

A useless Maginot Line in World War II.

It was based upon an older physical model; the protection of sensitive hard copy information entailed placing armed guards in front of a locked room containing a padlocked file cabinet. Info-guards of the Cold War. Only the good guys (Trusted Insiders) could enter the building, access the locked room, and unlock the secret filing cabinet. So, why not apply the same logic to information security? Maybe firewalls will fit the bill.

The concept is an old military one: fortress mentality. We keep the bad guys out by building the walls higher and higher and making the moats wider and deeper. For thousands of years this mentality has been a consistent theme. But no matter how high you build a wall, the bad guys can still fly over it, dig under it (as they did with the Berlin Wall), or drive around it (the Maginot Line). No, there is no perfect static defense.

While security modeling has traditionally attempted to keep the bad guys out, in both the physical and virtual worlds, businesses have always wanted and *needed* to let the good guys in to conduct commerce and encourage window shopping. The problem the store owner has is, "How can I identify the good guy from the bad guy?" It's tough, with some even resorting to constitutionally questionable stereotyping. The answer I remember from my teenage supermarket and drugstore jobs was to watch a customer's behavior. We used mirrors and secret codes; we'd have to monitor the potential offender's activity in the store while pretending to sweep up, then report it when appropriate.

The same problem has persists in the electronic world, and we have to ask ourselves the same question: how do we tell the good guys from the bad guys? A corollary question is, "How can building higher walls around my electronic place of business secure an open system whose fundamental goal is to encourage informational/data/commercial exchange amongst lots of people in various locations with different interests, behaviors, and agendas?"

In the original 1970s security models (*Ross Anderson's Security Engineering; the Bell-LaPadula Model; the Biba Integrity Model,* etc.), mediation of process requests generated audit trails of varying granularity. An analysis of these past-datum logs will show prior activities. One systems administrator from a government agency (who should know better) said to me in an open audience forum, "Oh, we have security. We check our audit trails at least once every two weeks." Clearly, there's a problem in both attitude and implementation.

However, that security model was based upon another antique premise: **computers operate in isolation – there is no such thing as a network.**

When the Trojans let down the drawbridge to admit the horse, they were "networking" with the outside world. When the Germans bypassed the Maginot Line, they created a network with the French, using Belgian routing. When people sailed over or around the Berlin Wall, the network connection was made.

When security pioneers began to develop security models, they took a similar approach, because the network had not yet begun to live and expand as an independent entity. And then criminal hackers arrived.

Based upon Fortress Mentality, our network defense program began. And the result? Use firewalls. Use passwords. Use Access Control Tables.

Do you know which security companies guarantee their products or will provide a warranty which states, if you use their products, they will accept legal responsibility for any losses you suffer if their products are compromised? Some won't release source code to permit verification on how well their products work. Even algorithms of dubious efficacy are carefully guarded, yet at the heart of many security initiatives.

Generally, security vendors do not and cannot guarantee their products. I don't like it, but I thoroughly understand it. That's where Analogue Network Security enters.

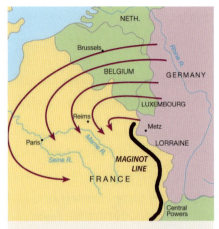

Internet security is like the Maginot Line; just pushing attackers above, under, and around our protective tech.

Hackers are good. Evil, criminal hackers are bad. I want this important distinction made clear, before we go any further.

Deterrence

Some security folks propose to renew the Cold War concept of deterrence, MAD *(Mutual Assured Destruction)*, in some cases.

I am not a fan. Never was.

It implies that the defensive actor is willing to take significant deterrent action when all else fails. That's called escalation, which is fine, if you have the political will and the ability to defend and gracefully degrade. At the private level, active defense is illegal in most places. Strike back, active defense, vigilantism; different spins on the same theme.

We just don't know the fine print in an escalatory conflict spectrum. Where is the tipping point between cyber and kinetic conflict? Is it a clear manifestation of policy, or – as are so many tipping points – the result of chaotic analogue functions? Where so many indefinable variables create instability, even the smallest system change inadvertently triggers an unexpected and probably unwanted action.

- *You can't go half-asymmetric.*
- *Our adversaries don't care about rules.*
- *Our lawyers do.*

However, I have asked lawyers and politicians for years to solve the following problem. (Thus far, they have not.)

In the physical world, if you attack me on the street, I can use any weapon at my disposal to defend myself. I can also, if capable, take away your knife, bat, gun, or

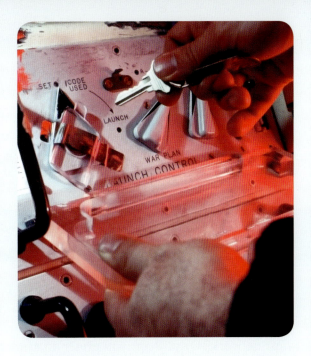

any other weapon and use it against you. The key point is, I am allowed to remove your weapon.

In this case, I also have a reasonable degree of attribution, versus the anonymity of well-crafted cyber attacks.

In the online world, however, that is illegal. The possibility of consequential collateral damage, or inaccurate attacker identification, is the oft-cited rationale for the current legal posture. I will later suggest a model on how, with global cooperation, I believe many such attacks can be mitigated before they become damaging. Additionally, like with Dridex C2 servers or Mirai infected IoT devices, the victims become part of the aggressor, against their will.

The Yardstick

How secure is your network?

Use any scale you want.

Perhaps, you like scales from 1-10, with 10 being completely, perfectly secure. On that scale, how secure is your network? Or perhaps you prefer an academic-style grading system. Does your network get an A? B-? C+ or an F?

I see so much cringing whenever I ask that question.

How do we measure security?

What is the risk of a particular network action, security choice, or hiring decision? Each one relies on some **degree of trust** which influences the macro-security of an enterprise versus the micro-security of a particular device or data-set. So, what scale do we use?

There are a lot of trust discussions coming up, I assure you.

> In so many cases, we tend to boil down our level of perceived security to a binary answer:
>
> ✓ Acceptable
> ✗ Not Acceptable

But what scale and what metrics do we use to get to that binary decision? That's fairly arbitrary, and certainly not an agreed upon reference or standard.

So, let's ask the vendors. *(Makes sense.)*

"Mr. Firewall, how long can your solution sustain a *[specific attack method and vector]* before the protective security fails? In weeks, days, or hours, please."

"Ms. Crypto, what guarantees do you offer that your key management system is bulletproof?"

"Mr. Anti-Virus, what is your guarantee that my networks will never be infected with your published list of malware?"

"Mrs. Vendor, can you please supply me with an EULA that provides performance and security guarantees instead of excuses?"

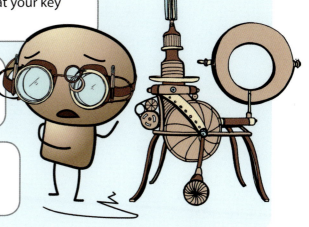

We can't measure security. Or, so goes the conventional wisdom.

I disagree.

I know this is a bit harsh, and I do understand the vendor position. But these questions are fundamental to finding a new approach to network security. In my honest opinion, metrics are key to this effort.

No, we cannot measure all aspects of security to the *n*th degree. But this book should help provide you with some new tools to measure many quantifiable characteristics of our networks.

These same arguments can well be made regarding software vendors and hardware vendors who depend upon software. Security is merely a vertical application.

The Guarantee

THREE THINGS:

1. No matter how many firewalls and access controls you install, passwords and policies you enforce, or upgrades and patches you apply, it's almost a 100% sure bet that you won't be 100% protected. *(There is no silver bullet, right? Besides, you can't patch a person, can you?)*

2. Security vendors don't guarantee their products. *(I don't like it but I DO get it.)*

3. We operate under the assumption that we cannot measure the efficacy of security products or protective systems.

I largely disagree.

So what yardstick can we use?

(We'll get to that in Chapter 3, Fractals.)

Cyber-insurance – a growing industry – should benefit from adding time dimensions to its risk approaches.

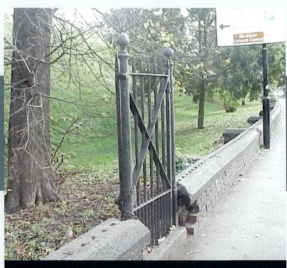

An awesome locked gate protecting an ancient Roman fortress in York, UK.

A Brief History
of Security Models

TCSEC (*Trusted Computer Security Evaluation Criteria*) or the Dept. of Defense's "Orange Book" from 1983.

It all began with a military funding effort from the Department of Defense and some very smart people who were hired to think about computer security. (Back then networks were still experimental. Think pre-dial-up.)

The outcome was the TCSEC, the first formal information security methodology. First offered as a document in 1983 and formalized 2 years later, TCSEC became the guideline by which we were to secure the commercial and government sectors from bad guys breaking into our computers. The way we told everyone to proceed was with a classification system from a fairly insecure D level, to the top, best of breed A-1, which included mathematical proofs plus years and years of analysis. There was a problem. One A-1 system, SCOMP, a mainframe security system, assumed on power-up that the guy flipping the switch was 100% trusted.

TCSEC employs the concept of the Reference Monitor via access controls to provide information protection. It was originally conceived by Ross Anderson (1972), embellished by Bell & LaPadula (1973) with huge help from security pioneer Dr. Roger Schell, and later interpreted as an integrity model by Kenneth J. Biba (1977).

I suggest that the interested reader examine other models: ISO/IEC 27000, RBAC, Zero Trust, Clark-Wilson. Don't forget newer data-centric approaches, including the use of blockchain technology.

With this approach and model, system requests are to be mediated by a so-called traffic cop - the Reference Monitor (below) – before executing.

Whether at the application layer, with the Operating System, or even at lower network and hardware levels, the Reference Monitor creates a range of problems for both the security engineer and the systems user.

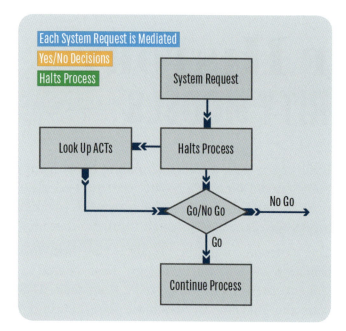

Remember, this was 1970-era tech.

The Reference Monitor slows down the system by requiring a process to be halted until the mediation is complete. Such a slowdown can be negligible if only a few processes are to be monitored. But, if a file opens, closes, and every process is included in the Rules Table, system performance can come to a seemingly grinding halt. Add networking and the grinding halt permeates throughout.

Security models generally call for the generation of an audit trail of system and process executions. The granularity provided by the audit trail can, at times, be too much and it creates immense, often unintelligible audit trails, again using up system resources and time. Today we call that big data, which many say is a good thing.

The Reference Monitor's inherent philosophical problems found in the *Orange Book* and other security models over the years, continue to hinder real world security practitioners.

In 1990, my company designed and developed COMPSEC II for the C2 component of Novell Netware.

Moore's Law roughly states that given constant dollars, the power of computing doubles every 18 months. Recent developments by IBM and Intel have suggested that this period might be reduced to less than a year.

Alternatively, along comes a disruptive tech that starts the process all over again. Think of it as a reboot of Moore.

1. TCSEC was aimed at standalone computer systems, especially mini-computers and mainframes. In addition, certain levels of physical security were assumed to be protecting the computing resources — such as fences, barbed wire, dogs, locked doors, and heavily armed security forces. Largely, TCSEC was for government and military use.

2. In 1987, the National Computer Security Center (NSA-centric) published the Trusted Network Interpretation, supposedly an approach to apply *Orange Book* principles in a networked environment. This effort was even more of a commercial failure as it offered few real solutions. After two years of study, the paper essentially came to the conclusion that we had no earthly idea how to secure a network.

3. Secured Operating Systems were the thrust of many TCSEC efforts. The NSA accreditation of a secure operating system is an exhaustive process that can take two or more years to complete. In the commercial world, this represents two or more generations of technology. Secure operating systems (for standalone environments) were often so restrictive in their operation that much needed functionality was stripped away. In the private sector, this was anathema. Internal staff need access to physically remote logical resources across external public switched networks.

4. Secure operating systems often required applications to be specially written for that secure O/S, according to a revised set of rules. This would necessarily increase the required efforts of software development geometrically.

5. Development of applications, which meet TCSEC specifications, can take just as long — an eternity in a world where Moore's Law reigns supreme. Obsolete, often useless applications become the rule.

TSCEC has some effective, real-world applicability and we must acknowledge its significant contribution to the thought and evolution of computer security. Other security approaches have been attempted over the years, but have generally been found to be lacking, overly-complex, resource intensive, and not abstract enough. They tended to be pin-point, surgical strike attempts at security versus an over-arching abstraction that can apply to multiple domains.

The problems with these models became increasingly clear as symmetric communications in distributed environments became the norm. Translation: the internet, intranets, email, and webification changed the rules virtually overnight. For all practical purposes, our approach to computer and network security has been static and limiting.

The current (some say superior) approach is the fourth revision of the evolving Common Criteria, a mixture of the U.S. TCSEC, UK's ITSEC, and Canada's CTCPEC. The value to vendors of investing hundreds of thousands of dollars for an evaluation is a subject of debate. Source code evaluation is reserved for only the highest certifications, making the program less than common.

As we learn more about Analogue Network Security, we may find that, in some cases, a perfectly acceptable way to secure some electronic assets of an organization will be to eliminate protection devices and technology.

Counter-intuitive, yes. Will it work?

We shall see.

ATTACK SURFACE

One of our book reviewers said his family of six *only* uses:

iPhones (4)
iPads (6)
Android Tablets (4)
Computers (6)
Media Servers (2)
Video Gaming Systems (5)
Televisions (5)
Blu-ray Players (4)
Cable Boxes (2)
Routers/Firewalls/Switches (2)
Wireless Access Points (2)
Children's Toys (4)

Now, multiply by orders of magnitude in homes, and by some almost-impossible-to-measure-factor in the enterprise.

SYMMETRIC SECURITY

Firewall technology was an early contender in internet security and its use continues to echo the fundamental premises of access-control driven TCSEC and its flaws: **keep the bad guys out — definitely a military mindset.**

Some firewalls and similar protective perimeter approaches are meant to protect the electronic inner sanctums of private networks from the ravages of the internet.

They were then discovered to be useful as protective devices on intranets within organizations to keep the valuable resources of various departments, divisions, campuses, and partners isolated from each other. Dr. Fred Cohen stated, "In this way, they have been, and will continue to be, valuable for some time. Barriers help, even if they are not perfect, because they allow you to focus other resources on the things the barriers don't stop."

The principle of the firewall was originally an extension of the "Build a Higher Wall" mindset. But, very quickly, some of us realized that the security models in use at the time did not match the real-world business models being practiced.

Just consider how much money the DoD and the NSA invested in contracts to companies whose task was to design the **ultimate** security protection device. Their goal was to connect their classified systems to the internet. Devices such as SNS (Secure Network Server) have been put into service in isolated cases - tens of millions of dollars later.

I look back on the good ol' days when information security was *so* darned *easy*. Well, maybe not darned easy, but one whole heck of a lot simpler. Really, it was. And there are lots of security professionals and IT managers who also recall how security used to be so simple. *(Simpler...)*

"Trusted workers" sat at text-only dumb terminals, which were hardwired to a mainframe where the data was processed and stored. A reasonably simple access control mechanism kept clerks out of the files where they weren't wanted. It kept salespeople away from payroll. This was one-way street, or uni-directional, security. Many of us remember the good ol' days of RACF, ACF-2, and Top Secret, along with their comparatively simple access control lists which were manageable in groups, function, or location.

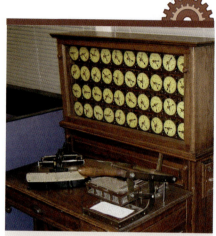

Herman Hollerith's tabulating machine, used for the 1890 census.

> **In the early days, security vendors chose from one of two basic binary defensive implementations:**
> - Controls denied permissions to users and had to be explicitly defined, approved, and set.
> - All users' activities were permitted and needed to be explicitly denied.

Think Windows for Workgroups 3.1.X, Windows 95, and protocol binding of the day!

But today? Today our security control needs are terrifically complex. We find that, instead of simple asynchronous connections to manage, we have to deal with dozens of different real-world operating environments that are simultaneously in use across multiple physical and logical locations, with conditions constantly in flux. See the list on the following page for some examples.

This list covers only a few of the possibilities! Complexify the landscape even further by 5! (that's five-factorial), given that each of us will have 5+ unique (and, to a degree, quasi-intelligent) internet devices in just a few years.

Common Synchronous Communication Endpoints Which Can Affect Security

1. Internal staff with access to physically local, logical resources.
2. Internal staff with access to physically remote logical resources across dedicated internal networks.
3. Internal staff with access to physically remote logical resources across external public switched networks.
4. Internal staff with access control to remote logical resources across external public switched networks.
5. Internal staff bringing remote data and information into the internal networks.
6. Internal staff publishing to remote logical resources.
7. Internal staff removing internal electronic resources and sending them to remote locations.
8. External staff requiring access to some, but not all, internal network resources across public switched networks.
9. External staff accessing remote resources.
10. Internal and external staff with access control to remote logical resources across external public switched networks.
11. External traveling staff requiring access to some, but not all, internal network resources.
12. Business partners requiring access to some, but not all, internal network resources.
13. Customers requiring access to some, but not all, internal network resources.
14. Customers requiring access to all public company publications, but not any internal resources.
15. Potential customers requiring access to all public company publications, but not any internal resources.
16. Anything mobile.
17. IoT ++++++++

COMMUNICATIONS

1 to 1: Fairly easy to secure.

1 to Many: Radio, TV, social media, blogs, websites. The only security is identity management at the source. You want everyone to read/see/hear everything.

Many to Many: Facility first, security second (or maybe last). We will revisit Many to Many in Chapter 8 (see "Fully Connected Networks"), as a view to solving DDoS.

Today, real-world security implementation must be symmetrical in nature.

Security must be implemented in two directions for each and every electronic nexus (and that includes the Internet of Things): the information going both **in** and **out** of the organization, the people accessing each of the multiple possible endpoints, moving information both **in** and **out** of each nexus, the myriad combinations thereof… my math skills hit a roadblock.

So, how do we install Fortress Mentality security mechanisms and models to reflect the business needs of symmetric processing?

Aha! Therein is the conundrum.

> The history of computer security has shown us why and how Fortress Mentality has failed rather than succeeded.

50 Years of Security

PROFILE OF A SECURITY MODEL

COMPUTER AND NETWORK SECURITY, INTERNET SAFETY, AND PRIVACY CONCERNS HAVE BECOME MAINSTREAM.

We live in a world where global cyberterrorism, information dominance, nation-state cyberwar, massive industrial espionage operations, perception management, fake news, and a creeping global surveillance society that strips individual privacy daily, are the new realities.

Cybersecurity is a global meme, from the data center to the smart phone, the power grid, SCADA/ICS systems, your autonomous car, intelligent refrigerator, and WiFi-enabled light bulbs that somehow communicate with the National Weather Service. *(Oh, boy. The internet of things. So cool.)*

Our jobs are clear.

All we have to do is make these new consumer and prosumer devices secure. All we have to do is make websites secure. All we have to do is keep the comm-lines and network connections secure. All we have to do is create a seamless, proof-positive identity management system that works everywhere, all of the time. All we have to do is…

I have asked many professionals over the years, in both public and private fora:

How well do security products and services really provide protection for untold trillions of dollars in intellectual property value, personal privacy, and

17

economic and physical national security? How many hundreds of millions of people have had their privacy and security violated through massive global data breaches?

I am not saying that any particular manufacturer of security products is derelict, or that they produce bad products. I mean to urge us to reconsider the overall approach we take with information and network security, as a professional industry endowed with the responsibility to keep much of humanity and its machinery running in smooth order.

We need models to achieve our goals. We need tools to do our jobs. We need these tools and models to protect our corporate assets, networks and enterprises, and personal privacy. We require strong models and products and services to protect the interdependent critical infrastructures: transportation, finance, communications, and power. The military, intelligence community, and governments (federal, state, and local) also require answers, tools, and modern approaches, to adequately protect their resources; for national security, public services, and day-to-day operations.

I hope that my thoughts on Analogue Network Security will offer a few practical abstractions and architectural concepts that can be built upon. In the search for strategic (versus tactical, read: vendor products) approaches to information and network security, I suggest we look for some basic, useful characteristics that more than six decades of computing have taught us:

ID Theft and privacy violations are known as Class I Information Warfare.

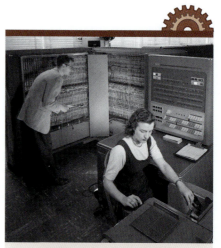

I use 1952 as the start of the modern computing world. Why? Because that's the year IBM introduced the first commercial vacuum tube mainframe, the 700 series.

SIMPLICITY. Should be conceptually simple and offer utility to developers, vendors, consultants, integrators, the customers, and all vested stakeholders.

UTILITY. Should have minimal interference in network operations or the ability of administration, management, and users to do their job. Some security models have negatively affected network efficiency and user productivity.

Think MLS (Multi-Level Security) of the 1980s.

50 Years of Security

Interoperability is Overarching: If we can't talk to each other about security with a common language, what's the point?

SCALABLE. Should offer security from the smallest network, app(lication), or single control process, to the largest of critical infrastructures.

MEASURABLE. Should be able to measure and quantify the effectiveness of security and support security budget decision making and risk.

QUANTIFIABLE. Quantifiable metrics should provide replicable mathematical tools to measure the integrity of solutions to system security problems.

PROVABLE. Should use simple, basic mathematics at its core, which are replicable in disparate environments by non-mathematicians.

SUPPORTS MANAGEMENT. Should offer mechanisms to allow management to make informed budgetary decisions on information resource and systems defensive spending and risk.

BRINGS RISK TO THE TABLE. We are security professionals, not accountants, financiers, or actuarial experts. But, we all need to be talking to each other with some common lingua franca. To date, our profession has brought few hard numbers to the analysis and concepts of security. I hope Analogue Network Security will help.

ADDS VALUE. Of course, the security model must offer something new to the practitioner, and something of value over, or different from, current approaches. Based upon the reactions of people I have spoken with over the years, Analogue Network Security has a chance of helping.

At DefCon 22, I hosted a small private event in a friend's suite. There was no location given on the 2,000 invitations - folks had to figure that out on their own. About 30 showed up and for 4 hours, we sat around a massive dining table discussing the principles of Analogue Network Security. Over the last decade, I made refinements in this manner, in several cities around the world.

So, based upon all this... what *do* we know about network security?

Synergy

> "Synergy means the behavior of whole systems unpredicted by the behavior of their parts taken separately." *(Buckminster Fuller)*

- ▶ 1 + 1 > 2, but how much greater?

- ▶ Combining an explosive metal and a poisonous gas unpredictably produces a harmless white powder: sodium chloride, NaCl, or table salt.

- ▶ Iron, chromium, and nickel have tensile strengths of 60,000, 70,000, and 80,000 PSI respectively and yet, combine to create an alloy with 350,000 PSI. This far exceeds the strength of its weakest link, but counter-intuitively and unpredictably even outperforms the sum of its components' tensile capabilities.

- ▶ Digital + Analogue (hybrid) network security? Let's see what happens!

Lessons Learned

In the U.S. alone, over the last half century or so, we've collectively spent endless trillions of dollars on impressive, often mind-boggling technology. Globally? An *IT*-load more.

During the same period, we have invested hundreds of billions of dollars on cybersecurity. That's a mere fraction of IT spending. A trillion or more dollars spent on constructing security products and deploying systems – some secret, some not-so-secret – and what do we have to show for it? We've tried to build the virtual walls around our computer systems higher and higher. We've tried to make our systems impenetrable. We've tried to adapt Fortress Mentality and Risk Avoidance in a symmetrical world.

1. The internet is not a friend of security.
2. Networks blew security all to hell.
3. Vendors do not, and cannot, guarantee their products.
4. There is no such thing as 100% security.
5. As a species, we humans are not smart enough to build a security system that is impenetrable. The two mutually exclusive goals of protection and open access sit at opposite ends of the spectrum.
6. We are not smart enough to build a secure distributed system that will both keep the bad guys out, and let the good guys in.

7. Based upon our collective experience, if we were smart enough to build an impenetrable security system, it wouldn't be particularly useful or functional.

8. If we were smart enough to build one, we couldn't afford it.

9. Fortress Mentality and its offspring, Static Defense-in-Depth, are merely speed bumps in the road to strong attackers.

10. Computer security is extremely difficult.

Trillions later, and it's still broken. Based upon those experiences, I come to the following conclusions:

The old approaches to computer security need to be put aside for bit.

Don't ignore them. Don't throw them out.

I will be arguing that an abstract strategic approach to synergetic digital and analogue network security thinking will bring us unpredictable results.

Let's take a trip to Warsaw, Poland, in 1995. That's where, I recognize in hindsight, my foray into Analogue Network Security began.

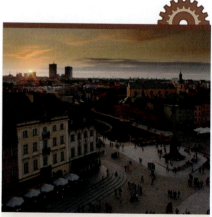

After being 97% razed, Warsaw was essentially rebuilt from the ground up after WWII.

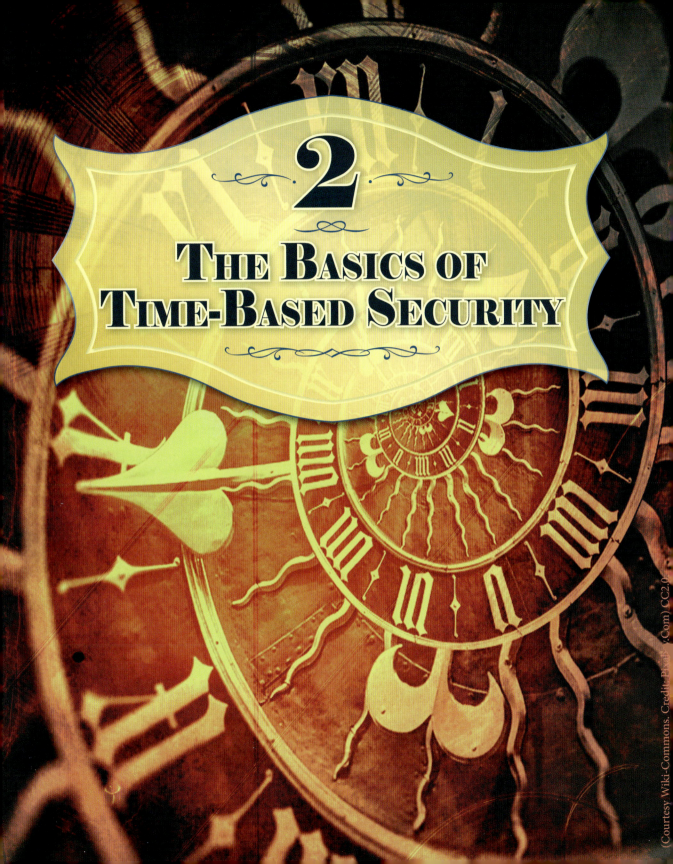

2
The Basics of Time-Based Security

Time-Based Security Genesis

Time-Based Security (TBS) began for me with a 21-hour flight to Warsaw in 1995. It evolved as a need to find a new approach to network security that had, to that date, been pretty much an epic fail.

My good friend and colleague, Bob Ayers (DISA) and I were the guests of a post-Cold War apparatchik security conference. We had scheduled a 1700h meeting at the hotel bar with our hosts. Shower. Nap. Time zone confusion. Downstairs at 1656h.

No one showed. Bob and I talked and had a beer. Or two. A cocktail napkin emerged and a pen scribbled. Bob's animation was contagious. He was describing his upcoming talk to the apparatchiks who were trying to blend their Cold War mindsets with modern western IT culture. He called it PDR, or **Protect-Detect-Respond**. *(Keep those letters in mind. We're going to use them in our first formula.)*

Over the next several hours, we sacrificed countless napkins to our scribbling, ate terrific sausage, and drank many *pivos* – beers. Our Polish hosts showed at 2215h, ready to party. We retired at 2245h, more than 30 hours after my trip had begun.

Over the next year, I took Bob's basic concepts and played with them, finally publishing *Time-Based Security*, first in 1998, reprinted in 2001, and OEM'd by several security companies of the day.

To date, I have had the opportunity to expand and edit many of the ideas in *Time-Based Security* while attending some outstanding information warfare and security conferences around the world. I got to evolve and actually document some new applications for the TBS abstraction. For what it's worth, I kept a lot of those ideas to myself, despite often speaking on Time-Based Security over the next fifteen years. Whatever the excuse, I didn't publish. But more importantly, a constant stream of concepts and ideas entered my mind and I always felt I was never ready to publish. I had to make it better.

Audiences were *sort of* getting it, and **Protect, Detect, and Respond** is now used as a marketing mantra for many security vendors.

Now, let's go rob a pawnshop.

The Pawnshop

Three figures, dressed in black, hooded and gloved, stealthily used the buildings' shadows as they moved down a darkened side-street in lower Manhattan.

After several weeks of close surveillance, this crew knew that their target – the pawnshop at the corner of 7th Avenue – had recently taken in some high-end jewelry. They knew the routines of the owner, had mapped the store layout, and knew under which counters the better goods were stored. They knew the make and model of the safe. And, perhaps most importantly, they knew how the security systems worked.

As the criminal 'team' approached the store, the *safe guy* said, "Time." All three checked their watches, synchronized to the second. "OK, go."

The *alarm guy* used a glass cutter on the door after first positioning a suction device to secure the circular cutout. (He knew the larger plate glass window had alarm tape, but the door did not.) He deftly removed the glass, reached in, unlocked the door, and they were inside.

"12 seconds. Let's go."

The *bag guy* went straight to the "good stuff," quickly placing items in a small satchel. The *safe guy* was in the rear office, deftly drilling a hole in its door.

"22 seconds."

Alarm guy had gone directly to the alarm system in the storefront, entering a series of numbers that disarmed it. During their weeks of surveillance, he had gleened the code simply by watching the owner enter the same

The Basics of Time Based Security

pattern each day. The one kink in the plan was the back-up security system in the rear of the shop, which he had not been able to actually see until they got into that office. But he knew it was there.

"35 seconds."

Alarm guy went straight to the panel, and while *bag guy* and *safe guy* did their jobs, he punched-in the same set of numbers used on the front panel, hoping that the owner had carelessly used the same passcodes for both systems. A red light flashed indicating the codes were NOT the same and a numeric readout started counting down from "20."

"We got 20 seconds till it goes." The others nodded, but stayed on task.

"55 seconds and I'm in," reported *safe guy*. The phone was also lit now as autodial was notifying the police.

"Plenty of time." All three were now grabbing the last of their bounty, including the premium goods and cash from the breached safe.

The phone rang twice. "1 minute, 15 seconds. That was fast." The phone rang three more times then stopped. "We got 90 more seconds, max! Hurry it up."

Alarm guy worked his way to the rear door, unlocked three physical locks and went out to scout the alley where they had parked their innocuous, already idling, dark blue sedan. All was good and they had "30 seconds left," meaning *finish up and get into the car… fast*.

"10 seconds."

The three moved to the rear door. Stepping into the alley, they dropped their "workclothes" on the ground and hopped into the vehicle.

"Perfect. To the second." They pulled out onto 6th, headed north, and disappeared amidst the Times Square traffic.

The Basics of Time Based Security

Ten minutes later, a squad car from the NYPD pulled up to the front of the seemingly sleeping pawnshop.

"What do you think?"

"I don't see nothing…"

"Let's take a look." The two officers got out of their patrol car and peered into the store.

"Nothing."

One cop tried the door but it was locked. Noticing the missing piece of glass, he said, "Hey, Mick, take a look at this."

By now the robbers were long gone, leaving no prints or clues. It took 2 minutes and 45 seconds to execute the well-planned crime.

It's a War Out There

During the Cold War, the U.S. defended its citizenry, with time. The idea (fear) was, that the planet was a mere 18 minutes away from thermonuclear extinction.

If the Soviets got it into their heads to send over a six-pack of MIRV, the U.S. had somewhere in the vicinity of 18-22 minutes to launch our thermonuclear response over the pole. The point wasn't to defend "we the citizens"; it was to kill as many Soviet comrades as we could in response. The 18 minute window was how long we had to respond before their nukes nuked our nukes. Yeah, a ton of people would die and then there was that 10,000 year uninhabitable planet issue to work out, but the real point was deterrence through MAD: Mutual Assured Destruction. Looks like it worked.

That's also what the Cuban Missile Crisis was all about: MAD and time. If missiles had been allowed to be placed in Cuba, it would have given our adversaries a distinct time-advantage. It would take perhaps 2-3 minutes, versus 18 or so, for nuclear tipped missiles to reach the U.S. mainland, and that was unacceptable.

War is all about time. *(Yes, military folks, Colonel Boyd and OODA are coming!)*

During the Gulf War, we measured the effectiveness of the land campaign against Iraq in hours; the so-called 100 hour war. History tells us about the Hundred Years War, too. How far was a day's march to meet the enemy in Napoleonic or Civil War days? How many days or weeks of supplies did they have on hand to keep the troops in fighting shape?

In high-speed wars, the generals want and expect real-time intelligence, use powerful technology to evaluate the data so they can make decisions, and transmit orders to the front-line combatants over fast and secure communications lines. Further, with the advent of the "digital battlefield", it has been jokingly said that soldiers will be so wired with technology and smart weapons, they will require a Master of Computer Science degree before they are allowed to shoot a kinetic weapon.

In fact, when we think about it, most human endeavors can be effectively measured in time. Think about that for a second. (I am sure there are exceptions, as there are to any generality, but time is absolutely critical for most anything.) Our personal value is measured in time; dollars per hour; salary per month or year. Rates of investment, annual percentage rate. Time is the constant element throughout. And cyber-wise, it's about bandwidth, just another way of measuring time: bits per second is the single biggest driving force behind the Global Network. Speed. Time.

Physical home and business protection is also measured in time and we see it as a staple in cops and robbers movies and in our earlier pawnshop example.

A crook breaks into a jewelry store (or home). The alarm goes off. It autodials the cops (20 seconds); the cops examine the call to make sure it looks real (20 seconds); the cops go to the scene of the crime, presumably not across the street from the police station (1-5 minutes). To be on the safe side, the robbers give themselves a maximum of two minutes for the whole heist. The quantifiable question is, how much can they steal in two minutes?

At the office, time is often the first tier of protection. You unlock the door, open it, and then run like heck to the supply closet so you can enter the security code into the alarm system. You have 25 seconds to do that or, in theory, the rent-a-cops come a running in a few minutes.

ATTENTION: Cyber Warriors!

Time has been a critical component of warfare for millenia. Analogue network security applies to cyberwar, as well.

The Basics of Time Based Security

JESSE JAMES

LET'S GO TO THE LATE 19TH CENTURY.

Back in the good ol' days of the Wild West, where trains and stagecoaches got robbed. Banks got robbed, too. Gold and cash and other valuables were kept in safes. Rugged, heavy safes. So, let's first ask the question:

Was the most technologically advanced safe from the mid-19th century secure?

Here are some of the answers I've gotten in an open forum:

"Sure it is! I can't break in."
"What do you mean by secure?"
"Somewhat secure."
"How secure is secure?"

Pressing the point, the answers tend to get a little more thoughtful:

"I could drill a hole through it."
"Jesse James didn't have drills."
"They had manual drills."
"So, they could blow it up."
"And blow up the money inside."
"Or shoot the lock."
"Brute force will work."
"Not really all that secure, is it?"

Most of my audiences come to the conclusion that, no, safes from the 1880's were not all that secure. Fortress mentality defeated again.

However, there is another realization that crosses the crowd: this awesome safe from 1880 is only secure from those people who won't hold up the train or the stage – the good guys. Bad guys will figure it out, no matter what.

Does that have a ring of similarity in our networks? *(Some things never change… and that's one of my points!)*

The Vault

Now, fast-forward about 140 years.

Inside a great, tall bank building in the City of London, is an incredible vault. Many banks have them. The shiny stainless-steel door is twelve feet high, eight feet wide, three feet thick, and weighs forty-two tons. Massive deadbolts lock the door into the concrete and there are steel reinforced walls surrounding the vault on its other five sides.

Deliberate thieves drilled through massive walls to reach the inner sanctum of the bank, netting $100M+. Nothing is secure.

"If the door is closed and locked properly, is this vault secure?"

The audiences to whom I pose this question typically think a bit on this one. That's one impressive vault I'm showing them on the screen. Then the questions start.

"What do you mean by secure?"

"I could compromise the electronic locks."

"I can't break in."

"You could always blow it up."

"With what… a nuke?"

"That's a lot of metal and reinforced concrete to get through."

"Is the door open or closed?"

"Is the bank manager trustworthy?"

"… Or can she be blackmailed?"

Soon enough the audience will come to the conclusion that this mega-dollar vault in the city is not secure either. It could be blown-up. Or perhaps attackers take a *Die Hard 3* brute force approach.

I have been told that many of the best vaults are made from metal that was found in crashed alien saucers and reverse-engineered in Area 51. If you have info, contact me.

The Basics of Time Based Security

So, I suggest, if we decided to go into the bank and rob it, we could bring in our dynamite and our oxygen-acetylene torches and we'd be home free and rich, right? Rob them blind?

"No!" the audience will immediately say. "No, they have alarms."

"Alarms? What alarms?" I question them, and they say that any bank will have alarms to see if someone is tampering with their safes. "So the safes aren't good enough, eh?" I challenge.

Some bright individual will immediately say, "of course not. You have to have alarms to make it all work right." She looks around for approval and a few nodding heads give her the support she needs.

"Then, what good is the safe?"

Huh? What good is the safe? No one is quick to answer that one.

Maybe a meek voice will say, "It makes the robbers' job harder."

"Exactly!" I shout. "When you buy a big safe, the manufacturer will add a sticker to the door or have a disclaimer in its specifications that says something like, 'This super-strong-stainless-steel door can withstand a direct oxy-acetylene torch at a temperature of 3,200C for a period of 93 hours. After that, all bets are off.' Or, it might say, 'This vault can withstand a blast created by 5kg of C4 at one meter; after that, all bets are off.'"

The audience nods knowingly.

"So what has the safe bought you?" I shout out the query.

"Protection!"

This time, a few other people answer in unison: "Time!"

"Yes!" I dance in their general direction. "Exactly, time!"

"Time for what?" I make them think once again.

"Time for…" Silence.

"Ah, time to…" Hesitancy.

"Time to set off the alarms!" Right again. These guys are good.

"So, tell me about these alarms…" The audience is getting excited now. Some are standing in the rear of the room or pacing and thinking. Others are sitting on the backs of their chairs. The room is alive with brain cells firing their synapses in rapid succession.

"The alarms detect…"

"The bad guys, right?"

"What kinds of alarms?"

"Heat sensors maybe…?"

"Sensors, yeah. Cameras? Motion sensors?"

"Microphones…trip wires…"

"Odor detectors to smell the bad guys!" someone offers enthusiastically and everyone enjoys a good laugh.

"Right, right, and right again," I say parading back and forth as everyone is shouting all at once now. We all smell satisfaction in the air. "Detection is the key here. Detection."

"So, OK, great. You got your sensors…but so what? Your bank is still getting robbed." I wait for answers.

"You gotta arrest them."

"Yeah, catch 'em in the act."

"You call the police."

"Or rent-a-cop."

"And what do we call that?"

"Response."

"Donuts first."

"An hour's wait." Lots of laughs.

"Reaction."

Reaction.

Good. Real good.

> So what do Jesse James, a pawnshop, and an ultra-modern bank vault have in common?*

Smash and grab and APTs are merely different time-based attack implementations. OODA is coming.

*I'm not telling, you should be able to figure it out.

IT'S ABOUT TIME

WHAT ALL OF THESE EXAMPLES HAVE IN COMMON IS A SIMPLE, INESCAPABLE METRIC: TIME.

For simplicity's sake, let's return to the pawnshop. The glass window. How secure is that pane of glass? How much protection does it offer? If we ask that question and add the time-domain as part of the question, the answer will be something like, "one hammer blow," or "one brick tossed from three feet." Fair? So, the protection value of the pawnshop defense – when measured in time – is for this example, 0.1 second. How does that measure up? We shall see.

The second piece of any decent physical security system is a detection component, which should be pretty damn fast – on the order of microseconds – but we'll call it 0.1 seconds for example's sake.

Then, there's the reaction system which alerts law enforcement or a private security force, who then have to physically respond to the report or alarm. In the pawnshop example, the thieves allotted 180 seconds for the alarm system to trigger and the cops to arrive.

Protection: Pane of Glass	0.1 sec
Detection: Sensor	0.1 sec
Reaction: Cops	180 sec

Let's call **P(t)** Protection (measured in time), and we'll do the same with **D(t)** and **R(t)**.

These three pieces yield us a simple, yet highly intuitive formula, that I have considered to be the bedrock of Time-Based and Analogue Network Security, since that long pivo-drinking evening in Warsaw:

$$P(t) > D(t) + R(t)$$

This says, "if the measured time afforded to me by a protection device is greater than the amount of time it takes to detect and respond to *(repair, halt)* an attack, then I have a secure environment."

This is worth a few minutes of cogitation. Once you "get it", it will almost seem obvious.

- If I can get my detection time really low, and I can get my reaction time really low, I lower my risk when things go bad.
- If I plan for known contingencies with highly automated, policy driven responses, my R(t) will decrease.
- If I get a human involved at every step, my R(t) goes way up and increases the chances for error.

The goal is:

$$[D(t) + R(t)] \rightarrow 0$$

...which can also be viewed as a Limit.

The time value of **P** is the common metric in many physical examples of protection. In banks, or for home security, the amount of security offered by vaults is measured in time. For example, how long will it take a given oxy-acetylene torch of a given temperature to burn through the metal wall?

THE AIR GAP

Some people call an air gap perfect security. But that hinders the whole *purpose* of networks in the first place: to allow businesses to seamlessly communicate and interact with as many other networks and people as they can for whatever purpose they choose. Plus, an air gap does not consider portable media and the ability of humans to find a way around impediments.

Be suspicious if anyone says "perfect security" and they aren't wearing a sarcasm sign.

See "Trust Factors" in Chapter 4.

Think of this fundamental analogue premise another way: Fortress Mentality suggests that new technology should increase P(t) and then you're doing your job right. However, what will actually limit an attacker's effectiveness is minimizing [D(t)+R(t)].

The Basics of Time Based Security

The defensive strength of road barricades, say, can be measured in kilograms-per-meter/second. *(Time.)* They can guarantee protection for up to such-and-such weight of a vehicle-impact at some speed. Beyond that, all bets are off. Warranty is null and void. These numbers provide a good metric base for choosing what kind of P-products, D-products, and R-products to use in a physical defensive system.

But not in our world. I could make a reasonable argument that, for the massive sums of money spent on network security products, we still have almost nil protection.

What we *have* done is construct a digital Maginot Line and the attackers merely bypass the heavily fortified defenses to attack through different vectors.

> Security simply allows an organization to do its job or conduct its mission efficiently without hindrance or interference by either internal or external forces.

Ask the Time

Try this. When you're geeking about security with colleagues or friends, add the word "time" *in context to* and *relevant to* the content of every question or comment.

"We see a 41% decrease in reports of phishing attacks at the workstation."

- "Cool. Over what period of time?"
- "Are those results consistent over time, or do they vary, and according to what criteria?"
- "What is the statistical sample?"

In our field, we don't tend to think in terms of common metrics. We also tend to avoid the question, "How is it measured?" Without a measurement baseline, many of the answers we accept today are downright silly.

DON'T FORGET – ASK ABOUT TIME.

Analyzing the TBS Formula

The **P-D-R approach**, known since 1998 as **Time-Based Security**, is the beginning of our analogue journey, and is comprised of two clearly analogue components.

==The first component is time. Is it analogue?==

We are really going to get into "WTF, Analogue?" in just a bit.

Is Time Analogue?

On your digital watch or mobile device, as the seconds tick away every…well, second… is time analogue or digital?

If you think about time as being clock cycles *(say 1,700,000,000 of them every second, or 1.7GHz)*, is time analogue or digital?

Okay, how about the sweep hand on a conventional dial-style watch? Is time there analogue, or do the precisely milled gears and teeth make time digital?

I can argue that it's all depends upon how you look at it; a sort of paradox, like wave-particle duality…but not so much. According to our current understanding of physics, the smallest divisible component of time is Planck Time, or roughly 10^{-44} seconds. That's quantum small when all laws of physics get exceedingly murky. (Besides, we can only measure down to about 10^{-19} seconds today. We have a long way to go before time approaches quantum-style granularity.)

Time is indeed analogue.

But we also treat time in discrete steps to make things conceptually easier.

So, for our purposes, let's first think of time as continuously variable analogue and secondly as cycles or flops.

With the second analogue component, inequality, there is no equivalence; there is no = sign. I'm using the > and < inequalities, which mean that the values can be anything at all within a specified range.

In our case, $0 < D < \infty$ and $0 < R < \infty$. The values of D(t) – Detection Time – and R(t) – Reaction Time – are only meaningful when measured. In this case, we measure between upper and lower limits.

The TBS principle is simple. P(t), or the amount of time a Protection device can guarantee its effectiveness even when under attack, must be greater than D(t), or the amount of time it takes to Detect the attack, added to the amount of time it takes to React R(t) to it. React can include mitigation and reconstitution, or it may be as simple as halting the offensive activity. That's up to you. The simplicity is a good thing.

P(t) > D(t) + R(t) is the basic TBS formula.

Infinity is our enemy. Infinity must be defeated before we can defeat any adversary.

Just a Moment ...

A caveat regarding the inequalities.

For example, D(t) must always be greater than '0' time units, because zero time begets instantaneity; that's unrealistic outside of the quantum level. If it's only one measly clock cycle, D(t) is still > 0 no matter how fast the computer.

Regarding infinity: Analogue Network Security is about bringing chaos under control by introducing myriad analogue ideas at different places in and around data and networks. Therefore, anything in meaningful improvement must necessarily bring D(t) substantially below infinity. Consider that today, without many of the analogue control concepts we're going to discuss, effectively, X(t) (any process) does have a limit that approaches infinity. I am simply stating that, without employing Analogue Network Security modeling, $[D(t) + R(t)] \to \infty$.

That is, in my opinion, why internet and network security is so abysmal, especially in regard to one of my most annoying pet peeves: Root. But I have an idea on how to fix that and bring Root under control.

(See "Let's Kill Root", Chapter 4.)

One *could* argue that as

$$[D(t) + R(t)] \to 0$$

...information security is now a simple affair. You no longer have to build up huge levels of protection. You need to concentrate on detection and reaction… which ultimately determines the amount of effective security you have. I am not saying to toss your firewalls, but conceptually, it's worth the mental exercise as we expose things a bit.

Now, let's change the inequality for just a second and consider what happens if…

$$P(t) > D(t) + R(t)$$

is modified to…

$$P(t) \geq D(t) + R(t)$$

This creates an equality I am uncomfortable with. It assumes a perfect equality that requires perfect execution and we all know that everything is perfect in *theory*. Just not in practice. Growing up in analogue audio gave me a great appreciation for a word I use a lot, even when it comes to networks: headroom. Headroom is that additional safe place above normal operating parameters, a sort of grace period/space. When you exceed your provided upper-limits, serious bad things happen to the analogue signal. I like the safety buffer. Period.

The network traffic metaphor would be, "I have a 1Gb/sec pipe, but my average daily traffic is only 500Mb/sec." In digital terms, that says you can double traffic and be fine. In analogue terms, two-times, twice, or double for headroom sucks. That's only 3db. We typically like 20-24db of headroom, which would roughly translate to a 1Gb/sec pipe nominally using only 50Mb/sec. But that allows for big traffic spikes. Ergo, analogue-based load balancing and network traffic shaping.

With my desire to build-in a lot of headroom with any sort of system design, I will adhere to $P(t) > D(t) + R(t)$ for current purposes. Ideally, and most difficult, is to provably increase $P(t)$ by as much as possible; orders of magnitude would be good.

Also note that, if $|D(t) + R(t)| > |P(t)|$, or conversely $|P(t)| < |D(t) + R(t)|$, is used, then security cannot be achieved. The use of absolute values is intentional here, as we don't want to introduce negative time into our analogue thinking for a while. And we *will* get there. I promise.

But first, let's get to the numbers on how much we expose ourselves.

THERE IS NO PROTECTION

NETWORK SECURITY IS JUST ANOTHER FORM OF CONFLICT: WAR.

Using Fortress Mentality in computer and network technology as a defensive method assumes that things *will* fail. After all, history says Fortress Mentality is only a deterrent. Can protective defenses, each a sub-set of a fortress mentality defense-in-depth approach, be relied upon? I argue, no, not enough; not with any degree of assurance or confidence high enough to create a metric.

Why Defense is So Damned Difficult

- Networks grow and change every day, thus changing their security posture endlessly… thousands of times per small time unit.
- Perimeters are, effectively, amorphous blobs of uncertainty. Think mobile.
- Connecting enterprise networks to partner organizations with unknown security necessarily weakens a network's defensive strength (as you will see mathematically).
- Organizations do not know every single network ingress and egress of their environment. Rogue modems, wireless, obscured network connections, USB sticks, and secret subnets plague organizations.
- Organizations experience similar opacity with third party networks. Which are current or out of date?
- Increasing complexity causes software and networks to fail regularly in unpredictable ways.

- Seemingly harmless applications often innocently create security vulnerabilities.
- New hacks (Zero-Days) appear daily and are used (or sold on the Dark Web) against leading applications, operating systems, and security mechanisms by organized crime and nation states.
- It takes time and effort to test and install new patches to enhance security, and they don't always work.
- Well-designed security mechanisms are all too often installed incorrectly and/or completely misconfigured.
- Administrators sometimes turn off security controls during audits and maintenance and then forget to turn them back on.
- You can't adequately test the protective value of a network with any degree of assurance beyond the exact moment it was tested. And here comes IoT!

How secure is a network? With all of the firewalls, IDS, IPS, and SIEM add-ons? I have no earthly idea… and you probably don't either. Despite the plethora of protective security technologies deployed in even the most security-conscious organizations, APTs have created breaches that have gone undetected for more than a year.

Yes, here D(t) > 1 Year!

One of our reviewers says, "We only have two options here, DEFENSE and OFFENSE," but I find his following thought to be even more salient for ANS considerations: "Beneath our DEFENSE we have: Identify, Protect, Detect, Respond, Recovery. (Pick NIST/CSF or any other model.)" We're guessing. And I'm guessing that a lot of you would like to stop guessing about your security posture… and would like to get a better handle on both the risk and the security.

What is the difference between Defense, Protection, and Prevention? I asked 100 people and got 1,000 different answers. My view is: Defense is an analogue spectrum, where both Protection and Prevention imply a binary success or failure.

Does this imply we should abdicate using protective security technology? How can we take this dearth of data and make it meaningful?

Bottom line, we as an industry have no reliable means to measure, or in many cases, semi-accurately gauge the efficacy of protective security tools and methods.

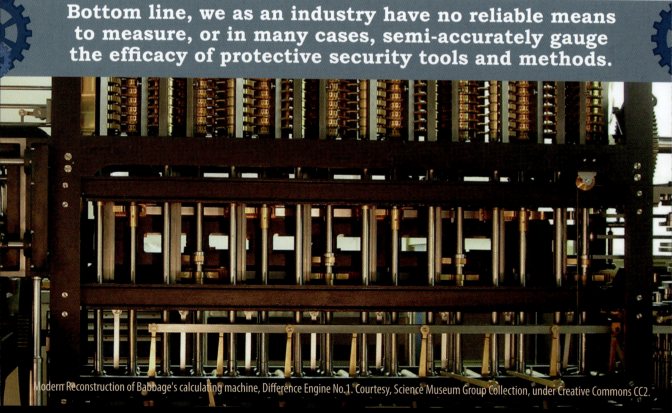

Modern Reconstruction of Babbage's calculating machine, Difference Engine No.1. Courtesy, Science Museum Group Collection, under Creative Commons CC2.

E(t) Phone Home:
EXPOSURE

According to Time-Based Security, we now know two things:

> P(t) > D(t) + R(t)
>
> *and*
>
> P(t) is indeterminate

We do not know, and probably will never know, if our protective technologies work at all, or if they are merely acting as a temporary Maginot Line, pushing hostile security attempts to different vectors. Currently we cannot assign a value to **P(t)**.

Let's assume that a bank has no protection mechanism at all. Maybe the vault door is wide open. However, to deter crime, the bank has wisely put a number of well-designed detection and reaction components in place. The D and R are well defined, measurable, and replicable. The question we now ask in this situation is: given **P(t) = 0** *(where P(t) cannot be a*

Sort of like trying to push escaped air back into a balloon.

negative number, obviously), does it not follow that **[D(t) + R(t)] = E(t)**, in the worst case?

For example, assuming zero protection, how bad is my exposure to network compromise and data loss?

E(t) meaning Exposure Time here.

Another way to phrase the question is, **"How much damage can the intruders cause in the amount of time it takes to effect (D + R), or E?"**

In the pawnshop example, when we added the **D(t)s** and the **R(t)s** together, we found the bad guys had something less than 3 minutes to make off with as much loot as they could before the cops arrived. The store can then – based upon the known contents at risk – determine quantitatively how much risk that worst-case scenario represents in terms of dollars.

Now, as I have done hundreds of times, ask yourself a similar question:

> **"Given a reasonable cyber adversary who has done his homework, if your D(t) + R(t) = 10 minutes of unrestricted access, how much damage can be done to your networks or data?"**

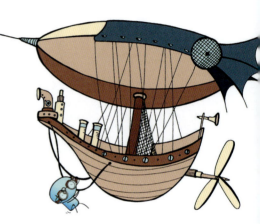

The answer has been universal: **"We're screwed,"** to which I have amended the technical term: **S.O.L.**

Next, let's play with dividing by time and see what happens.

An Extremely Extreme, Yet Unwise Case

Think of putting a server on the internet with no firewall, no passwords, no barriers at all. No patches. No nothing. Except, highly effective detection tools. *(Don't come after me because I can't define those detection tools. This argument operates off the idea that, in this **hypothetical** world, we have much better detection mechanisms than we actually have in the real world today.)* So, what can the TBS formula tell us then, if we either choose to use no protection or have no way of measuring the efficacy or strength of that protection?

We see that,

$$\text{If } P(t) = 0, \text{ then } D(t) + R(t) = E(t)$$

Not having a protective mechanism, $P(t)$ no longer automatically dictates the security of the system, does it? There is none! The system is not protected, at least in the classic Fortress Mentality sense of the word. The protection is a function of **D(t) + R(t)**. That defines protection. And **E(t)** is that metric.

To extend this thinking:

$$\text{If } P(t) < [D(t) + R(t)], \text{ then } E(t) = \{[D(t) + R(t)] - P(t)\}$$

Meaning, if I can assign some number, or range, or limit of $P(t)$ with some level of confidence, and both **D(t)** and **R(t)** utilize reliable metrics *(in that hyper-better detection technology world)*, then my **E(t)** is reduced by **P(t)**.

Will this ever be achievable? Yes. But only if we think in a more analogue way than we do today.

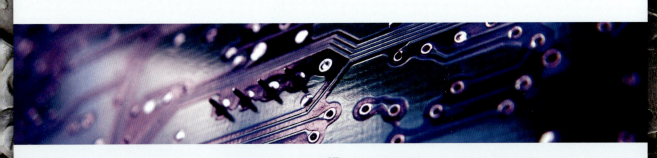

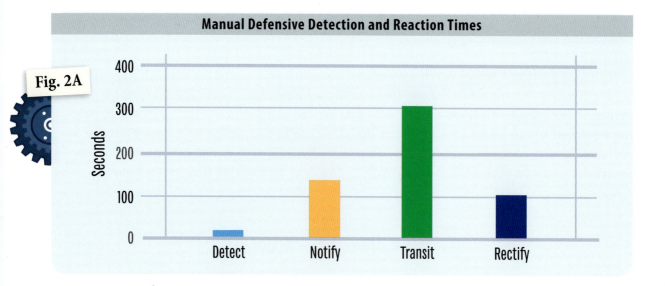

Fig. 2A

REACTIONS

In the well-budgeted security world of disaster recovery and business continuity, companies spend a great deal of time and money planning for the (largely binary) Acts of God and how to reconstitute normal services quickly.

▸ How can we keep the transaction processors operational when the hurricane flattens the data center?

▸ How long does it take to become operational after the highway overpass tumbles on top of our building in the midst of a 7.4 earthquake?

▸ When downtown Chicago (or NYC, etc.) basements flood, how can the call center service our customers?

▸ How can QVC keep selling parasols to its California clientele, when its Florida broadcast facility has been struck by lightning 300 times in the past hour?

"Welcome to Our Company. We are sorry - our security administrator, Dick, is home with his family for the weekend. All criminal hackers and online miscreants are respectfully requested to restrict all attacks to between the hours of 9-5, Monday thru Friday, EST. We thank you for your understanding."

The Basics of Time Based Security

In the Detection/Reaction process in Fig. 2A (*previous page*), an administrator is the human involved in the process and also represents the step with the greatest room for error because it increases **R(t)** unacceptably. Most people hesitate to make the tough decisions quickly. Thus, especially in those cases where **P(t)=0** (or so we assume) and the goal is to limit **E(t)**, for a human reacting to solve a problem by punching the correct key on the administration keyboard, ten seconds can be entirely too long.

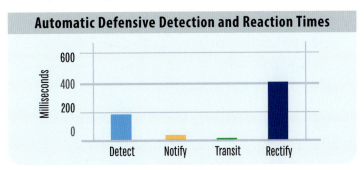

Remember the government security manager from earlier, whose idea of security and response was to manually examine his audit logs every couple of weeks?

To increase the defense of the network, an automated response mechanism (*see Fig. 2B*) is certainly a choice that Time-Based Security encourages, but this is only viable if the appropriate responses are predetermined, based upon a set of input conditions. (For those thinking *SkyNet*, ANS & AI come later!) Thus, if a denial of service attack is under way, a pre-prescribed set of responses should be considered and programmed into the Reaction process. However, if automatic reaction is chosen, one coincident response should be to contact the appropriate humans. In this case, they are side-chain, or OOB, and alerts of the attack (or other security violation) and the actions taken are automatic and without human intervention.

Security should then know exactly what the system did to protect itself, and what state it is in the moment an authorized human takes over. The Administrator can then, with greater leisure, manually invoke other reactions, shut down the automated responses or even try to strike back at the offender. *(Oh, if only...)*

If implemented properly, **R(t)** remains small, and the human element does not degrade **R(t)** or the defensive process. Creating an automatic Reaction process is critical to efficient TBS as it also enforces policy. But, even more importantly, the Administrator (or Root) must be similarly empowered to make tough decisions.

- Is the attack real?
- What was the goal of the attack?
- Is the attack still occurring?
- Did the Reaction Matrix come to the proper conclusion and act accordingly?
- Was the attacker thwarted?
- Do we need to perform a damage assessment?
- What further steps are needed to protect the organization and its resources?
- When can we get the systems back on-line?
- Is further disconnect and systemic shutdown in order?
- Lastly, who is behind the attack and can we nail them?

An issue to be considered is whether automatic responses should tend towards the false-positive or false-negative. A false positive detection/reaction could unintentionally interfere with normal business operations which is not on the highly-desirable list. But false-negatives can permit certain events to occur without a defensive response. Policy and risk decisions must be the deciding factors.

Assume that, based upon a certain detected event, a Reaction Matrix (or suite of options) says to disconnect a subnet of the organization's infrastructure from the rest of the enterprise, in order to protect its assets. The people within that division might not exactly be happy about being disconnected from the world, but that particular reaction was chosen to isolate the attack and limit potential damage. The so-called 'sacrificing of a pawn' to protect the king is a well-understood and rational strategy in any form of conflict – and applies in network security, as well. In this case, it's not so much sacrificial, as it is a Graceful Degradation, until Remediation is complete.

The Basics of Time Based Security

Again, all can be measured in the TIME domain.

Which is the *best* of the two bad options? Plan for this!

OK, I do tend to use Administrator and Root somewhat interchangably to account for myriad installations and policies. If it's "my bad", so be it.

Depending upon the business, the policies and tolerance for risk, shutting the whole "thing" down, although perhaps painful, can be superior to what would happen if it stayed up while under attack.

Administrators must, now more than ever, be empowered to make these sorts of tough decisions that affect business operations. They must be empowered by the top management in the organization – and supported when they act according to policy. Security administrators are historically placed in an unenviable position: they are held accountable when things go wrong, but not given the authority to take drastic (re) actions without the blessing of the CISO/CIO/CTO/CEO/Legal/Compliance or even the Board of Directors.

Any such additional human intervention in the Reaction process is anathema to effective Time-Based Security. Management's empowerment of the front-line network administrator to conduct rapid triage is necessary to limit R(t) and effectively increase the defensive posture of the network. It may be a tough pill to swallow for old-time managers, but a necessary component of TBS.

Physical "TBS" Metaphors

Upper management needs help understanding security and models. So, here are a few little metaphors to cut and paste when you're trying to explain these concepts to the bean counters.

Depending upon how long the intruders take to do their job, which probably exceeds the **D(t)** of the sensors, their activity will be sensed. Now, the last step is to build in a response, **R**. Some possibilities for detection and response in the physical world are found in the charts below.

PHYSICAL DETECTION

Alarms	"D" Time	Trigger Event
Door Alarms	~15 secs	Incorrect code entry
Window Alarms	~0.1 sec	Electrical discontinuity
Sound Alarms	~0.235 sec	>58 db/SPL
Motion Sensors	~0.7 sec	0.2 fps
Heat Sensors	~1.2 sec	95 F/10 sec
Vibration Sensors	~0.45 sec	0.32 kj

PHYSICAL REACTION

Reaction	"R" Time	Reaction Method
Loud Alarm	~125 secs	Sound
Alert Alarm Co.	~3.5 secs	Hard-wired
Alert Alarm Co.	~22 secs	Dial-up on telephone
False Alarm Analysis	~75 secs	Off-site at Alarm Co.
Call Police	~18 secs	Dial-up on telephone
Police Respond	>120 secs	Dispatcher voice

From the available options, our physical security system designers choose the appropriate detection and response mechanisms to implement while keeping in mind that the sum of their times must be less than the time value offered by **P**, which has been specified by the vault or safe manufacturers.

Now, let's consider a smaller facility; perhaps an office, or even your home. Alarm companies will come wire-up your house to "protect" against burglars. **In reality, such companies aren't offering any protection at all.** They are providing detection and reaction services. They wire your windows and doors to detect an intruder and alert the police.

In the physical world when you want to enter your *secure and protected* office in the morning, the same logic applies. You put your key in the lock and then open the door. The detection mechanism wrapped around the door (or perhaps a sonic/motion detector) now knows the door is open, but it doesn't know if you're a good guy or a bad guy. So it waits. When the system was installed, you were probably told that you have 15 or 20 or 30 seconds to run like heck to the alarm box hidden inside the coat closet and enter the correct password or code sequence. If you remember that there's an alarm, and if you succeed in entering the correct code within the prescribed amount of time, the detection mechanism now knows who you are (theoretically) and will turn off the reaction mechanism. (It won't call the cops.)

If, however, you forget to enter the code, or if it's a bad guy dumb enough to break into a facility with a big [Alarm and Protection Company] decal stuck on the windows, the detection device will wait the programmed amount of time and tell the reaction mechanism to do its thing. Likely (and it's happened to me countless times) an [Alarm and Protection Company] employee will call. He will ask for a verbal code and, if you're a legitimate employee, you will scrounge through your wallet or purse and nervously recite it to him. No cops or guards wildly waving guns will show up immediately.

Depending upon the chosen reaction mechanism, though, maybe no call will come to your office, and instead you *will* find yourself face-to-face with a Magnum .357. Explanations have to be fast… and good!

Think about protection, P, now. Storefronts are "protected" by panes of glass; negligible protection at best. **So, for security, these stores rely far more upon detection and reaction systems, than protection technology.**

To revisit our personal lives, remember that residential windows and locks alone offer minimal protection. Let's say that a hypothetical home security system employs a yard pressure gauge (perimeter). When it senses something more than 20kgs present, it might turn on interior lights as a deterrence factor and/or it may increase the sensitivity of other home security sensors (e.g., SIEMs). Thus, if a sonic alarm detects unexpected disturbances at the doors or windows where it should be nearly silent, the system might self-activate (react) for faster communications to the Alarm and Protection Company. In addition, pets might wear ID collars or get implants to avoid false alarms (ACL rules).

Home alarm systems offer a variety of detection-reaction mechanisms to suit the lifestyle of the occupants along with *nearly* real-time mobile notifications, but home protection is still only 1/8" thick (glass pane).

As you are probably thinking by now, **"What happens if I have no protection? What do I do?"**

DIVIDE BY TIME

Let's make up some stuff based upon what we have covered on Time-Based Security basics. Some analogue security ideas. Maybe they're OK. Maybe not. They are just some ideas that I hope, if of value, others can build on.

First (funny) assumption: You actually know where the "crown jewels" are located in your networks. *(For explanatory purposes, we won't discuss the copies, backups and archives.)* Second: you have some reasonable idea of the size of the crown jewel dataset. Err on the small side.

BW stands for Bandwidth of the channel. The size of a database is |DB|. In the following example, we will assume that both the internal and external data throughput and upper limit is 1GB/sec.

We apply:

$$\frac{|DB|}{BW} = \max EXF(t) \text{ (data exfiltration time)}$$

If the financial folks have some sense of the value of the data in question, answers start appearing. Like: If the crown jewels are 1TB in size, and worth 1/2 the value of a company valued at $50M, what fiscal effort should be put forth, over what period of time, to protect that dataset from improper access or distribution? Using EXF(t), one question pops right up: should more effort and resources be applied to more detection and reaction technologies than conventional defensive/protective approaches?

Let's say that this 1TB dataset is not needed for high speed access on a regular basis. A law firm's files; trading or bank data; PHI, PII, IP and code... the usual suspects.

Over the network's 1Gb backbone:

$$\frac{1TB}{1Gb/sec} = 10,000 \text{ sec}$$
(just under 3 hrs)

Now, let's reduce the bandwidth to this dataset *(given we know where it is, of course!)* to 10Mb, because we don't need it often.

$$\frac{1TB}{10 \text{ Mb}} = 1,000,000 \text{ sec}$$
(1.65 weeks)

For fast guesstimation and bar-napkin approximation, I decree one byte = 10 bits, including data and overhead. We're talking orders of magnitude here, not <7% errors.

TCP/IP Overhead + Ethernet Tagging + IPsec, Session, and Application Overhead leaves us with 87.7% available data transmission. Over HTTP, another 25% can evaporate quickly. So, divide by 10 is close enough.

OK? Cool.

Padding

An entirely different approach may have some value, and actually has been one of the arrows in the crypto-world's quiver: data padding buffering. In a world where data storage is arguably close to free, dataset size is almost a non-issue.

$$\frac{|DB|}{BW} = \max EXF(t)$$

$$\frac{1GB}{1Gb/sec} = 10 \text{ secs}$$
(data exfiltration time)

But, if the high value data is padded:

$$\frac{500GB}{10Mb/sec} = 50,000 \text{ secs}$$
(~14hrs - plenty of time to detect)

By padding certain select datasets with what I imagine could be simple options in databases and, of course, keeping increased detection in mind, does a measurable reduction in risk, of a factor of 50, warrant consideration? *(Just think of the many ways to "scramble" the padded datasets further with a cryptographic approach. The more obfuscation, the better.)*

COMPRESSORS & LIMITERS

In the analogue audio world, compressors and limiters are used to control the dynamic range of signals.

In this case, in order to keep things from getting too loud, we limit the dynamic range (the min-max for audio loudness/volume) of the signal, so that it will always be between specified upper and lower limits. Compression became "necessary" with the popularity of car radios. Because of road noise, the quiet sections of the music had to be increased to be heard, and the loud sections were turned down, resulting in almost the entire song being played at the same volume.

What does this have to do with security?

Let's examine a process called bandwidth limiting. A normal network design goal is to provide as much bandwidth for maximum data throughput. In this example, however, let's add a reaction matrix from TBS

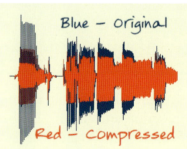

This wave demonstrates the pinching effect of audio compressors. In Chapter 6 you will see its similarity to "Squeezing the Loop" in OODA.

A limiter is essentially a compressor, reducing the loudest signals to a maximum limit, and not permitting any audio level to reach 0.

The Basics of Time Based Security

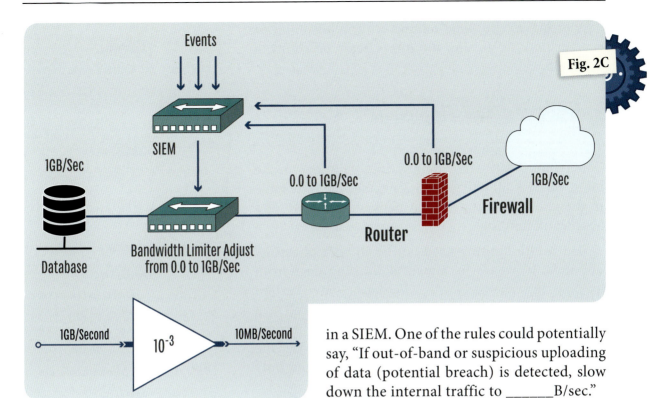

Fig. 2C

In fact, firewall vendors might find it useful to add bandwidth limiting to their next, or next-next, Next Gen devices.

in a SIEM. One of the rules could potentially say, "If out-of-band or suspicious uploading of data (potential breach) is detected, slow down the internal traffic to _____ B/sec."

Instead of the binary decision to totally shut down all traffic, this approach *(mapped above in Fig. 2C)* provides high degrees of granularity. Does this mean all traffic is slowed? Maybe. That would be part of the design of the Reaction Matrix. The bandwidth limiter could be designed with sufficient granularity to choose which protocols and ports are affected by any decisions from the Reaction Matrix or human administrator.

What is the measurable advantage with this approach? It goes back to risk. In Time-Based Security:

Let's assume we have measured and accepted that $E(t)$ is 1 sec. *(Just to make the math easy.)*

$$P(t) > D(t) + (R(t)$$

$$\text{If } P(t)=0, \text{ then: } E(t) = D(t) + R(t)$$

A breach to the cloud follows a formula similar to current-limiting in any dimmer circuit powering a lightbulb.

$$BW = |DB|/Time$$

Maximum data extrication rate is 1GB/Sec. In one hour, 3.6TB would be potentially extricated. The table to the left demonstrates what happens when we add bandwidth limiting.

Bandwidth limiting need not be all encompassing, nor must it always be aimed at limiting data from leaving internal networks. Perhaps, only certain domains, departments or locations are suspect in a security event. Therefore, adding bandwidth limiting to routers offers an opportunity to decrease the potential Exposure measured in data, instead of only in time.

Bandwidth compressors are conceptually the same, but have a lower limit that is greater than "0" bits per second. Maybe I'm wrong, but it seems to me that the compressor is useless for our purposes because, wanting maximum control, the limiter provides an adjustable bandwidth of:

1GB/sec

Time	//	Data Extricated
1 sec		1 GB
1 min		60 GB
1 hr		3.6 TB

100MB/sec

Time	//	Data Extricated
1 sec		100 MB
1 min		6 GB
1 hr		360 GB

90% reduction in data extraction

10MB/sec

Time	//	Data Extricated
1 sec		10 MB
1 min		600 MB
1 hr		36 GB

99% reduction in data extraction

1MB/sec

Time	//	Data Extricated
1 sec		1 MB
1 min		60 MB
1 hr		3 GB

99.9% reduction in data extraction

$$\text{"0" Throughput} < \text{Actual Throughput} < \text{Max Throughput} < \infty$$

...whereas a compressor would never be able to stop traffic altogether, since it's lower limit is always greater than zero.

3
WTF... Analogue?

Tide Predicting Machine No. 2, public domain, U.S. Government, used 1910 to 1965.

The Brain

They used to say we only use 10% of our brain. Forget that. It's wrong. Neuroscience is in its infancy… just learning.

The brain is, however, the greatest approximation machine we can conceive.

The brain computes poorly, but averages stuff amazingly well. Computers compute well; we are just learning how to make them approximate.

ANNs (Artificial Neural Networks) attempt to approximate the way the brain works. There are lots of competing models, but they all have one thing in common:

Analogue-ish-ness.

Lots more on analogue synaptic weighting and how it applies to security later.

This is all about **synaptic weighting** in both neuroscience and the physical representation of brain-like behavior.

The Brain is far from being a computer.

ANALOGUE 101

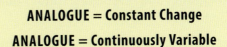

ANALOGUE = Constant Change

ANALOGUE = Continuously Variable

Technically, analogue means continuously variable. That is, there are no discernable (depending upon scale, or granularity) stairsteps of consequence.

After leaving the audio industry where analogue reigned supreme, I ventured into the nascent days of the digitally driven personal computer field. Thankfully, my foray into digital audio had prepared me a bit for this.

I was the only one in the company who spoke analogue engineering, yet found myself managing the *marketing* of machines and peripherals. As one might expect, I was often called upon to help out the purely digital folks, and one day, the sales V.P. – who didn't know bits from shinola – came to me and quietly asked, "What's the difference between analogue and digital?" My mouth moved before thinking. "Round wheels are analogue. Square wheels are digital."

With my new title, V.P of Round Wheels, I explained how audio is really nothing more than complex sine waves.

WTF, Analogue?

One of the best examples of a sine wave, is the volume of your favorite record coming from a set of speakers. Imagine this as a graph: *voltage* on the vertical y-axis representing the sound volume with *time* on the horizontal x-axis. The oscillations (ups and downs along the x-axis) that occur in a given time period represent the sound's *frequency*. More oscillations means a higher frequency and fewer means the frequency is lower.

> The sine wave is the curve pattern of the math function of the same name. It represents a repetitive oscillation based upon amplitude and frequency.

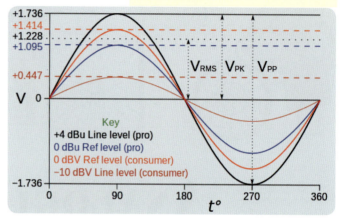

To create the sound, the analogue electrical signal in the power amplifier is converted (or, transduced) to analogue electromagnetic energy in the speaker coil, which can then move the speaker's cone (the cardboard or piezo bit), which in turn moves the air in analogue patterns of sound that finally descend upon the human hearing apparatus. In analogue receipt, the brain then does its own analogue synaptic weighing and averaging, and voila: we can perceive the Beatles!

Another physical example of analogue functioning is a continuously variable transmission, which has no gears. The belt moves up and down the tapered cylinders instead of using more traditional discrete gear shifting.

Continuously variable is the key. Digital is discrete. Right? Soon, the entire staff knew the difference between analogue and digital.

WTF, Analogue?

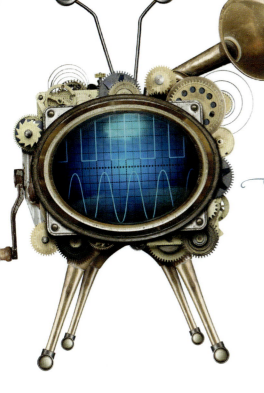

Square Waves
ARE ANALOGUE
(in disguise)

A SQUARE WAVE IS SUPPOSED TO BE, WELL, SQUARE. BUT IT ISN'T! NOT IN THE LEAST. We mentally picture a pure square wave when ideating circuits.

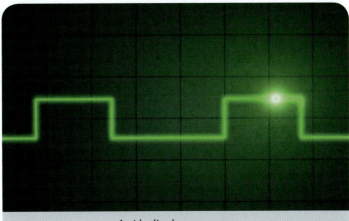

An idealized square wave.

Chip manufacturers have an entirely different set of digital problems at high speeds and nanometer proximity. Quantum effects get in the way all over.

A square wave purports to show an instantaneous change in voltage from (nominally) 0 to 5 volts, for example. Yet there is no such thing (outside of quantum weirdness) as instantaneity. The change actually takes some amount of time, as shown on the next page in Fig. 3C. The ostensibly vertical leading edge of the wave is actually at an angle, with an analogue increase of voltage over time, appropriately called *rise-time*.

==But square waves are even more analogue than that!==
A high speed rise in voltage always causes an overshot. The initial voltage spike will cause the wave to rise above the target nominal 5 volts, fall a little below 5 volts, then 'ring' with analogue variations until settling at the appropriate voltage.

Ringing is also the reason some audio amplifier/speaker combinations sound like crap.

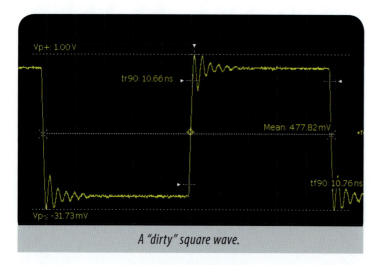

A "dirty" square wave.

Ringing in digital circuits is the manifestation of certain inherent instabilities. Using simple circuits, much of the ringing (or, analogue noise) can be filtered out so that a much cleaner signal is achieved. This results in higher speeds, lower voltages, and fewer errors.

I know I am pushing the point, but hell, it's my book. Even the smallest thought might trigger a reader to make a huge breakthrough! This may not, but it's yet another important view of the digital-analogue duality I see in networking.

IS SPACETIME ANALOGUE?

NASA Research on x-ray and gamma-ray data shows that spacetime is smooth down to distances one billion times smaller than the nucleus of a hydrogen atom. We're in Planck range here. Other than at that deep level of granularity, it's all pretty analogue.

Digital Is Not Binary

I HAVE COME TO HATE BINARY THINKING. Our attachment to it has definitely screwed us up. In court, lawyers routinely ask yes or no questions – to which there is no sane yes or no answer – of a witness, who is still forced to give a binary answer.

Binary means ON or OFF.

Why are we learning to behave like a computer? Shouldn't it be the other way around? Just sayin'...

Let's say I ask you a simple question: Do you like country music? Before you respond, what exactly does that mean? Is there a defined yes or no answer? Or is there a spectrum of possible answers: early country, country rock, only Lynyrd Skynyrd, pop country top forty, or maybe Kid Rock? Or, do you give country a 2 out of 10, but classic rock a 9.5? **There is a spectrum of possible answers.** *Not* binary.

"That kid has Asperger's Syndrome." Well, what does that mean? Is Asperger's a binary condition, as in you either have it or you don't? No, it's actually a spectrum disorder that sits within another, the Autism Spectrum. The severity of the symptoms varies. They are continuums, which is an analogue concept.

In our field, "Is your network secure?" is a **Gotcha! Question**, with no believable, binary answer. What the hell does **secure** even mean? In the context of Time-Based Security and other Analogue Network Security approaches, perhaps we can find a glimmer of a metric.

We live and work and play in a digital world, but does that mean we have to transform humanity into digitally compatible carbon units? It's pretty easy to argue that the computer industry has attempted to make people adapt to the needs of the digital machine without much in the reverse.

I get it. We're experimenting, much as we do with robots. Robots that attempt to mimic human anatomy are creepy. Robots that look like… well, robots, are cool.

Point is: what is wrong with attempting to defy the binary-digital dogma of existing security approaches by introducing analogue functionality? If you accept that an analogue revisit of security might be of value, I implore you to give up on binary knee-jerk responses. Really think about it!

- Add "what-if" conditions to every question-answer set.
- Add subtlety, vagueness, and grayness.
- Add granularity to the discussion.
- Consider the **scale** you are using.
- Are there binary preconceived beliefs, biases, or operating tenets that trigger binary response?
- Respond as if 0 and 1, yes and no, do not exist.
- "It depends" is a powerful analytical response.
- Think fuzzy.

What if your light switch also has a dimmer? Is the light *on, partially-on,* or *dimmed*?

MAN VS. MACHINE

Computer: Back pain from poor ergonomics.

Monitor: Better than paper tape or Nixi tubes. Eye strain manifests 20 years earlier than sans monitor.

Mouse: Point-and-click is cool. Carpal tunnel, not so much.

Mobile: Looking down at a mobile screen adds kilograms to the strain on the vertebrae. Imagine all the millennials with Hunchback Syndrome in 2050! Just sayin'.

My wife just asked me, "What's the largest tree in the world?" My brain rattled between Sequoias, Banyans, and Mushrooms. "Define what you mean by 'largest.'" We ate a lot of Google data coming to an agreeable working definition. We should do a helluva lot more of that in everything we do.

Is It Analogue?

In any conversation of import, think about the difference in results with both analogue and binary thinking. You will be surprised at what happens.

Simple Question	Analogue Thinking	Binary Thinking
Is the network secure?	Define security, parameters, environment, and the granularity of the time function.	Yes.
Is her hair brown?	The CMYK value is an average close to 43, 65, 92, 44.	Yes.
What is the length of the coastline?	It depends on the measuring device and where the start and endpoints are defined.	1000 km.
What would Yoda say?		Do or do not. *(Hey, it's Yoda!)*
Will a lawyer screw you over?	> 0, but indeterminate at all times.	Yes, of course they will.
How far over the speed limit will get you a ticket?	Depends on the cops' moods.	The law is the law, nothing over the speed limit is tolerated.
Are movies a curve?	We see movies as continuous, fluid movement.	Created with frames per second, with each still frame flashing by quickly enough to yield analogue perception of movement.
Are you certain of your beliefs in deity?	Agnosticism: I'm not (and cannot be) 100% sure.	Atheist / Theist: I'm 100% sure.

THE MIN-MAX APPROACH

In my old audio days, the parametric equalizer was a thing of beauty. It was the ultimate audio waveform shaping tool, with more control than ever, using purely analogue electronic circuits.

As with the design, testing, and maintenance of any system, it was standard procedure to "exercise" each

circuit. That meant quickly twisting knobs in various combinations, testing the full spectrum of the circuits, and their extremes.

The Min-Max approach was normal for us. It is so analogue and so easily represented, as in time-based security and other analogue methods.

> -24db < Set < +24db
> *Signal Strength*
>
> 300Hz < Set < 1800Hz
> *Center Frequency of Signal Strength*
>
> 0.4 < Q Set < 90
> *Bandwidth & Bandpass Characteristics*

All this says is that the amount of amplification for a specific center frequency with a variable bandwidth defined by Q, ranges from -24db to +24db, for a total Min-Max of 48db. From this, it's easy to conceptualize with this analogy of an automotive engine:

> 0 < Idle Set < Max RPM Pre-Failure
> *Engine Speed*
>
> 0(t) < Set < 10,000(t)
> *User Logon Load*
> *(measured in Users Over Time, of course)*

So, is this immediately of value to the security and network engineer? Remember that much of Analogue Network Security is about a change in our traditional methods of strategic thinking.

Earlier, I suggested adding the variable of "time" to network and security discussions, both in the questions and the answers. **Let me further suggest that we add another question to any discussion: "What are the Min-Max conditions?"**

IS IT BLACK OR WHITE?

In fact, it's neither. Black is the absence of all color in light *(or the mixture of all colors physically)*. White is the absence of physical color, but the perfect combination of all frequencies in the visible electromagnetic spectrum. Absolute zero (0° Kelvin) is not achievable; nothing is truly black or white. Instead, everything is a shade of gray.

This fact gives us another perfect example of a Min-Max approach using analogue-speak.

> Black < Shades of Gray < White
>
> 0 < Shades of Gray < 1
> *(or vice versa for non-light)*
>
> White < Shades of Gray < Black

Lesson Learned: When people say, "It's either black or white," choose to take a closer, more granular view. It could be a fractal!

The Ladies' Room

Whether at a sports or entertainment event, here in the U.S., we know that the lines to the ladies' rooms are **always** longer than those for the men's rooms. This discrimination is due to poorly conceived political correctness and the infinite wisdom of elected officials and architects. Their attempts at gender equality are *epic fails* due to binary thinking.

> "For equality, all restrooms shall have the same number of square feet and facilities."

The analogue metric of time was not factored into the original equation, and thus, as genteelly as possible: visits to restrooms generally take women longer on average (hence the lines). Of course, there *are* public venues, restaurants, etc. worldwide which do not face this problem because the restrooms are unisex. I honestly do not know how this has not become a global standard, but I am sure there are some historians who could fill me in.

Let's say, all things being equal, that there is an equal representation of male and female attendees at a given event. If everyone – on average – required the same amount of time for a rest stop, then an equal number of square feet and facilities would make sense.

However, ladies just simply need more time since their 'restroom visits' involve more steps, the desire/need for privacy, etc. What does the math say? A few assumptions for example's sake *(next column)*:

1. Men require "X" time, with less need for privacy.
2. Women require "2X" time to complete their tasks.
   (Number chosen for example only… no hate mail, please.)

$$M(t) = \frac{W(t)}{2}$$

Thus, with equal facilities provided, the extended line for ladies was all but pre-ordained. All I did here was consider 'time' to be the primary variable, and use that in calculating the unfair advantage men have in most of these public settings.

Let me suggest, that when confronted with many common-place situations, which on the surface appear to defy common-sense, try applying time as the common denominator. You will be surprised at how many confounded situations become clear with such an approach.

APPLYING MIN-MAX TO NEGOTIATIONS

In Singapore, I wanted to have a few dress shirts made. There are hundreds of tailors, so I just guessed and picked one. "John" handed me a water and asked me for my budget per shirt. I retorted, "What are the cheapest and the most expensive options, and why?" I wanted to understand the entire spectrum of possibilities, then weigh them based on taste, material, details, and budget. Bob's question addressed a spectrum that was too broad for me to give an answer without more information first.

Choosing at random is very analogue, eh? No fundamental basis for the choice. Pure guess, in a Bayesian sense.

(Bayes' Theorem is a way to quantify uncertainty, to calculate the probability of any given future outcome or conclusion. Essentially, you start with a guess.)

$$\$0 < \text{Shirt Price} < \$\infty$$

Which approach is right? Neither. It's a matter of what kind of answer you are looking for. Replying with, "I can spend $10 per shirt," would have given me a very narrow answer and fewer options from the tailor. I knew John didn't want to waste anyone's time, including his own.

I prefer to know the upper and lower boundaries within a defined environment.

THE FASTEST COMPUTER

The U.S. and China lead supercomputer development where millions of multi-core processors and GPUs are grouped to create insane speeds. The U.S. A21, and competing Chinese efforts with exa-scale (10^{18} or 1,000+ peta-flops) computing, should be online shortly.

That's more than 400 times the speed of 2007's computing Top Dog, with a mere 0.28 peta-flops under the hood. Zetta-scale computing (10^{21}) is estimated to arrive in 2030. What's the upper limit? Or is a quantum-von-Neumann hybrid the way to go? But I really don't care about that. I just have a question to ask.

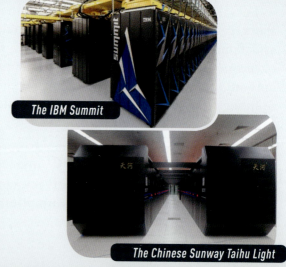

The IBM Summit

The Chinese Sunway Taihu Light

==What is the fastest that a non-quantum computer can process, calculate, store, retrieve, and transmit data?== You might think the answer has already been stated earlier, but I mean EXACTLY: What's the *smallest* time unit in a modern computer?

How about in an iPhone? Or in an Xbox? What will be the smallest time unit in a computer in 2030 or 2040?

The answer is the same everywhere: one clock cycle. With a purely reductionist view, one clock cycle is the current indivisible digital unit of computing measurement. The speed of the data processing is measured in cycles per time unit, like a 3.8GHz processor or a 300 baud modem.

Using Time-Based Security concepts, the theoretically best-case scenario (which is impossible in the real world) of Detecting and Reacting to an event is:

> Limit > 1 cycle D(t)
> and
> Limit > 1 cycle R(t)
> *therefore*
> Limit (Dt + Rt) > 2 cycles

In this optimized and idealized limit, this also means that the maximum exposure to the target data is 2 clock cycles, a *meh* data breach by any standards.

Let's just take this to a little logicum-absurdum: How much data can you lose in 8 clock cycles?

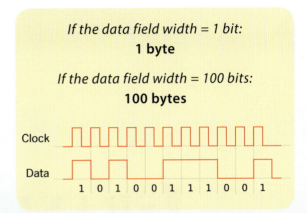

In the future, will we combine massive multi-core computing with massively wide storage registers and communication paths? I don't know, but wider *words* offer one possible approach to faster computers – and more data loss in a given period of time!

Detection requires processing time in the real world, as does reaction. Obviously we cannot detect an event or react to an event in only one clock cycle.

Or can we? What about using wider words in a Detection/Reaction Protocol? With a little analogue thinking... maybe.

> **Throughout, I will be making constant reference to "thinking in an analogue fashion," in an attempt to make binary-ism anathema to your security efforts.**

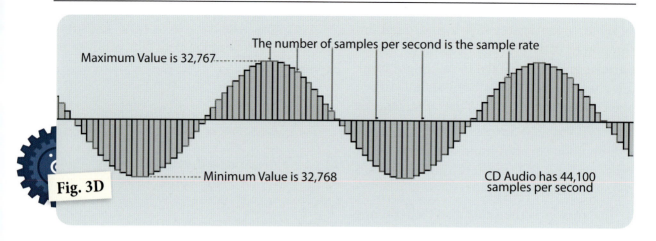

Fig. 3D

Granularity
in Digital Audio

When IT and network security folks talk about **granularity**, it is often referencing how detailed administrative functions can be made. Does a rule-set affect the entire user population? (Call it A.) Or was it designed for specific groups or locations, a subset B within the original A, or $B \subseteq A$.

Granularity refers to the level of detail in a set of given data.

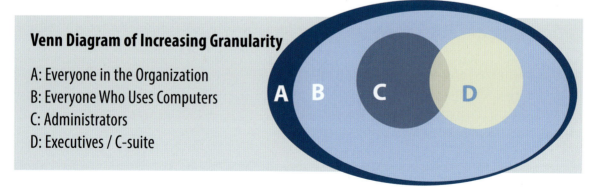

Venn Diagram of Increasing Granularity

A: Everyone in the Organization
B: Everyone Who Uses Computers
C: Administrators
D: Executives / C-suite

Let's look at granularity with a time function added and see what happens.

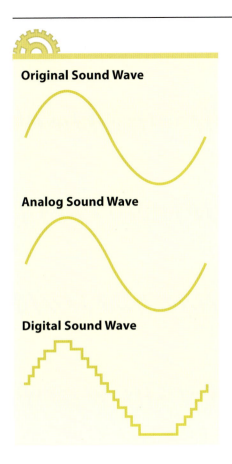

Original Sound Wave

Analog Sound Wave

Digital Sound Wave

An audio signal is analogue, but the digital representation of that same signal is anything but smooth or continuous. It's stairstepped! *(Note that the x-axis is time, and the y-axis is intensity – or volume – of an analogue audio signal.)*

Two digital representations are made in the process of digitization, and they both contribute to the overall sound quality. The first is called the sampling rate *(see Fig. 3D on previous page)*. How often (**time!**) is a sample or snapshot of the analogue volume taken? The more often a sample is taken, the better quality and reproduction of the higher frequencies. CD audio, for example, is sampled at 44.1KHz, thus providing close to sonic purity for signals below the Nyquist frequency (or at least to the upper threshold of human hearing, approximately 20KHz).

If we sampled at 22.05KHz, (half the CD's rate) then the upper frequency would be only about 10KHz; less sonic purity because of less granularity. In this case, the granularity of the sampling process determines the frequency response (**another time function**) of the audio signal. (FM was superior to AM radio in part because of the wider frequency response in their allocated spectrum.)

The second digital representation in sampling is the **bit depth** of the specific sample. The more granularity, the better the signal from a greater dynamic range and signal-to-noise ratio. An old Atari video game from the 80s used 8-bit PCM (Pulse Code Modulation) audio. Today, the pros use highly granular 24-bit depth with the general prosumer standard at a less granular, but eminently acceptable, 16-bit.

As we discuss security, remember that granularity is an oft-overlooked analogue variable despite its daily use.

You Can Add Them Easily

One of the really cool things about analogue is that you can add (combine/mix) two or more analogue signals quite easily. Let's think audio here, since I am supposed to know that stuff.

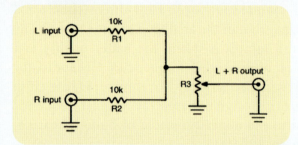

Two audio signals enter on the left. A super-simple resistive summing network (yes, network!) mixes the two in equal amounts because R1 = R2. R3 is the volume control, and the output adds L + R into a mono signal. You can just as easily mix dissimilar frequencies.

When we mix these simple A and B waveform signals shown below, to the right, we get signal C. In audio this would be two very clear tones heard at the same time, a more complex waveform.

Now, look at color for a moment. Mixing two or more colors is just mixing frequencies of source or reflective light, creating complex electromagnetic waveforms. Fourier analysis can filter and isolate narrow frequency bands of a complex waveform.

These powerful tools make for enhanced detection of otherwise, potentially hidden information. Below, we see a stereo audio complex waveform. The taller bits are louder than the shorter ones. Is this Beethoven or Hendrix? A penetrating scream echoing for seconds?

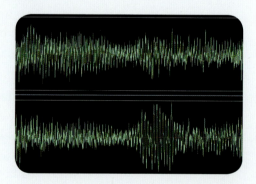

As we explore Analogue Network Security, we will be combining (mixing) different dynamic data streams and filtering them to enhance detection in depth.

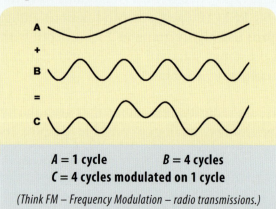

A = 1 cycle   *B* = 4 cycles
C = 4 cycles modulated on 1 cycle

(Think FM – Frequency Modulation – radio transmissions.)

Smoothing Functions

Have you ever watched high speed slow motion videos of water balloons bursting, bullets piercing watermelons, or milk hitting a countertop? These are filmed at high rates like 1,000 to 25,000 to nearly 200,000 fps in order to capture the desired amount of detail when played in slow motion. YouTube it!

When you watch a movie on TV, in a movie theater, with your old 8mm projector, or streaming, is the video analogue? In other words, is the video a continuously variable, uninterrupted experience or is it the opposite, flashing on and off? Despite my persistence to think analogue, the answer is no! It is the latter.

We experience video as analogue, but it is actually digital. Video is broken up into frames, thus the measurement fps, or frames per second. The human eye-to-brain circuit smoothes out the edges – the sudden transitions from one frame to the next – so that we only sense continuous smooth motion. Averaging.

75

Pixels also operate in much the same way. If we look at an image from afar on a computer or television screen, we see something more realistic and smooth than if we zoom in on a smaller area. In fact, the further we zoom in, the more the originally smooth picture reveals itself as a set of gridded multicolored squares.

The pixel is the smallest digital visual element. The more pixels you have per square inch, the better the image will look at large sizes without excessive pixelation.

We humans do this smoothing function automatically, but in audio we must do this manually. To the right at the top of the box, we see a noisy signal. Basically, this means that there are lots of little variations which have no bearing on the meaning of the lower frequency analogue information. A smoothing function *(we call them filters)* can be applied to the noisy wave to remove some portion of the variance. This makes the signal more usable.

Our eye-to-brain system averages perception into something meaningful – an analogue experience! – with its own smoothing functions. We allow the preponderance of our sight to be quite hazy, since we also naturally focus on only a tiny portion of our visual field. Luckily our brain can integrate data very quickly as we need to adjust focus. *(Think reading.)*

But at some point, zooming-in causes the resolution to be so bad that we cannot interpret anything meaningful from the data. It can be useful to step back and take the analogue view.

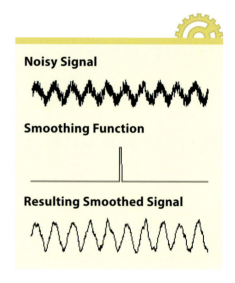

Business decisions are often heavily influenced by trending, without the need for exact figures.

WTF, Analogue?

THE POWER
OF PERCEPTION

During the Vietnam U.S. military draft, a patriotic doctor reported my color blindness to the Air Force, causing them to aggressively recruit me for my prized medical disability. I would be a human bomb sighter used to spot camouflage over the jungles of Southeast Asia.

My color perception, greatly influenced by brightness, texture, and proximity, is vastly different than 'normal' people - the middle of the bell curve. (That's 68% of *normal*. Also, as you will care later, 1-Sigma.) I grew up seeing things no one else could see, but I was missing a great deal of the beauty that others could appreciate.

When an entire population's color perceptions are measured, the bell curve is a fair, first-cut representation of probability distribution. Color-challenged folks are on the left, and those with super color vision (known as tetrachromacy) are on the right.

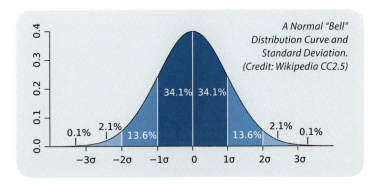

A Normal "Bell" Distribution Curve and Standard Deviation. (Credit: Wikipedia CC2.5)

Perception is a funny thing. The green and white image below is almost painful to look at; all those distorted lines and boxes seem to be in constant motion. The brain is simply trying to make sense of the addition of two dots to each square.

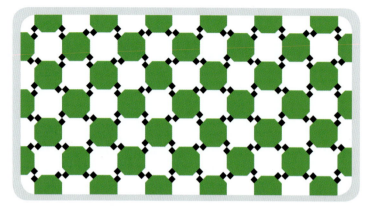

Our brains attempt to average and approximate things in order to get as close as possible to understanding the world around us, rationally, from a plethora of sensory inputs. Our averaging engine filters out all the useless stuff unless we need to focus on it. As mentioned earlier, the human eye-to-brain circuit only focuses on a small portion of our field of vision. The rest is fuzzy or unseen, but the experience is exceedingly adaptable as we flutter our eyes and attention with saccadic movements..

My evolving thoughts on network security are similarly a matter of using a different mode of perception. I find I am more comfortable adding an analogue view to the current predominantly static, digital one. It helps bring clarity to many compelling security problems.

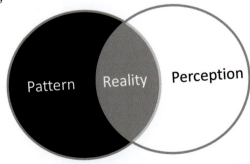

Flatland

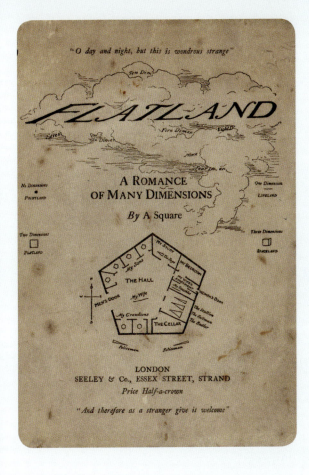

If you have not read the brilliantly insightful 1884 book by Edwin Abbott, *Flatland: A Romance of Many Dimensions*, then **stop!** Do not pass go.

I can give you the gist. It's a world of 2D intelligent creatures. Citizens of Flatland – males, females, priests, etc. – are differentiated by their perimeter shapes: super pointed, square, circle... They are a happy people.

One day at a 2D picnic, the Flatlanders (as they are known) suddenly see something they cannot explain! This is what they see:

> A small dot.
>
> The dot gets larger.
>
> And larger, becoming a small circle.
>
> Then the circle gets bigger and bigger.
>
> And bigger, still! It's still a perfect circle.
>
> Then it grows smaller and smaller.
>
> The circle becomes a dot again.
>
> The dot gets even smaller.
>
> And disappears.

The Flatlanders are so confused. What did they see?*

Flatterland by Ian Stewart and *Spaceland* (go 4D!) by Rudy Rucker are mind-messing "must reads," too, IMHO.

*SPOILER ALERT! A 3-dimensional sphere was passing through 2-dimensional Flatland.

Trending

Trending is the tendency to move in a particular direction.

Do we really care that a particular Famous Person Who's Famous for Being Famous generated 1,340,567 likes, shares, or retweets during May, and that this number increased to 5,319,902 in June? Or, will a simple trending curve *(yes, analogue)* gives us a better view of the information we want?

Business decisions are often heavily influenced by trending without needing to consult the exact figures. This is especially true when dozens or more of both independent and dependent variables (subjects, topics, objects) must be evaluated in a decision-making process.

Humans can input and process a tremendous amount of information using visual aids: graphics, charts, pictures. We continue to evolve competing methods of displaying vast amounts of data in a meaningful way. Our brains are extraordinary approximation engines and we excel at processing continuous streams of analogue information coming in through all of our sensory inputs.

With a well-designed visual analogue representation, the brain can process *the big picture* (strategic) and then choose where to drill down and focus on more granular data (tactical). Stock trending existed long before LinkedIn, Twitter, Facebook, etc.

Another example: I give a lot of presentations. I always request a cheap, but large enough, old-fashioned, ugly analogue clock, set to the correct time with a fresh set of batteries. It's so much easier to grok the amount of remaining time I have with a quick glance at an analogue data source versus a digital one where *(even super simple)* math is required. It's a distraction.

But maybe that's just old, analogue Winn.

The Big Picture. The Executive Overview. Ballparking.

An easy, everyday way to grasp this concept? Think about all the features available on digital maps: zoom, street view, rotate. When you want to see your house, you zoom way in so that you can see much greater detail than when looking at your entire neighborhood. Zoom way out and you've found Management Porn Nirvana. ("I don't need the details...")

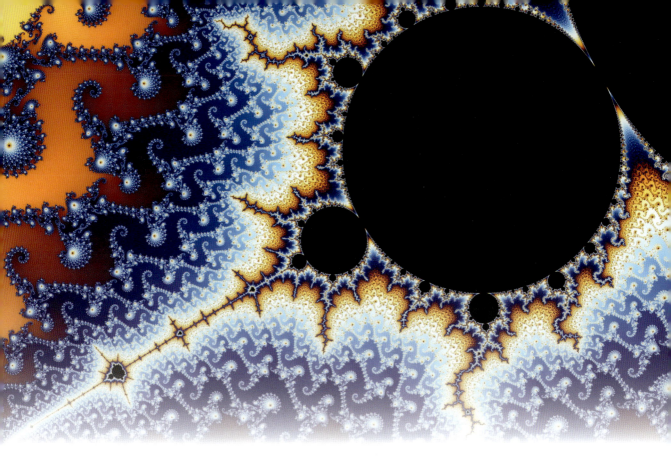

FRACTALS

WHAT THE HELL DO FRACTALS HAVE TO DO WITH NETWORKS? Gimme a second... Hold on! Oh, right, we were talking about granularity and different ways to look at security.

Question: How long is the coastline of Iceland? I had no idea, but the CIA World Factbook *(which is a tremendous resource from time to time)* said 4,970km.

But, isn't that answer incomplete? I don't know what that number means on its own. For example, is there a difference in shoreline length between high tide and low tide?

I don't know for certain, but I am comfortable assuming the 4,970km is an average of the normal upper and lower limits.

More importantly to me – in an analogue way of thinking – is the question, "What is the resolution of the measurements?" Or in mathematical terms, what is the coastline's *fractal dimension*?

A fractal is by definition a curve whose complexity changes with measurement scale.

In the case of Britain, a measuring stick of 200km *(yes, a very big yardstick)* yields a coastline length of 2400km. But when measured at a resolution of 100km – a greater amount of granularity – the coastline increases by 400km *(see Fig. 3E)*. Various sources put the actual number between 12,800km and 18,000km when measured in scales like 1:10,000, as seen on physical surveys.

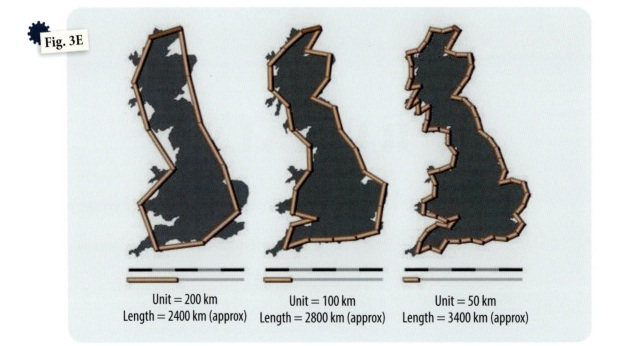

Fig. 3E

Unit = 200 km
Length = 2400 km (approx)

Unit = 100 km
Length = 2800 km (approx)

Unit = 50 km
Length = 3400 km (approx)

Rule of Granularity: The smaller the measuring stick, the longer the length.

In theory, then, as the unit of measurement gets smaller, the length approaches infinity. This formula is a simple analogue view we will see over and over.

$$\text{As } M \to 0, L \to \infty$$

As the granularity of measurement, M, gets smaller, the length, L, approaches infinity. Now, think about big data.

The picture below is an example of fractals found in nature. Beautiful as a colorful piece of art, it's a natural watershed network of run off, streams, rivulets, tributaries, and wider navigable waterways.

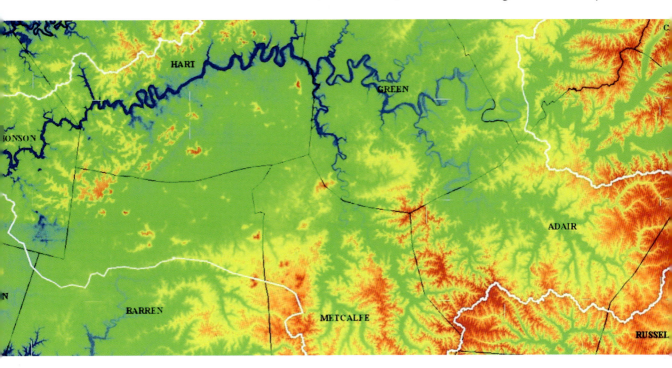

How many of all those small twists and turns go into the measured length? At a certain point, an answer becomes pretty meaningless.

As with networks.

Static vs. Dynamic

Heraclitus said, "Everything changes and nothing stands still," which someone later shortened to: "The only constant is change." This is another one of my mantra-based hot buttons.

Change is fundamentally about a difference, or a delta, over a designated period of time.

- Kilometers per hour
- Miles per second
- Gravity 32m/sec/sec (acceleration is the rate of change of velocity)
- Hot dogs eaten per minute
- Revolutions per minute (RPM)
- Warp speed 6.2

Static is only an idealized condition that does not and cannot exist. Ever. Static means zero-motion, which also means zero-heat and zero subatomic motion. Absolute zero is similarly unattainable. I believe the same of networks. There is always some traffic if the power is on.

The belief in "static" is just as crude as in "binary." Dynamics – constant variability – are what enable Analogue. Yet, in network security, we still think in terms of absolutes:

> **Bob has access to the Finance server.**

I suggest that we think in more dynamic terms, and add the time domain to our modeling.

> **Bob has been given access to the Finance server until...**
> 1. He leaves the company and his access is revoked.
> 2. Bob is suspected of <Bad Thing>.
> 3. His time-based security access expires.

The greater granularity in the definition of Bob's access rights, allows for more detailed controls which can be put into place. Nevertheless, a simple binary function is what we generally live with today.

Analogue thinking says, "add more variables" to your questions and answers!

SECURITY BY STATIC VS. DYNAMIC PROCESSES

THE FOLLOWING REALLY BOTHERS ME ON SO MANY LEVELS. Do you have any idea how hard it is to get a new social security number in the U.S. if your identity has been stolen?

When I call up any of my financial institutions and they want to remotely verify my identity, I am shocked that well over 75% of the time, the proof-positive, definitive authentication of my identity is such open-source information as, my date of birth and social security number. Checking an ID at a bar is better security!

Social security numbers were originally never intended to serve as a *de facto*, unique identification code for Americans, but that's effectively what they have become. When the banks' and the feds' authentication procedures are based upon a single, static identification code for a person's entire lifetime… well, that's just dumb. One static identification number for life? No mechanism for a replacement number even if your life has been ripped apart by identity thieves or the security failures of those we trust to protect our PII? Completely binary, over a period of 80 or so years that within themselves involve constant flux? Dumb and *dumber*.

When I refinanced my home with Chase, within 48 hours I received an unsolicited credit card from a third party bank that I did not even know. *Winn reacts: Cancel credit cards. Chase provides credit monitoring. We survived OK.*

In the next two years, my Chase credit card info was breached 3 more times, that I am aware of. In each case, I had to go through the dance of updating auto-pays, relinking accounts, re-verifications, and then see what I missed when something doesn't get paid in a few months.

A traditional (static & binary) credit card has a fixed, non-variable number associated with the person and the corresponding account. Once again, ignorance personified. The companies have responded to this by saying, "Oh, check out our new chip cards!"

CALL FOR LAWYERS

Can you please lobby Congress and the SSA to create a far easier system to reissue a new SSN in certain cases?

If banks can issue new credit cards, the U.S. government should be able to issue new SSNs. How about spending some serious effort on fixing this low-hanging fruit problem before it becomes more of a national tragedy?

The June 2015 Chinese hack of federal employees' databases is only the beginning.

And while they may be a notch up in physical transaction security, online and backend databases still *see* a static number. Did I already ask, "How dumb…"?

RSA SecurID tokens generate authentication codes at fixed intervals which usually must be used in conjunction with a user's PIN. Above is a prototype of the Hidden MasterCard, a credit card built upon this same idea that dynamically changes the card number and the security code each time it is turned on.

Besides, if a single layer is your only defense, you've got a lot more problems. Note, I said defense, not protection.

There has to be a better way, but my banking friends won't do it. The excuses are interminable and bank-profit based. The tech is pretty simple actually. Apply ever-changing dynamicism like the time-based security approach pioneered by Security Dynamics in the late 1980s, now known as the RSA SecurID token.

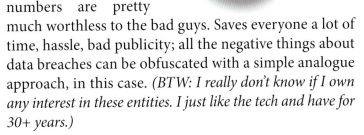

From a data breach standpoint, it's a no-brainer. With a dynamic system where the numbers are not static, the purloined credit card numbers are pretty much worthless to the bad guys. Saves everyone a lot of time, hassle, bad publicity; all the negative things about data breaches can be obfuscated with a simple analogue approach, in this case. *(BTW: I really don't know if I own any interest in these entities. I just like the tech and have for 30+ years.)*

Same thing with system access to company networks. Which is more secure *(whatever that means)*? A static password tied to associated fixed-fields databases, or an ever-changing, non-repeatable access code that is not stored in any database because it's always different, tied to a corresponding time-based engine?

The time-based aspect to this approach is, in my honest opinion, spot on. Perfect? Never! But, the bad guys go after the low hanging fruit first, before tackling tough technical approaches.

Bottom line: I like dynamic access mechanisms a whole lot. We should be using them just about everywhere and they need to be designed into more IoT deployments. **So analogue!**

Electronics 101

One of the most basic electronic circuits is that which makes a light bulb emit light.

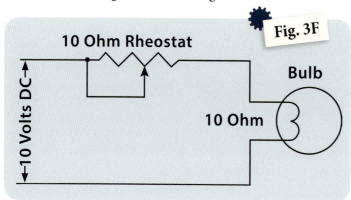

Fig. 3F

Yes, you should know some of this. After all, it's the basis of *all the things*.

This circuit could use either AC or DC as the source voltage. The rheostat (potentiometer or dimmer) controls the amount of voltage that reaches the lamp, and thus the amount of current that flows through the filament. Everyone knows Ohm's law.

To illustrate this, look back at Fig. 3F. If the rheostat is turned all the way to the right:

Ohm's law states that the current through a conductor between two points is directly proportional to the voltage across the two points.

$$I = \frac{E}{R}$$

- ▶ The applied voltage is E = 10V.
- ▶ The lamp has 10 Ohms of electrical resistance (R).
- ▶ The current (I) passing through the light bulb will be 1 ampere, the maximum amount of current that can flow in this circuit, and the brightest the bulb can be.

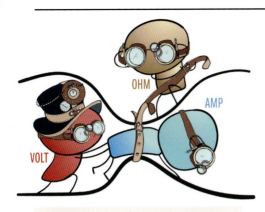

Voltage (E) provides the pressure, resistance (R) puts up the fight, and current (I) is what remains.

If the rheostat is turned all the way to the left:

> ▶ The applied voltage is E = 10V.
>
> ▶ The lamp has 10 Ohms of electrical resistance.
>
> ▶ The rheostat adds 100k Ohms of resistance.
>
> ▶ The current passing through the light bulb will be limited to 0.00009999 amps, the minimum amount possible in this circuit, and the bulb will be just about as close to *off*, as possible.

I will continually point out, as we explore the non-binary nature of things, that absolute 0s and 1s should be increasingly difficult to accept on faith. In the above example, there is no such thing as **zero resistance** or **total resistance** in any circuit. Idealized, this is another min-max condition that should be familiar from Time-Based Security.

> **0 < Resistance < ∞**
>
> *and*
>
> **0 < Voltage across bulb < 10V**

Now how can we apply this fundamental analogue electronic concept to network security?

We will get there once we find the Missing Link of Electronic Theory.

Do you think it will be analogue or digital?

Analogue
Computers in History

I'm *not* saying we should retreat and abdicate a couple hundred years of digital development. I *am* saying that we should discern the analogue approaches of yore that can add value in our purely digital world, especially when it comes to the abysmal security posture we find ourselves in today. I can easily foresee a future of hybridized analogue-digital integration everywhere.

Let's take a trip through history, shall we? These are the Analogue "roads less traveled" of computer history; you won't find the Colossus, Pegasus, or PDP10 here!

Think Hybridization.

Greece, circa 100-200 BCE

Antikythera Mechanism

This ancient analogue computer was designed to predict astronomical positions and eclipses for calendars, astrology, and setting the cycles of the ancient Olympic Games.

Difference Engine

This was originally built by Charles Babbage in the mid 19th century. This model was built in 2002 and resides in the London Computer History museum.

United Kingdom; designed 1786, built 1823-1842.

Kelvin's Tide Predictor

A mechanical analogue device for computing the tides, designed and built by Lord Kelvin.

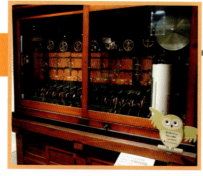

United Kingdom, 1872-3

Ship Gun Fire-Control Systems

Enabled remote and automatic targeting of guns against surface ships, aircraft, and shore targets via analogue computing.

UK, 1916

Norden Bombsight

An analogue computer constantly calculated the bomb's trajectory. This was based on current flight conditions linked to the bomber's autopilot which allowed it to react quickly and accurately to changes in the wind or other effects.

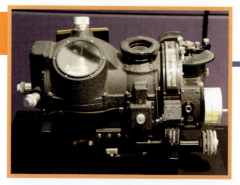

United States, 1920s-50s

Flight Control Analogue Computer

1949

WTF, Analogue?

AKAT-1

Poland, 1959

This machine was the breakthrough achievement of Jacek Karpiński's career; the world's first transistor-based differential equations analyzer.

Slide Rule

Developed in 17th century, popular in 1950s-60s

My early math and electronics calculations were done on analogue slide rules. Since they wouldn't fit in pocket protectors, we wore them on our belt, along with miniature oscilloscopes.

CSI 6F13 Naval Training Device

USA, 1970

Heathkit EC-1

USA, 1970

An educational computer that made basic analog calculations. I built one of these and learned early on that machine language and I did not play nicely.

The Inequality
of it all

I guess the bottom line should be obvious.

Digital is all about exactness. Absolute measurable precision. *(Within very precisely defined limits, of course, such as square wave rise time and damping.)* Comparing the value of two bytes results in a binary response: Yes, they are the same - equal. No, they are not the same - unequal.

In the ways that I view analogue anything (electrical, mechanical, etc.), equal does not exist for many reasons. Let's use voltage as an example.

Tons of modern gadgets are powered by +5V energy sources. Is +5V a binary condition? When you look closely, with the appropriate measurement tools, the actual voltage could be, e.g., +4.801V or +4.941V or +5.110V. This is called tolerance, and circuit designers allow for a range of acceptable analogue tolerance for specific applications and performance criteria.

Analogue measurement is an approximation based upon the granularity required and the accompanying sensitivity of the measurement gear. Meaning, if I think in purely analogue terms when I design, in this case, a circuit, I will specify an acceptable tolerance range for the power source. Thus, it really doesn't matter in the least if the battery puts out anywhere from, say +4.7V to +5.3V *(made up numbers)*, because the circuit infrastructure (chip) allows for such variances. Somehow, it seems to me, we've missed some opportunities by trying to be so darned exact.

Optical computers offer many analogue-ish advantages over traditional von Neumann processes. Light adds, subtracts, and interacts in single-steps at tremendous speeds, but has its own set of limitations. Great for some applications. Others, meh. Follow this nascent field!

Can two analogue pieces of data ever be equal? My argument is simple: it all depends upon the number of decimal points of accuracy you're looking for. For batteries, perhaps a 12% variance (+/- .3V possible range from a nominal +5V) is sufficient. No need to label them as "+4.78V Batteries on Sale!" In old audio terms, we called this, "Close enough for rock'n'roll."

To fly a spacecraft and land it on an asteroid... well, that requires a whole lot more places to the right of the decimal point. The accuracy must be insanely spot on. And so it goes; in the analogue view, for greater accuracy, we need more zeroes (granularity) when we play with uber-nano-small and screamingly *fast* stuff. Likewise, we need more zeroes to the left of the decimal point in order to meaningfully talk about the Cosmos - the unimaginably large.

Back to our world... how accurate do we, in the world of security, need to be?

1. We will never get it all right. The goal is a higher degree of precision, not perfection, since that is impossible.

2. If we don't at least try to do something new, we'll never, ever get at least one thing right.

3. What are you trying to measure and with what level of accuracy or granularity? Context and scale are critical to understand before making decisions.

C-SUITE GUYS:

Please stop harassing security geeks for exact answers. There just aren't any. Please don't ask, "are we secure, yet?" Answers are merely approximations that exist only for a moment in time. Next moment, new answer.

On the Quantum Nature of I.T.

In the quantum world, things can be viewed as either waves or particles; a rough analogy to analogue versus digital. Which one is right? Neither and both. Quantum weirdness, for sure.

It comes down to what you are trying to measure – or observe – depending upon your needs.

My Analogue Network Security concepts do not supplant the digital realities of 1s and 0s; they just, hopefully, give an alternate way of viewing network security behavior. Quantum security is way beyond the scope of this inchoate effort, but the metaphors have had pronounced influence on the way I think.

I have truly found that oscillating (an analogue function) between Binary-Digital and Analogue thinking offers more systemic and strategic views than merely one or the other.

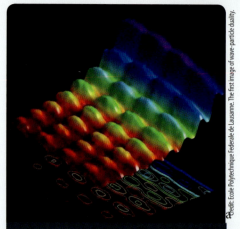

This colorful tableau is the first experimental demonstration of wave particle duality. In my mind, I replaced Wave with Analogue and Particle with Binary-Digital.

With all the hype of quantum superiority comes an ironic twist: quantum computing promises to be extraordinary at averaging and approximating probabilistically (analogue answers). Leave it for now, to von Neumann architecture, for exactitude.

...OK, fine. I'll move on.

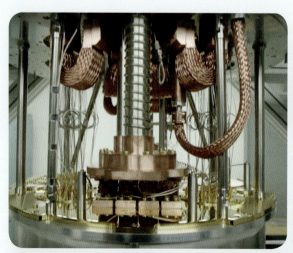
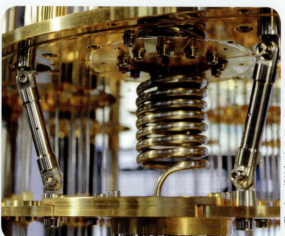

Quantum computer on the left. On the right, a quantum computer with analogue springs.

4
Let's Kill Root

The Buck Stops
with Root

What is the dirtiest four-letter word you can think of? *User* is a popular choice. *Spam* gets mentioned. *Bots* and a few others, perhaps.

No, I'm thinking of **ROOT**, the mechanism that gives Single User Master Control over all the things. It is literally the single place from which all controls reside. Because of this, security folks assert that those with root have god-like powers.

Whoever has been given root control is the one assigned the responsibility, and in some cases, the accountability for any activities that have taken place under their root privileges. Technically, the person with root has access to all of the data and all of the resources under that root's umbrella.

Former U.S. President Harry Truman famously took responsibility for his actions. He did not believe in "passing the buck," which had come to mean passing responsibility and/or blame onto others.

In security, the buck stops with root.

Root. Single User Account. Default. Low Level Admin. Master Admin. I am not trying to conflate them; IMHO, they all represent controls with a lack of oversight. More coming…

A reference to a poker practice in the American Old West of placing a marker (often a buckhorn knife) in front of someone else, indicating you don't want to deal.

I found it sort of awakening to see just how much root is in our lives. Everywhere!

- **Your mobile device.** *(How many billions are there?)* You swipe a pattern or a code and you have an All Access Pass. Somehow, we consciously chose to build an incredibly useful and powerful suite of technologies and tools which reaches into all areas of our lives, yet we let **Default = Single User Account**, jailbreaking notwithstanding. An estimated 100 million of these devices with mere binary control get lost or stolen every year.

- **Server root in the enterprise**; Oh, there are so many. From databases to mail servers, to Office suites and patch management controls. Perimeter controls, routers, firewalls, AD, VoIP, backup, and countless enterprise appliances use root. Root then assigns limited rights to subsets or functions based upon the organizational structure of the month. Then we have anti-virus, CAs, ID Management, DLPs, DNS, DR, Incident Response and Reporting - and the list of root-based security tools is just as daunting.

- **OS X, Windows, and Linux** offer some degree of separation between the all-powerful admin (root) account and limited-rights user accounts. This permits, for example, a number of family members with differing rights to share a computer.

- I have seen lots and lots of awesomely **cool IoT devices.** They are controlled with **single user, binary root-based security.** So, bad on us.

- **Industrial Control Systems (ICS)** are meant to keep power, telco, water, and other physical critical infrastructures working correctly. Broadly think of ICS as the smarts behind large engineering projects like dams, power systems, water, sewage treatment, and transportation, to name a few.

- **Think of cloud accounts like Facebook, Pinterest, social media galore... and the endless interactive online lives we lead across millions of servers globally.** Each of those accounts is binary - and root. One level and access to all of the data, all of the resources, and all of the associated rights are compromised.

- **Mobile banking is getting less binary,** thanks to some ANS-style (e.g., FB_t, 2FA, OOB), approaches which some banks deploy quite well **(see** *My Bank* **later).**

- **My wife's car actually has separate admin and user accounts.** *(I was impressed!)*

RANT: Facebook Lite

I have often wondered (then un-wondered when I think of it from Microsoft's point of view), why I need the full-blown version of Word. It offers a bazillion options, crashes regularly, and sometimes inexplicably takes on a mind of its own. Why can't I get *Word Lite*? Just give me 1% of the total functionality that I actually use and need, e.g. VI, edlin, text edit.

And, while I'm at it, why shouldn't social media sites, for example, force users to manage two modes? Admin with full rights to really screw things up (access to billing and personal information, etc.) and User mode, for day to day stuff, where public humiliation is better when reduced to only what you post, but then questions your every choice with an intelligent agent:

"Suzi… are you sure you want to post that bikini pic? Nick, isn't that chugging pic a little too sophomorish to post? Might come to haunt you when you apply to college or for a job."

Real-time, interactive, intelligence to help youth and users make smarter online choices. (See Chapter 8 for a suggested Fake News and Social Media solution.)

==Global lawmakers, heed this as you begin regulation debates!==

Another way to view root is to ask, what systems do not employ non-binary root controls? Sadly, barely a few, in my experience.

Because root offers largely unfettered access and control, plenty of scary security scenarios are easily imagined. They are rooted (couldn't resist) in three general modes of failure at the root level. (Remember: the greater the E(t), the greater the possibility for damage.)

The three causes of root failure or compromise:

1. **An insider with root access. Ouch. That can really hurt, no matter which of the three types of insider is at fault.**
   - The Malicious one, with devious malevolent purpose.
   - One who is exploited by a 3rd party. (Via bribery, extortion, blackmail, e.g.)
   - The arrogant, apathetic, or careless one. Oops. Just a mistake. (Didn't double check. Clicked too fast.)

HOSTILE ATTACK vs. ERROR

There is little difference between a hostile attack and an error.

Any sufficiently advanced cyber-attack is indistinguishable from an error.

Any type of error can be introduced in design, policy, architecture, implementation, configuration, updating, clicking, or typos.

> 2. **A technical attack that looks for known vulnerabilities to exploit.**
>   - The abuser may buy or develop zero-day malware, or even use brute force and big data attacks.
>   - Privilege escalation, just like in *Donkey Kong*, is the goal.
>
> 3. **Social engineering is attributed to being the most popular and successful attack vector to gain escalated and root privileges.**
>   - Some estimates suggest 90+% of successful attacks begin with some form of social engineering.
>   - Same result as #2, except, in this case, it's hacking the human first, in order to subsequently abuse the tech.

To temper your expectations, I do not believe in perfect security; that's much too binary. As I have explored analogue ideas, I have come to realize that security is analogue: the simple answer is security can be measured; it is nothing more than approaching a functional (real-world) limit, similar to the approach of many risk-based, physical security strategies.

Risk will never be 0 and security will never be 1. I am, however, hopefully going to give you some workable ideas on how to make security approach a 1 in certain cases. The rest I leave for you to figure out.

In the next little bit, I have a few thoughts about controlling root privileges with greater granularity in applications, devices and networks. Of course, I'm going to add in some analogue ideas and a *sprinkle* of time.

I Have Trust Issues

More specifically, I have an issue with the way the security industry views trust.

> "She's a trusted employee." "They are trusted partners." "I trust my staff will always do the right thing." "The code has been reviewed so we can trust it."

C'mon, really? Are you saying that trust is an either-or condition? *(Binary, that is.)*

Do you trust your partner with your life? I'm talking absolutely, totally, with 100% control over whether you live or die. Would you give him or her "the switch" on your life? Under what circumstances? During a cozy dinner or during a disagreement? Would you trust them 100% in all possible situations? For instance, if your child's life was at stake? Or if the choice was to end your life in order to save the lives of 10,000 people? Would you trust him or her 100% with your life if the lives of complete strangers hung in the balance? What then?

Should we also have absolute trust in our senior military leaders? Role models, entertainers, athletes, politicians, or faith leaders?

Being human is not binary.

Criminals operate with trust relationships, perhaps handling them with better alacrity than we "good guys." "She's OK. I'll vouch for her." "Vinny's cool. He's Colleen's cousin." The penalty for losing trust can be swift and severe.

Business operates on trust. And security, too, is supposed to function on a basis of trust… but I disagree with the finality of the two extreme binary boundaries of =="Yes, I trust…" and "No, I don't trust."== I have come to approach trust as yet another analogue function, as I just have trouble with complete absolutes. *(You have probably gathered as much from my occasional rant on the topic.)*

Rather, I look at trust as a place, or a condition, that resides between two extreme non-achievable boundary conditions. My working axiom is all trust functions are > **0** and < **∞**. In my analogue view, a now familiar min-max condition appears again, which I have arbitrarily set:

> **0 < Trust Factor (TF) < 1**

View trust as a spectrum of fuzziness. **0** Trust sits on the left, absolute trust or **1** on the right, and both are unattainable. I have absolutely zero tolerance for absolutism. In reality, trust is fuzzy, foggy, and dependent upon many dynamic, situational variables. Or, one can view Trust as a limit, as in:

$$\text{for } x \in (0, 1) : \lim_{x \to c} f(x) = L$$

Here, f(x) can approach L by making x sufficiently close to c. In that case, the above equation can be read as the limit of f of x, as x approaches c, is L. A limit can approach both **0** and **1**, unachievable conditions, but notionally necessary.

WINN'S TRUST POSTULATE

One can never be 100% positive about trust; it is an analogue function. Therefore, neither 100% or 0% trust is achievable or meaningful. There is always an exception. Ergo, think of min-max as mathematical limits or defined, unreachable boundary conditions. You can get close, but never really make it.

In security, however, we still fall back on the flawed binary assumption that trust is absolute. The PGP encryption scheme uses Trust at its core. If Phil trusts me, and Phil trusts Diane, is that sufficient for me to trust Diane? How concatenated a trust chain is reasonable?

That's not for me to answer. If limited to enterprise identity management, I would argue that the PGP-style trust model has value for a trusted central authority that periodically updates itself. In the real world, though, when a trusted CA (Certificate Authority) is hacked out of existence, Trust, by caveat, must be **TF < 1,** but in such extreme cases, **TF → 0** becomes the rule.

I am similarly not so optimistic when we're talking about security administration. Root is a (tangled and broken) binary function, and we give away root to trusted insiders because we have no choice; that's all the vendors supply. Yes/No binary trust for admins and Root. In most cases, admins and C-Suiters have no clue how risk can be quantified and mathematically increased. Either the admin is trusted to do their job or not.

Trust is so much more than the one-dimensional view we employ today. Trust is not only a value of the potential for hostile acts; it is a value for the amount of trust we have in the integrity of our employees and partners. How do their actions, behaviors, and reactions respond to pressure?

> ▶ Are they mistake-prone?
> ▶ How likely are they to click on compellingly stupid email attachments?
> ▶ Are they susceptible to social engineering?
> ▶ Are they good-intentioned airheads? (It takes all kinds...)

In today's absolutism view from HR, someone is either trusted or not. We know that binaryism doesn't

Look at what we try to teach folks about social media. Just because Henry claims to be a good friend of Sonja, so what? Does that mean you automatically transfer trust? Is trust transitive? Think carefully before deciding.

Does the Board, CEO or CISO of any organization truly have 100% absolute trust in one or more employees who have the proverbial "keys to the kingdom" (root access)? Does the Board have 100% confidence in the CEO?

We tend to act like we do, but if we are honest, we silently don't have 100% trust in *anyone*.

It's all a big gamble (or risk), and, in some cases, admins and C-suiters are even lying to themselves. The concept of a trusted insider is pure lip service. How many APTs, data breaches, and major security incidents begin life as an enticing email?

See *Hiring the Unhireable* on RSA-TV: https://youtu.be/C_9cdzLi6-o

Neural processes will automate a great deal of this, once the initial conditions and biases are set.

work, but HR dichotomically expects their absolutism to be accepted, absolutely. This is where dynamic confidence and trust scores come into play. The analogue view says, no one is perfect (1) and, in any typical hiring situation, a complex set of variables must be weighed in order to find the best fit, > 0 and < 1.

==When we provide Root, we should better understand the risk== associated with each choice made by that "trusted" person, and, in this case, access rights given. In the following matrix, (*Fig. 4A*) I am using 14 arbitrary criteria. There is no magic in the number 14. Having too many criteria does more harm than good.

Granularity adds a more analogue view. Pick the criteria you want to use, as this example is for general illustration only, so you can build a fast XLS and enter your own criteria and weighting factors to see what happens. Perhaps engineering will want to employ a different set of criteria than those used for the sales, finance or help desk staff. Trust Value: it's up to you to design, using an age-old, proven technique.

Fig. 4A

Meauring Trust		Case #1	Case #1	Case #2	Case #2
Criteria	Value > 0.0 to < 1.0	Weighted Factor	Weighted Value	Weighted Factor	Weighted Value
Technical Competence	0.95	75.00%	.713	6.00%	0.057
Past Job History	0.85	10.00%	0.085	5.00%	0.043
Recommendations	0.9	6.00%	0.054	2.00%	0.018
Vetting Level 1: Tech	0.97	1.00%	0.010	5.00%	0.049
Vetting Level 2: Background Check	0.86	0.00%	0.000	5.00%	0.043
Social Media Behavior	0.65	0.00%	0.000	5.00%	0.033
Years on Current Job	0.5	1.00%	0.005	15.00%	0.075
Miscreant Illegal Behavior	1	1.00%	0.010	19.00%	0.190
Psychological Profile	0.67	1.00%	0.007	8.00%	0.054
Belief Systems	0.77	1.00%	0.008	3.00%	0.023
Weakness/Frailties	0.6	1.00%	0.006	9.00%	0.054
Commitment	0.78	1.00%	0.008	11.00%	0.086
Life Goals	0.7	1.00%	0.007	3.00%	0.021
Career Goals	0.7	1.00%	0.007	4.00%	0.028
Total Trust Factor	0.779	100.00%	0.918	100.00%	0.772

The "Value" column *(see Fig. 4A on previous page)* is the employer's assigned value to each criteria on a min-max scale of 0 < Value < 1. Then, adjust the relative importance using your chosen weighting factors for each criteria, which must total 100%, of course. In Case #1, the arithmetically weighted factors emphasize technical skills with almost total disregard for anything about their personal attributes. It appears that this position requires great technical dexterity, but little privileged access. Thus, the Trust Factor (TF) in Case #1 is .918.

To make this operable and useful inside of an organization, a self-consistent internal policy on Trust Factors is required. Do you give root access to someone who scores a TF of only .918? Or do you insist on a minimum of .95? Or .98? That is entirely up to each organization. All I can suggest is to maintain a self-consistency throughout the process and remember that these are relative numbers, not absolutes.

In Case #2, the criteria appears to be more traditional, with a weighting towards stability and prior acts being more important than skills. All other things being equal, this person's TF is much lower, .772, largely because s/he has a past with miscreant illegal behavior. Is that a deal breaker? Up to you.

Many companies would use a prior bad act as an immediate reason not to hire a person. But, as I have suggested strongly in my treatise, *"Hiring the Unhireable"*, in order to get the skilled people we need so desperately, binary exclusion (aka discrimination) is self-prescribed failure.

Who is more likely to get hired? Depends on the job and policy. Weighing the relative importance of Trust for your own defined criteria gives us another analogue component for building a security model. I think you will find more real world flexibility in your security-risk decision making instead of the demonstrably failed current binary Yes/No modality.

Please do keep this in mind: the same principle applies at the network-to-network (inter-networking).

These same approaches work for code: do I trust the developer? How much code-review has occurred, and who did it and how much do I trust him/her? Has the API been updated and how does that affect TF in my weighting?

BILLY BALL & SPORTS

The Oakland A's famously relied upon numbers to run a baseball team. How much predictive trust is needed to put a pinch hitter into a 1-1 game, with 2 outs in the bottom of the 9th? Billy Ball says to apply the historical numbers - *trust* them - and not to go with the gut. Consider basketball and football (all versions). Some people predictably and probabilistically will perform better in certain situations.

Generally, the batting, running, or tackling skills will likely outweigh poor interpersonal skills. A sales person doesn't need to be able to code an app, but he better be good with people.

Binary Trust decisions, especially those surrounding us carbon units, should be eliminated.

Let's Kill Root

TF .918 = a 91.8% probability of success or an 8.2% probability of failure.
TF .772 = a 77.2% probability of success or a 22.8% probability of failure.

Fig. 4B

**Single Alice Examples of Trust Factor/Risk:
Time = Infinity**

	Alice	Alice	Alice	Alice	Alice
TF	0.90	0.95	0.70	0.60	0.10
Risk	0.10	0.05	0.30	0.40	0.90

Another way to view TF is as Risk *(Fig.4B above)*. And we will see just how valuable both approaches are as we become more analogue in our thinking.

While Trust Factor and Probability of Failure (Risk) are inverse, don't take these definitions too literally. They are meant to provide guidelines. Be very careful of rounding errors. Is a TF of .918 that much better than .910? Or .912? What about .901 or .867 or… ? It's all about your choices of scale, granularity, and how you interpret them.

Depending upon your chosen values for the matrix, you may find that every single person resides within the range .9 - .999. No matter; it's just a relative scale. In this case, you might choose to widen the Value range to see more .2 and .3 values and make .9 harder to achieve.

By adding the glint of probability, you will find the next sections, perhaps, a bit more intuitive.

Binaryism is a slippery slope *(well, a precipice)* as is arbitrary discrimination (binary), because of the subjective evaluation of humans.

Is the kid with an "A" who scored 95% really all that different from your kid who scored 94% but received a "B?" I hope that you become insanely uncomfortable with binary answers.

Trust Factor is a spectrum. Just like with electromagnetic energy, hearing, and autism, for example. The range is from completely untrustworthy (Approach 0) to unwavering trust (Approach 1). Nothing is ever perfect or null.

WARNING!

Trust Factors can be exceedingly useful when comparing trust assessments in the human domain… but only within a specific constraint: The same criteria must be used consistently across an organization or group to have any meaning. Each value assignment and weighting factor is somewhat arbitrary and subjective, so please don't try to turn this into an unyielding binary output. It's merely meant to be a functional approximation, based upon other assumptive approximations. More Bayes.

Turn the dials, so to speak, to see how your output, TF, changes, as weighted input values change. Analogue neural-like. These analyses do provide a spectrum for trending, tendencies, and a method for self-correcting when overemphasis on specific criteria skews common sense results. (e.g., too much emphasis on social niceties, drug use versus the need for explicitly uncommon skill sets).

If Company A uses a different set of weights and criteria than Company B, their respective Trust Factors won't translate precisely, since the metrics are relative, not absolute. They can be used as a guide of course, but imagine trying to compare the length of an object if my yardstick is 3" shorter than yours? My five yards will not be the same length as your five yards. *(Remember fractals.)*

Keep Trust Factor (probability of failure) in the front of your mind, as we will need it again soon.

WANTED:

I hope some brilliant math-person will prove me wrong and come up with an insanely insightful inter-organizational transform.

Ada Lovelace, the first computer programmer; 1815-1852.

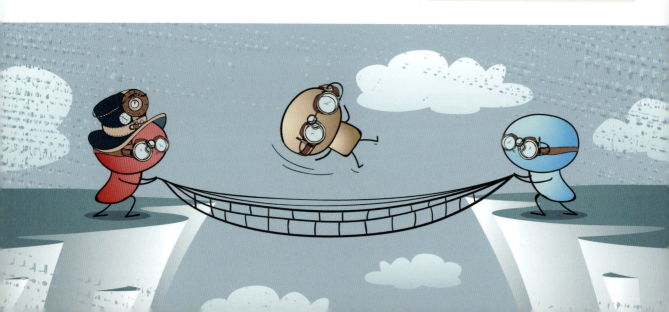

The Case of the Sole Admin

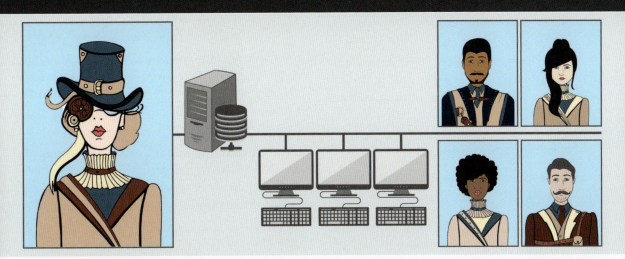

Let's see what Boolean logic can do for us. A binary root-based decision works like a standard light switch, no matter whether it's at the human, network, or code level: on-off, zero-one, high-low. This is typically how networks are designed, implemented, and administered.

And yet, we wonder why we seem to be totally screwed. Why do APTs take years to be discovered? Why is it that the first clue that millions of U.S. government worker's PII was stolen, came only after their details were already posted on Reddit?

The traditional binary approach to security *is really that bad*, but has remained the *de-facto* model since the early 1970s.

For now, we will use Admins and Users as examples, but don't get stuck in that framework. We are really talking about Subjects and Objects.

- **HUMAN:** Root, Admin, SubAdmin, SuperUser, User, Guest
- **NETWORK:** Tier 1, First Hop, Intranet, Subnets, VLANs, LANs, Workgroups, Mobile
- **CODE:** Applications, Libraries, Calls, APIs, Links, Macros, Embedded, Steganography

Logically, they are all equivalent; either Subjects or Objects that interact in some way.

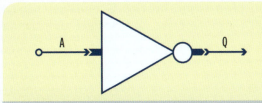

INVERTER aka **NOT GATE**: If input A (Alice) is high, then output Q is low. If A is low, then Q is high.

Think of any decision from Alice as flipping a "rule" switch on or off: adding a name, changing a config file, editing a function... anything that any admin with root privileges to system resources can do. (*As well as anything that any average user can do as the single user admin/root on mobile devices or in poorly configured PCs.*) This is done billions of times every day. The NOT gate merely represents a choice, since changing the input A also flips the output Q.

If "A," then "Q."

(Where Q is the positive high, 1, or true output of a particular action by A with security implications.)

That's the prevalent binary world view. A Single-Pole Single-Throw switch *(yes, a light switch!)* is another way to look at the result of a single binary decision. But what does this same picture look like with a little analogue tossed in?

In the previous binary switch example, $D(t) \to \infty$ and $R(t) \to \infty$, because I didn't add any detection or reaction in either of these decision operations. Therefore…

> Since $D(t) + R(t) = E(t)$,
> $E(t) \to \infty$ *as well!* **Infinite exposure time.**

Thus, because the amount of time that Q (in this example, a protection control) is enabled, and the operative axiomatic presumption, of course, is that absolutely perfect protective security cannot exist.

In plain terms, because Q remains enabled (high), and there are no detection or reaction

> $Q(t) = P(t)$
> and for protective security to be effective,
> $P(t) > D(t) + R(t)$ and $Q(t) \to \infty$

mechanisms, any compromise or abuse of the rights of Alice (the admin) implies unrestricted access to Q in perpetuity, or in analogue terms, $E(t) \to \infty$.

The many nation-state level attacks going undetected for months and years, I would argue, are due to an overemphasis on our industry's historical bias for protective binary thinking. Which doesn't work.

I will, in a few pages, attempt to convince you that Defense in Depth is dead and should be replaced by Detection in Depth.

In the real world, how many admins do you have?

The Case of the Multiple Admins

More admins are better than fewer admins. We need more overseeing manager-types to make sure the lowly users are doing what they're supposed to be doing and nothing more. Right? Wrong?

Now, let's get uglier. Let's look at how many people share administrative root capabilities for a particular function within a hypothetical enterprise.

- Alice works 0800h - 1700h, M-F, for 40 hours a week.
- 3 Alice clones are needed to fill in the other 128 hrs per week. Right? Or is it all on her?
- Alice's boss has the admin rights, too, to keep Alice honest, of course.
- So does Jill from the "Other Tech Dept.," as she has enough political clout to demand access rights, too.

That's six folks with admin root access. For 24/7 coverage, a company needs to have roughly 4 people to cover a specific admin function. Then a couple of backups. Ouch! At the simplest multi-admin level of two – Alice (A) and Bob (B) – the OR logic gate is appropriate.

They are logically equal. If either, or both, Bob and Alice take an action, the output goes high, says yes, turns on, sets a condition; Q = High = 1. This is ever so common: two admins with equal power and who don't, in this case, have to ask permission or get approval from each other or anyone else (in this logical domain); in other words, an OR gate. This is key to both the understanding and confusion of where we're headed: probabilistically, Alice and Bob are considered to be independent variables.

This OR gate has only two inputs, meaning both Bob and Alice, two separate and independent people, have Root control. Now, look what happens to our Trust Factor as a result of this.

- Current technical authentication implementations
- Applying analogue Trust Factors

Let's say both Alice and Bob have been determined to each have a Trust Factor of 0.9. If **TF(A) = 0.9** and **TF(B) = 0.9**, then, independently, they each represent a 10% risk, or probability of error (oops!), or miscreance (gotcha!).

However, with the OR function, and "adding" two independent events probabilistically, we find we can actually measure the increased risk to the enterprise, or at least to a specific portion of a network.

TF(A) * TF(B) = TF (A * B) = 0.81
or inversely,
Risk has increased from 10% to 19%

For the C-Suite: By giving even *one* additional equally-trusted person root access (to any object in the network), your risk has nearly doubled.

Depending on how much additional subsequent SSO (Single Sign-On) access is provided, similar risk can propagate throughout systems.

The usual set theory notation for OR with independency is:

$$P(A \cap B) = P(A) \cdot P(B)$$

if A and B are mutually exclusive

The Probability of A or B equals the product of the probabilities of both A and B. (A times B.)

Meaning either Alice or Bob can make a change without the permission of the other. The combined multi-admin Trust Factor (probability) of error is determined by multiplying the individual Trust Factors and arriving at a total risk.

For four admins with equal control and vetted to equal weighting, we can use a 4-input OR gate with the same Q output.

$$0.9 * 0.9 * 0.9 * 0.9 = 0.6561$$

Risk increases proportionately to the probability of independent event failure. So, even though you have four reasonably trusted folks, all vetted at a Trust Factor of 0.9, your business process and architectures collapse the trust and increase the risk, remarkably.

With a view from probability, we get:

$$P(A \cup B \cup C \cup D) = P(A)+P(B)+P(C)+P(D)-P(A \cap B)-P(A \cap C)-P(A \cap D)-P(B \cap C)-P(B \cap D)-P(C \cap D)+P(A \cap B \cap C)+P(B \cap C \cap D)+P(A \cap C \cap D)+P(A \cap B \cap D)-P(A \cap B \cap C \cap D)$$

We grew and grew networks, scaling them to incredible heights and phenomenal depths, gave people almost unfettered access with SSO-like controls, yet Root lived on.

It's the frog in the frying pan. By necessity, we need more than one admin for dozens of specific functions. We have, by choice, or arrogance, or ignorance, substantially increased risk by adding more admins in the ol' Binary way.

I don't know why we have missed this. In my opinion, the I.T. and security industries have failed magnificently.

This OR gate model is where we still are. Yeah, this is 'state of the art' tech. Sorry to vendors who think their product solves all the things. I am only at the very beginning of attempting to create a more integrated security amalgam… *'cause just patchin' and hopin' ain't workin'.*

Credentials Management Folks:

If you forget to revoke the creds for anyone with - in this case, root privileges - and you add a new person, too… well, please, do the math.

THE 2-MAN RULE: 101

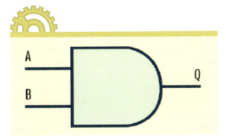

2MR Disclaimer: Okay, before I get beaten up for "exclusionary sexism," the 2MR is also known in some places as "4-Eyes" and other places the 2PR, or the 2 Person Rule. I chose to use the 2MR for maximum historical context and understanding, while knowing that the convention may certainly change. During research, the use of the word "man" is quite varied; from complete inclusion of everyone in mankind, to humanity, and to perhaps the more sexist "woman." My wife and I discussed this at length, and this was our choice. When I see you at a Con somewhere, tell me your thoughts.

The obvious solution to using OR gates for multiple admins is to use AND gates, instead. Right?

Both inputs A and B must be **high** or **1** (arbitrary units) to get the output Q to change to **high** or **1** from its normal/default **low** or **0**. In the simplest case, that means both Alice and Bob must agree. Just like some checks must be countersigned to be valid.

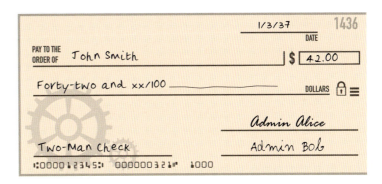

Or two independent keys are needed to open a safety deposit box. Note, I used the word independent again. The two keys are independent, but they only work when there is mutual dependence. They must BOTH be present to open the box.

The Logical notation for AND is:

$$A \cap B$$

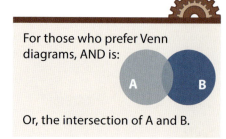

For those who prefer Venn diagrams, AND is:

Or, the intersection of A and B.

==Another way to visualize the 2-Man Rule with AND logic is with the logical switch method==, as described by Claude Elwood Shannon (father of information theory). Both A and B must be closed to enable the inverting buffer to change the state of Q.

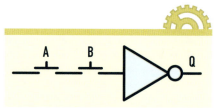

In the following view of a 2MR situation, the AND function spreads linearly across a time scale on the x-axis from left to right.

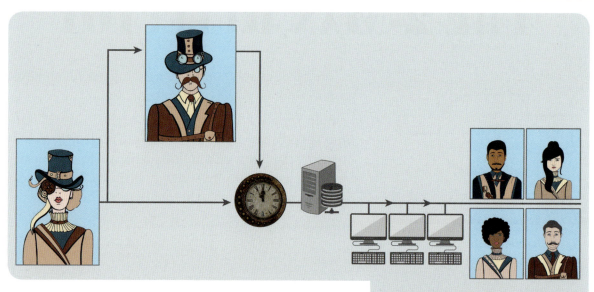

Alice Set Time = 0
0 < Bob Time < ∞

There is no specifically-enforced time mechanism. Bob might be able to approve Alice quickly, or he might be out and about, unreachable. Then, Bob's approval time gets bigger and bigger, and Alice's Set is not approved by Bob and therefore, does not go into effect. At least, not until Bob gets around to it. In order for Q to go high, both A and B must occur in any sequence, with no time boundaries. A and B must agree. Simple, yes?

Consider the Trust Factor of a 2-Man rule AND gate:

$$P(A \cup B) = P(A) + P(B) - P(A \cap B)$$

This Bayesian view of probability of the two dependent events equals the sum of each independent probability, less the probability of the union of the two.

So, if both Alice and Bob are trusted 90% as TF(A) and TF(B), look what happens with two equally trusted admins or processes:

$$P(0.9 \text{ and } 0.9) = P(0.9) + P(0.9) - P(0.9 * 0.9)$$
$$= 1.8 - 0.81$$
$$= 0.99$$

Whoa! What happened? ==When added logically, two people or processes of equal trust actually *increase* the Trust Factor significantly.==

Another way to view the same data is with the OR-gate, the current method, with multiple admins. For example:

$$P(A \cap B) = P(TF(A) * TF(B))$$
$$= 0.9 * 0.9$$
$$= 0.81$$

Given that the TF of each are equal, the probability is 81% that things will be OK. By simply inverting we get:

Am I right? Is the AND gate the solution to multiple root or approval controls? Before moving on, let me suggest you take a break, and figure out the fallacy (if there is one) in the above premise.

$$\text{Risk} = 1-(P(TF(A) * TF(B))) = 1-(0.9 * 0.9)$$
$$= 1 - 0.81$$
$$= 0.19 = 1 - P(A \cap B)$$

In ANS language, there is a 19% chance something could go wrong.

The 2-Man Rule: 201

So, you do see the problem with the two man rule I proposed?

What happens if Alice and Bob sit next to each other, as illustrated above? The AND condition is satisfied. In this case, the results are dependent on both Alice and Bob approving the action taken.

What happens in the different security case on the next page, though?

The AND condition is not satisfied, because Bob cannot be found.

==The problem is that, once Alice (or an "Alice" process) is initiated, the output, Q, will not be realized until such time that Bob approves!==

It comes back to time. Yes, here we go again. Time is the variable that gets in the way every… ah, time.

You can also think of Alice and Bob as being processes or decisions in an application or in network-wide requests. They are all logically equivalent.

Now, what happens if Alice and Bob have different Trust Factors? Do the first two cases have equivalence or not?

1. Alice = 0.9   Bob = 0.8
2. Alice = 0.8   Bob = 0.9
3. Alice = 0.5   Bob = 0.96
4. Alice = 0.96 Bob = 0.5

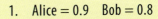

One of our content reviewers wants to be sure the reader knows that "you also have to consider the possibility of both of the people colluding to produce a nefarious result."

What about examples 3 and 4? Same "Q" output, right? Well, this is where things get sticky.

Allow me to next introduce some other analogue concepts that will hopefully make sense out of this seeming illogic, and will perhaps, offer an approach to a solution.

5 Feedback

Old manual typewriters were the ultimate haptic feedback system.

Feedback

In the world of hardcore engineering – which became its own formalized discipline during the Industrial Revolution – one concept kept rearing its head over and over again. This concept was hard-learned when early mechanical systems would simply disintegrate or fly apart; when engines would enter runaway conditions; when turbines would self destruct.

Yes, this essential concept at the very heart of (dare I say) every successful engineering project in the last two centuries, except, unfortunately, network security. The concept of Feedback.

Let's explore this.

Centrifugal governors were invented in 1788 by James Watt (yeah, that Watt), to control the speed of an engine. The "proportional control" system is, abstractly, a ==linear feedback system==, and such mechanisms vary speed, pressure, flow rate, or other variables to maintain operation within acceptable limits.

> The considerable engineering successes of ancient Rome, Greece, and Egypt left scant records of formal engineering processes.

> The term "Balls to the Wall" is believed to come from the centrifugal governor steam engines, which used spinning ball-bearings to adjust a valve, limiting the amount of steam entering the engine. As more fuel was put into the engine, more steam was produced, adding pressure. Centrifugal force of the spinning ball-bearings pulled them outward toward the wall of the housing, thus activating a lever and valve to limit the amount of steam. Balls were forced to the walls of the governor assembly and we got ==mechanical feedback== to avoid runaway conditions.

Feedback

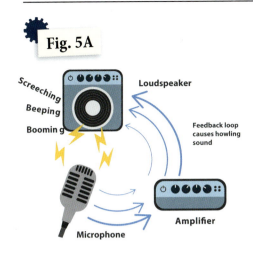

Fig. 5A

Infinity + Control Systems = Chaos

Fig. 5A is a specific type of feedback loop (positive) that causes ear piercing squeals at concerts or during boring speeches. In this case, the upper bounds of acceptable acoustic pressure at the microphone and speaker diaphragms have been exceeded, often accelerated by frequency synchronization, or resonance; thus the seemingly single frequency squeals we hear. ==Positive feedback tends towards infinity,== but is realistically limited by the performance capabilities of the hardware.

Fig. 5B is a simple circuit for an amplifier used in audio, video, radar - almost any analogue engineering discipline where signals need to be boosted (amplified), or gain-controlled in some manner. In order for any amplifier to work, there must be a feedback mechanism to reduce the gain from theoretical infinity (unattainable, but it's another limit function), to a manageable level. This is perhaps the simplest feedback circuit description, to which most complex ones can be reduced, with analysis.

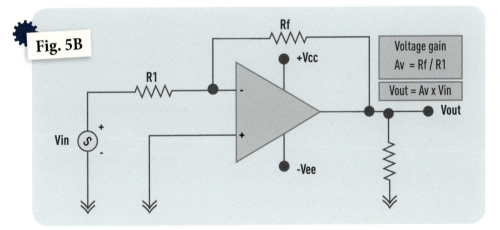

In other words, in order ==for any **NETWORK** (amplifier) to work, there must be a feedback mechanism== to reduce the **RISK** (gain) from two unattainable theoretical limits: Zero and Infinity. The job is confining the upper and lower limits to acceptable and manageable levels.

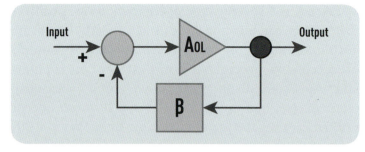

This diagram is the idealized abstraction for a negative feedback system in any domain.

Attempting to reach infinite gain creates instability (to say the least; indeed unpredictable chaotic behavior), therefore, a gain-limiting governor or feedback is required.

The three feedback mechanisms we've seen here span mechanical, acoustic, and electrical. However, keep in mind that when we speak of feedback, there are two kinds. Negative and positive.

NEGATIVE FEEDBACK

Negative feedback in this context, is not about unfavorable critiques. Negative feedback occurs when the output of a system is fed back through the input, except it is inverted (or 180 degrees) out of phase with the primary input.

Note: For now, polyphase systems are out of the scope of this discussion.

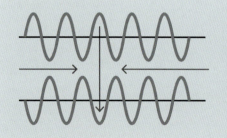

Out-of-Phase signals cancel each other other out. Just to add time-based confusion, the phase relationship of the output to the input is determined by the processing delay of the IC itself. That could be a slight delay, meaning only the highest frequencies would be affected by phase shift. Time considerations should go into any design process involving feedback.

The amplifier circuit described on the previous page (*see Fig. 5B*), is one example. Because analogue signals combine so easily, taking the inverted output of an amplifier and adding it to the input signal, reduces that amount of gain - amplification - in a given circuit, as per Rf/R1 *(Fig. 5B)*. Without any feedback, an electrical

Viral videos and fake news, for example, are shared over social media, creating dynamic shifts in opinion, action, and popularity through **positive feedback**.

That's a perfect example of self-actualizing cognitive bias in a networked social environment.

In the 1980s, VHS beat Beta in the "format wars" for this very reason. Initially, there was the general perception among consumers that since there were more manufacturers building and selling VHS machines than there were for Beta *(Sony being the ONLY Beta manufacturer)*, then there MUST be more content for VHS available.

Media developers also decided to focus on the seemingly more 'popular' VHS format, which made VHS content vastly more available at neighborhood video rental/purchase stores. Self-actualizing positive feedback. And since VHS content availability grew (porn allegedly had a huge effect on VHS winning the format wars), more consumers bought more VHS machines… and the positive feedback crushed Beta for the consumer market.

amplifier, for example, approaches infinite gain, which creates an awful and unusual cacophony, in the case of both acoustic and electronic audio.

POSITIVE FEEDBACK

Similarly, positive feedback here does not refer to the human realm of confidence boosting or learning through reinforcement. This kind of positive feedback can wreak havoc on physical, acoustical, and electronic systems *(as in Fig. 5A)*.

Positive reinforcing systems tend toward instability and chaos pretty quickly. Electrically, positive feedback is used to keep 1s and 0s distinct from each other, by digitizing analogue signal ranges.

Positive feedback can be a hardcore engineering nightmare. When troops march across a bridge, they are instructed to "break cadence" or fall out of step. The aim is to avoid time-synchronized forces that can cause the bridge structure to begin resonating through the positive feedback of the soldiers' march.

In 1940, the Tacoma Narrows Bridge (Galloping Gertie) collapsed shortly after construction was finished. In this case, the "cadence" was the wind providing a periodic frequency that matched the bridge's natural structural frequency - yes, resonance. Ultimately, though, the bridge failed due to aeroelastic flutter caused by the positive feedback in the bridge-wind dynamic system.

Courtesy: Barney Elliott; The Camera Shop, Under Fair Use Doctrine.

LET'S NOW GLUE A THING OR TWO TOGETHER, ADD A LITTLE FEEDBACK, AND SEE WHAT HAPPENS.

Feedback in Nature

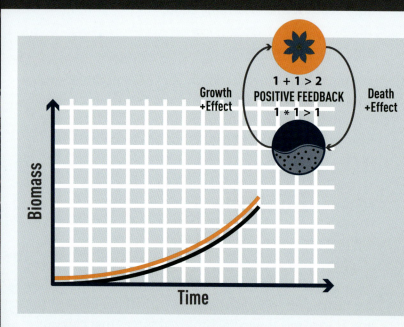

A few examples of positive feedback systems in nature:

▸ Plants grow and die, creating biomass for the next generation of plants, thus increasing *their* viability and, if successful, continuing the cycle.

▸ Environmentalists posit that manmade pollution is accelerating climatic shift; essentially, a positive feedback system.

▸ Deforestation.

Feedback is about establishing an equilibrium in a given dynamic (versus static) system. We see nature employing feedback mechanisms to keep everything in balance with self-regulating systems.

Economic bubbles are also the result of positive feedback. The oscillations between boom and bust are one byproduct of unrestrained capitalism, whose critics say, "may sometimes create a positive feedback loop, in which a small number of individual accumulations of capital grow ever larger, eventually becoming so few, as to limit effective competition, thus ceasing to strictly be free-market capitalism. In this regard, pure capitalism is unstable." What is missing from many systems that employ any type of feedback is "damping," which is used to temper the "ringing" discussed earlier.

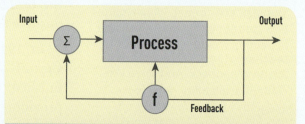

The simplest generalized abstraction of a feedback mechanism, with a direct input to affect the process, also.

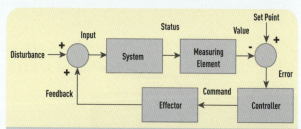

A more complex, real world example of how a typical ICS (Industrial Control System) uses feedback.
Note: the input "disturbance" is any dynamic signal.

Nature's SCADA & ICS *(we'll be looking at these systems in-depth in the next chapter)* are absolutely essential for life and for a functioning global society. Consider the following feedback mechanisms:

- Human body temperature. The hypothalamus of a human reacts to temperature fluctuations and responds accordingly. If the temperature drops, the body shivers to bring up the temperature and, if it is too warm, the body will sweat to cool down using evaporation.
- Touch. Tactile feedback. Haptics. (e.g., "clicky" keyboards)
- Learning.
- The photosynthesis in plants speeds up in response to increased levels of carbon dioxide.
- Global warming. Ice Ages. Back and forth.
- Higher oil prices cause an increase in gas prices. Consequently, people drive less, so demand is decreased. This brings equilibrium to supply and demand.

If we apply the concept of nature's built-in oscillations with more of an analogue view, we might not always be panicking to make impossibly difficult binary decisions. Answers need to be more flexible over time.

I still find it remarkable that almost every engineering discipline on the planet, and in space-faring endeavors, relies upon well-managed feedback systems; information security - not so much. In fact, not at all, with some minor exceptions. Feedback should be built-in as an architectural requirement in any dynamic system, such as data and control networks. But it's not. Analogue Network Security, however, relies on feedback throughout all applications, from code, to humans, and from applications to inter-networking, in all three domains.

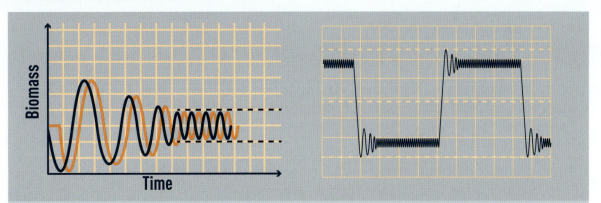

The chart on the left plots population of predators (dark blue) and prey (orange) over time. If the number of prey decreases, then some predators will starve, and their numbers will decrease. The initial population swings are "damped" over time and iterations, ending with, all other things being equal, an equilibrium. The graph on the left illustrates that, as you may recall from Chapter 3, pages 5-6, this is the exact same process that generates square waves.

SCADA & ICS

Stuxnet (~ 2010) blew up a lot of Iranian centrifuges. It essentially defeated the internal feedback loops designed to prevent the spinning speed from attempting to reach infinity. *(Analogue upper-limit.)* The attack worked and the centrifuges went SNAFU. Stuxnet set a standard for attacking infrastructures' SCADA and/or Industrial Control Systems (ICS).

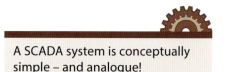
A SCADA system is conceptually simple – and analogue!

SCADA – Supervisory Control and Data Acquisition – systems are what keep today's kinetic-based worldwide infrastructures from self-destructing. Dramatic, but true, nonetheless.

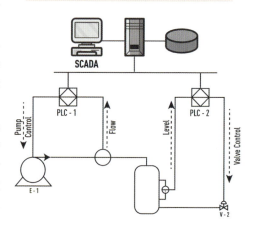

Programmable Logic Controllers (PLCs), are at the core of most SCADA and ICSs. A PLC is essentially a small, special purpose digital computer used for automation, as in factory assembly lines, amusement rides, and other physical processes. PLCs utilize both digital and analog inputs and outputs.

Feedback

In the olden days, feedback was controlled through abstractly equal electromechanical devices, such as relays, which were slower, larger, power-gobbling, and difficult to maintain. Modern PLCs are nothing more than Boolean logic embedded in hardware.

We currently live in more of a SCADA-world than you might think.

First published in 1948, **Cybernetics** by Norbert Wiener is one of the most ground-breaking books ever. Treat yourself.

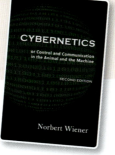

SCADA-Like Negative Feedback in Our Personal Lives

- Thermostats. These devices sense ambient temperatures and adjust cooling and heating systems to dynamically adapt as dictated by the chosen temperature.
- Toilets. The ballcock in a toilet rises as the water rises, and then, it closes the filler valve.
- Motion detectors for rooms or property lighting are also time-based.
- Home automation systems rely upon both human and cyber trigger events.
- Driverless cars and trains use multiple high-speed feedback loops.

And of course, enterprise and infrastructures are looking at moving SCADA to the cloud, moving the intelligence and PLC functionality to distant servers. We shall see how many of the use-cases listed to the left will move to the cloud.

Oh, wait! WHERE'S THE SECURITY?

Okay, moving on.

SCADA in Business

- Brewing beer (et al)
- Waste treatment plants
- Flood control
- Rail switching
- Traffic control
- Oil and gas refinement
- Drilling
- Agriculture
- Food processing
- Auto manufacturing
- Actually, just about all manufacturing...
- Packaging
- Robotic warehousing
- Heating / cooling (green stuff)
- Power distribution
- ... ∞

Dutch Dikes

I love Holland (The Netherlands). I am honored and privileged to know incredible Dutch security pros, from hackers to enterprise partners to my infowar and cyberterrorism associates and government leaders. Lots of friends, and always awesome food.

In 1953, destructive North Sea Floods inundated the country, killing almost 2,000 Dutch. Twenty days later (yes, days!) the government began efforts to protect the country from similar future catastrophes. Called the Delta Works, and sometimes known as the 8th wonder of the world, this massively dynamic project is perhaps the largest man-made feedback network ever created.

*(I look at the Delta Works or a Jet Engine as being a **closed system**. Please keep this in mind, as it will become more critical in the way we look at securing networks.)*

With constant monitoring of weather data, water conditions, soil saturation, and pressure, and adapting those sensors to a network of dams, levees, and sluices, the Delta Works is designed to protect The Netherlands from a "1 in 4,000 years" storm. The complex, nation-wide feedback mechanisms control the amount of water inside the Delta, and sample weather, water depth, flow, pressure, and other variables to manage the balance between the North Sea and the protected lands.

In centuries past, windmills have been a core component of Dutch flood control, acting as water pumping stations in the extensive canal systems. Centuries of feedback-based engineering on a grand scale, indeed.

Time & Clocks

Notation	Seconds	Value	Time	Value	Time	Value	Time	Value	Time
10^0	1	0.02	Minutes						
10^1	10	0.17	Minutes						
10^2	100	1.67	Minutes						
10^3	1,000	16.67	Minutes						
10^4	10,000	2.78	Hours						
10^5	100,000	27.78	Hours	1.16	Days				
10^6	1,000,000	277.78	Hours	11.57	Days	1.65	Weeks	0.03	Years
10^7	10,000,000	2,777.78	Hours	115.74	Days	16.53	Weeks	0.32	Years
10^8	100,000,000	27,777.78	Hours	157.41	Days	165.34	Weeks	3.18	Years
10^9	1,000,000,000	277,777.78	Hours	11,574.07	Days	1,653.44	Weeks	31.80	Years

Fig. 5C

Before we dig in, look over the chart in Fig. 5C above. Use it as a handy dandy reference for fast approximation of huge numbers of seconds. To keep it simple, I'm going to use scientific notation for many time-based criteria and metrics. Please use this chart to see just how much impact a single order of magnitude change in time has.

When normal folks think about clocks, they look at their wrist, their phone, or perhaps a nearby wall. It's about "the time," here or elsewhere in the world.

Feedback

When computer guys think about clocks, we think more about the speed of the clocks that govern the speed of circuits, as in the following simple example from an antique Z-80 processor.

See "How Fast Is A Computer?" in Chapter 3.

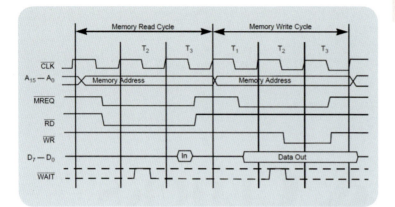

Ignore the details. The point is, the Clock Rate *(top row)* is set by the hardware design and external oscillator. Some instructions, such as "Wait" may only take one clock cycle, but other processes take many clock cycles. These are continuously running clocks that are part of the synchronization of data and systems.

The stop watch, digital or analogue, is an "incrementing clock." The time count goes up in defined increments. The more granular the increments, the finer tuned (and more analogue) the clock's precision.

A decrementing clock lets me know how much time I have left or, in other cases, how much time until some time-critical event occurs. Remember the countdowns that were in the movie *Independence Day*?

This is a picture of a Decrementing Clock from TV shows in ancient times.

In my notional Decrementing Clock, when **DC(t) = 0**, an event occurs; here, if there is a "high" input, it creates an output trigger of "high," or "1." Not much different than a bell going off when the oven timer says the turkey is done. Or your iPhone buzzing when your 6 hours and 22 minutes of allotted hotel-room sleep time is over; alarm clocks decrement time, too.

Feedback

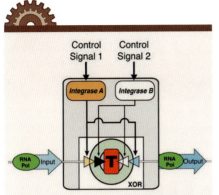

In 2013, researchers at Stanford invented the "transcriptor," a biological equivalent to the transistor, that can emulate basic logical operations using Boolean Integrase Logic (BIL). They can also act as amplifiers. Tremendous opportunity for computing when power is not readily available.

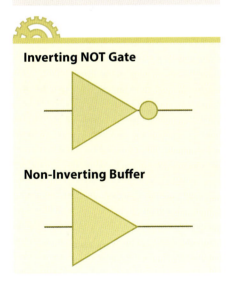

Inverting NOT Gate

Non-Inverting Buffer

In our early audio days, we were ecstatic when FETs, (Field Effect Transistors) became readily available. Fundamentally, they function on the same principles.

MY IDEALIZED CLOCK

I've used clocks in both analogue and digital applications, designs, and architecture, for a long time. For Analogue Network Security I wanted to use a standard, if somewhat idealized, clock. Here's what I came up with.

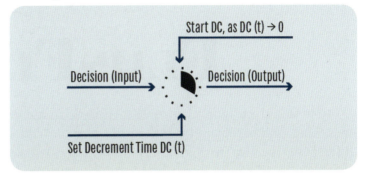

Logically, this is really no more than an inverting NOT gate, or a non-inverting buffer with a time function internally controlling the logic.

Some readers may recognize a similarity with tri-state buffers. True enough, with the addition of the decrementing time-based control before the buffer-logic is enabled.

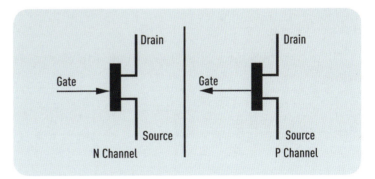

In the above FETs, the source and drain are the inputs and outputs, while the gate turns the current flow on and off. It's a switch that works in either direction.

NEXT? WE'RE GETTING INTO SOME FLIP-FLOPS.

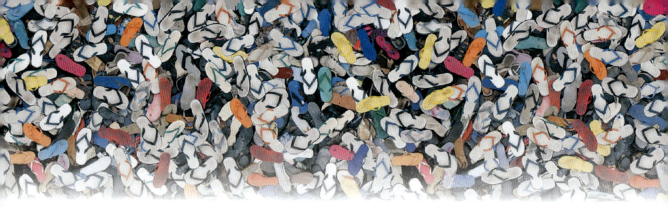

Flip-Flops

I want to add one more element that will help us revisit the 2-Man AND Problem from the prior chapter with a different perspective *(see Fig. 5D)*. A flip-flop, also known as a latch, is a Boolean logic circuit that has two stable states and can be used to store information.

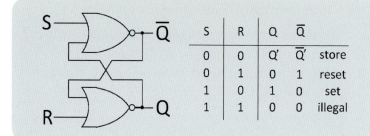

S	R	Q	Q̄	
0	0	Q'	Q̄'	store
0	1	0	1	reset
1	0	1	0	set
1	1	0	0	illegal

- When S - or Alice - is high, the Q output goes high (1), and Q' (the opposite of Q) goes low (0).
- If R - or Bob - goes high, then Q and Q' are reversed.

Fig. 5D

I'll use a simplified Flip-Flop circuit for clarity, as below.

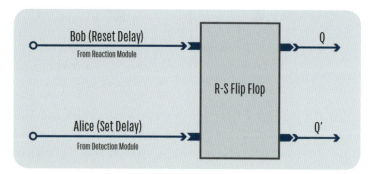

This circuit "remembers" a bit of information (just one bit, not a byte), until such time either R or S are changed.

This is a Flip-Flop. Or, one bit of memory.

STEP IN TIME: BOOLEAN RELAYS

I grew up on relays. We used to build recording studio switching matrices on the cheap by repurposing old AT&T telco stepper relays.

Talk about reliable… even if we *did* find them in a garbage bin on the corner of 47th Street and 11th Avenue at midnight, in front of the old AT&T switching building. (*Statute of limitations, please. And, for much of that chicanery, I was under 18. Ah, youth.*)

The cool thing about telco steppers was that each single switch could represent any of the numbers from 0 - 9. Instead of just a binary condition of on or off, these steppers allowed us to easily work in decimals and build fairly complex switching networks with minimal effort and little or no cost. The point is, we unknowingly, purely from being broke-ass kids building studios on zero budgets, hybridized analogue-ish and binary switching technologies.

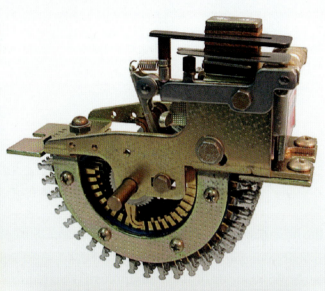

This is a 10-position stepper relay used in old telephone switching networks. Each stepper "remembered" a number from 0 through 9.

Today, you would simply concatenate 10 of these circuits to digitally emulate that old piece of metal above.

BUT THEN, ALONG COMES THE MEMRISTOR.

Memristors

The memristor is an analogue memory device. Sort of.

In the analogue electronics world where I grew up, memory was made up of active components that required a power source; like a tube, transistor, FET, or early logic TTL circuit. (Think CMOS and any chip.) There were three fundamental passive components: the resistor, the capacitor, and the inductor, ubiquitously used in clever combinations in both analogue and digital circuits.

We thought we understood analogue (and digital, for that matter) electronics reasonably well. But in 2008, HP said they had built the memristor, first theorized in 1971 as ==the missing link in analogue electronics.==

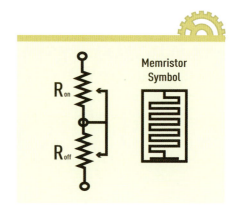

To understand the significance of the memristor, first some basics. The most common electrical formula is called Ohm's law.

$$I = E/R$$

The amount of current (I) that moves through a conductor is linearly proportional to the ratio of the voltage (E, electrical pressure) applied to a load (R, resistance) in a closed circuit.

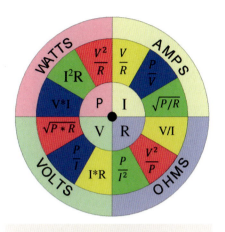

We lived and breathed these simple, interrelated formulas.

Arguably, the second most common electrical formula is about Power.

> $P = I * E$, or equally valid, $P = (E^2)/R$

The power (P) in watts, is linearly equal to the product of the current and voltage.

For example, a 60-watt lightbulb in a 120 volt (U.S.) system conducts only .5 ampere of current. In a 240 volt circuit, the same lightbulb would draw only .25 amperes, but the same amount of power. Linear analogue simplicity. Lower wattage means lower electric bills and less heat waste (greener), which has been possible with the introduction of the terrifically more efficient transducers we call LEDs or OLEDs. They transduce (change) electrical energy into light.

So far, so good. As mentioned earlier, and prior to development of the memristor, the other passive fundamental electrical components were the capacitor and the inductor, both of which are measured as a function of time. The capacitor resists changes to voltage (over time), and the inductor resists changes to current (over time). Thus, even the simplest of circuits can be "tuned", like an old radio dial, to the correct frequency, or time, by the relationship:

> $F = 1/t$

Or, at 1MHz, each cycle (any constantly repetitive waveform) will be one microsecond in length. Think analogue bass and treble controls for audio, and hue for old color TVs. But something was missing...

Here's where it gets both cool and a bit head-scratching, depending upon how you look at the *missing link* of passive electronics.

The memristor is a resistive memory device whose resistive value (measured in ohms) is entirely dependent upon the value of the last current to flow through it and, like the capacitor and inductor, is valued as a function of time.

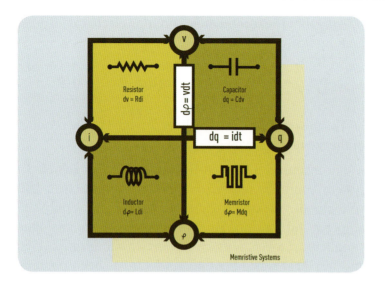

In the simplest case, when a voltage is applied to the memristor, current flows. Then, the power is turned off. Whatever value of resistance the memristor had when the current was flowing will be retained (remembered) until a new current is applied. This way, the memristor can be a switch of two values: On and Off. Nice, neat, and binary.

But the memristor may hold additional promise - like "remembering" 3, 5, 10, or more discreet values in a single "bit." ==Discriminating 10 discreet values in a single bit improves capacity by an order of magnitude.== Each bit could then represent values from 0-9. *(Like in old stepper relays, or chapters 0-9 in this book.)*

So, now I have to ask the question: Is a memristor analogue or digital? For now, I'm going to go all Schrödinger on you and say, both. It depends upon how you look at them.

A base-10 differentiation in the same amount of physical space as a binary or base-2 system, is a huge improvement. One slightly erroneous way to look at this is with dimensions. The more dimensions, the more complex and the more analogue.

> **Memristors function quite similarly to a human brain.**
>
> "Unlike a transistor, which is based on binary codes, a memristor can have multi-levels. You could have several states, let's say zero, one half, one quarter, one third, and so on, and that gives us a very powerful new perspective on how our computers may develop in the future.
>
> Such a shift in computing methodology would allow us to create *smart* computers that operate in a way reminiscent of the synapses in our brains, synaptic weighting with feedback and feed-forwardness.
>
> Free from the limitations of the 0s and 1s, these more powerful computers would be able to learn and make decisions, ultimately getting us one step closer to creating human-like artificial intelligence."
>
> – Jennifer Rupp
> (Professor of Electrochemical Materials at ETH Zurich)

Granularity should also come to mind.

A circle becomes truly analogue where the circumference is perfectly round. Think *zoom* on a digital image of a circle's arc. At one point, if you zoom enough, you will end up with a single pixel - the digital reductionist is alive and well. It's about perception. That's another Limit function, in case you were wondering.

Digital	1 and 0
Memristor	Some number of discreet values, between 2-10
Base Ten	Ten values per character
Hex	16 values per character (2 bytes = 1 word. $16^2 = 256$)
Greek	24 values per character ($24^2 = 576$)
English Alpha	26 values ($26^2 = 676$)
Alpha Numeric	36 values ($36^2 = 1296$)
ASCII	256 values (8 bytes = one word)

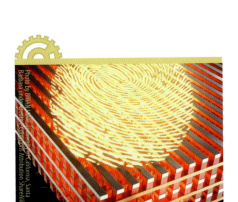

Memristors are now being used in cybersecurity to create non-cloneable (immutable) hardware by exploiting their analogue nature. A memristor circuit essentially becomes a complex Black Box, where the output is terrifically hard to predict; it looks probabilistically random, but is also reliably deterministic. In the coming age of AI vs. AI cyberwar, a metamorphic memristor network is a great hybridized approach for additional time-based security.

(June 2018, University of California, Santa Barbara.)

More memristor coolness. Memristors are an inchoate science. What level of granularity will be developed over the next decade? What about 100 (10^2) discreet values per device? Or more? I have no idea.

But, in my mind, the memristor is truly an analogue-binary chameleon composed of quantum duality: it can be viewed as either analogue and digital, but not both, depending upon which side of the resolution and granularity world you happen to choose.

This is "granularity." Back to the resolution of a wheel. A four-sided wheel (square) has low granularity and a pretty awful ride. 8 and 16-sided wheels (polygons) are improvements in granularity, and smoothness of ride. A Circle is essentially a polygon with lots and lots of small sides. (Smoothing functions, averaging, approximations.)

Analogue-ish.

THE BASIC BUILDING BLOCK OF ANALOGUE NETWORK SECURITY:
The Time-Based Flip-Flop

Let's have some fun gluing these ideas together and then look at how they apply in solving the 2MR conundrum. Please keep in mind, this section is fundamental to ANS, and it is critical that you understand it in-depth before moving on; so I suggest spending a little extra time here to make sure I get it right for you. And maybe you can spend a few extra minutes to truly grok what happens at each point in the logic, so future chapters will make sense.

First off, this is how we left the 2 Man Rule (2MR):

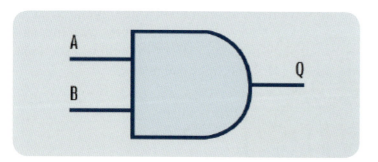

OK, here's an engineering question. How the hell did homo sapiens, like 8,000BCE, build structures with ~1.2 Million Kg (1300 ton) pieces of precisely machined rock. Check out Baalbek. I don't know the answer.

The problem with the 2MR using AND logic is that once Alice (or an Alice process) is initiated, the output, Q, will not be changed (from 0 to 1 or vice/versa) until such time as Bob approves!

Now, let's look at how the 2MR can be viewed with feedback. Remember, Alice and Bob can be calls, routines, outputs of decision trees, network traffic communications, or human activities. The abstraction is the same. In this example, we initially mix 3 ideas.

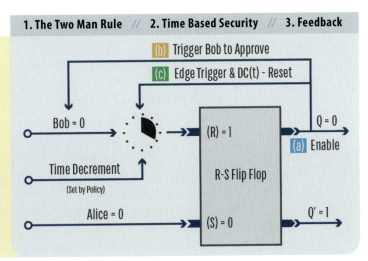

1. Alice = S = 0 = low.
2. Bob's input is Lo, or 0, and the R-input of the flip-flop = 1 = high. (Initial stability)
3. Q = 0 (Q' = 1, and is useful in many applications.)
4. Decrementing Clock Time = DC(t) = X.
5. From a memory standpoint, the initial state represents a bit 0.

The next step is determining one of many possible initialized conditions. I chose just one, for example's sake.

Before Alice, or any processes, can do anything, the initial conditions must be stable. Starting a dynamic system at a predefined level of equilibrium makes things so much easier!

Next, let's go to the next page and have Alice set things in motion.

Feedback

1. Alice makes a decision and "sets" S high.
2. Q goes high, which does the following:
   - The action triggered by Q going high connects to a subsequent circuit that *does* something. I like to view Q(t) = 0, as you will see shortly.
   - Bob is notified, through some communications channel, that his approval has been requested at some start time, where DC(t) > 0, and the reaction time R(t) is determined by the method of notifying Bob and by the actions he takes. (In a non-human automated process, this can be measured in either clock cycles or time, but R(t)>0.)
   - Using edge triggers, this feedback loop does two things. First, when Q goes high, the positive edge triggers a Decrementing Clock which has been told to start counting down from its time-value as assigned by policy, where the value can be DC(t-start) > 0 and is decrementing as DC(t) → 0. In a decent design, this instruction should only be a few edge triggers away at most. Second, when Q goes low, the negative edge will reset the decrementing clock to DC(t-start), from whatever decremented value might have occurred in the last cycle.
3. The Decrementing Clock time, DC(t) → 0, with whatever "ticking" granularity the designers choose.
4. Once Bob has been notified, where D(t) > 0, Bob then has to react, where R(t) > 0, as well, even in the case of automated response where we want R(t) → 0.

The Time-Based Flip-Flop (TB-FF) is a basic building block of ANS, applied here to reducing the risk of, for example, root access, or initializing unauthorized or unapproved mission-critical processes. This works in the physical domain, too.

Notice here that the feedback loop to Bob now represents a familiar formula:

> **Bob's Decision Making Loop**
> $D(t) + R(t) > 0$ and $> Q(t)$

Looks like Bob is the Protection in this system. There are only two possible outcomes permitted in this gated configuration (*and refer to the TB-FF Truth Table in Fig. 5E, too*).

Fig. 5E

TB-FF Truth Table

Alice (Set)	Bob (Approve)	Decrement (t)	Q = Enable
0	0	OFF	0
0	0	t > 0	0
0	0	t = 0	0
1	0	OFF	1
1	0	t > 0	1
1	0	t = 0	0
1	1	OFF	1
1	1	t > 0	1
1	1	t = 0	1
0	1	N/A	0
0	1	N/A	0
0	1	N/A	0

Feedback

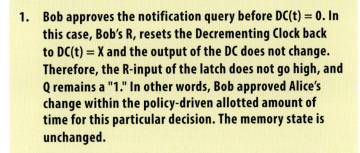

1. **Bob approves the notification query before DC(t) = 0.** In this case, Bob's R, resets the Decrementing Clock back to DC(t) = X and the output of the DC does not change. Therefore, the R-input of the latch does not go high, and Q remains a "1." In other words, Bob approved Alice's change within the policy-driven allotted amount of time for this particular decision. The memory state is unchanged.

2. **Bob is out to lunch.** Bob doesn't get the notification. Bob doesn't care. Or maybe, Bob does not explicitly approve of Alice's decision, which, in any case means that when DC(t) = 0, the clock has fully counted down and the DC output goes high, which also does two things:

   - It resets to DC(t) = X
   - The DC output goes high on the R-input of the latch, S returns to low, or "0," thus flipping the output, Q from "1" to "0," revoking the actions (permissions, etc.) made by Alice. The memory bit is flipped.

Alternatively, Time-Based Flip-Flops can be designed to prevent an action from taking place until both (or more parties) are in agreement, within a prescribed time period. Much more on this in Chapters 7 and 8.

Before going on... please review this a bit. Sit back and cogitate. It will only get more complex from here, and **I really want you to *get this* before moving on.**

Let's look at this with slightly different wording.

We want two people, or processes, to agree on a decision. If we don't use this approach, our Exposure Time, $E(t) \to \infty$. That's where we are today and it doesn't work.

With a Time-Based Flip-Flop (TB-FF) feedback based 2MR mechanism, our exposure time is defined by policy, by **$DC(t) = X = E(t)$**, in 2MR and TBS thinking.

With TBS, we want our feedback loop to be negative, taking us from unstable infinite conditions, $E(t) \to \infty$, to a more manageable state of a pre-defined policy-driven equilibrium of **$E(t) = D(t) + R(t)$**, which resides in the feedback mechanism itself.

Have I said this before? Infinity is the enemy of security.

The time-based approval and revocation model might bring measureable degrees of stability and equilibrium to code, networks, and security, as never before.

By using this approach, the dangers of root control, or single-process decision making without any oversight, can be hugely reduced, provably so. If I reduce anything from infinity to a manageable, real number, the improvement is infinite or indeterminate. (Think divide by "0"...) So, to bring things into the realistic, we can choose some real, arbitrary time period as our maximum for $E(t)$. Let's assume that any current policy-driven operational oversight or audit takes 10^7 seconds, or about 4 months to detect, which is not an atypical amount of time an APT can go unnoticed.

This is me, Winn, on the day I got married, agreeing to abide by the 2PR (2 Person Rule) with my very soon-to-be wife, Sherra.

If a new, ANS-based policy calls for Bob to approve Alice's human interactions, say, within 24 hours of notification, which should be arbitrarily small and → 0, then $E(t)$ improves by more than 10^2, or by a measurably provable 99.72% over the current 10^7 seconds oversight procedure. Not bad for a few lines of code.

This simple 2MR case is only the beginning. Consider that additional feedback-based approval complexities can be added as needed. In code, there may be several OR conditions that would precede a Bob approval. Perhaps a Bob1 and Bob2 are required, so a secondary TB-FF would be added in the primary feedback loop to meet those design requirements. Get as complicated as you want in code, network, or human process, but simplicity is king.

There's more: **I want to add a bit of the element of risk, so we can see what happens with the TB-FF.**

My Wife's Car

My wife has one of those new-fangled automatic-this-and-that SUVs. I won't drive it much because it's like driving 500 computers at 120km/hr and I prefer my antique, manual 6-speed rotary sports car. I have two FM stations pre-set. I'm good to go.

Nonetheless, her Collision-Avoidance (C-A) system is way impressive. Driving along the highway, we are notified of cars to the left of us, cars to the right of us, all to help keep us from doing stupid stuff. Then I got to thinking how much her car's C-A system reminded me of the decades of failures we have experienced with network security. Follow my logic, please.

I was taught to drive by looking hither and yon before a turn, a lane change, or any maneuver that could impact another vehicle. A couple of fast sanity checks to verify there is room - and enough time - for me to make a cogent decision and take an associated action. I need to quickly approximate versus precisely compute the distances and speeds involved to make a safe, time-based decision.

With C-A systems, however, it can be very tempting to *trust* the computer-driven (ICS style) notification as being 100% accurate. In the case of a false positive – "There's a car there!" – no harm. However, a false negative can be life threatening if the driver trusts the C-A with absolute, 100% binary trust. A few autonomous vehicle incidents illustrate the imperfection of binary reliance at this point in CA systems evolution.

So, I got to thinking and saw a time-based analogue feedback parallel to what we are talking about here.

I want to make a lane change.

The C-A system tells me that no car occupies the space where I want to go. (Now, we start time, with $T = 0$.)

I have two choices.

1. I completely trust the C-A and make the lane change without further verification; no feedback. This is the equivalent of network security today. A single, binary decision point, the results of which, in this case, determines whether I will be involved in an accident or not. I provide no balancing or verifying input as to whether the decision is correct or not.

2. I "sort of trust" the C-A, but now, with $T = 0$, and an unknown Trust Factor (because nothing is **100%**, or **1**), I choose to verify what the C-A tells me. I turn my head to visually examine the road; enhanced situational awareness in security-speak. There is no car there; the safety is verified, and I switch lanes. That's $D(t) > 0$.

In analogue terms, blindly trusting the C-A means that I have an absolute 100% trust in its efficacy, and I am completely comfortable to let it make life and death decisions for me. Because there is no subsequent verification, $D(t) + R(t) \to \infty$, and therefore $E(t) \to \infty$. That's a bad thing.

In case #2 above, we have a different condition:

> - My desire to change lanes.
> - The C-A says it's safe.
> - I choose to look around, which is invoking a verifying feedback loop.
> - Based upon that feedback loop, $D(t) + R(t)$, I make a much more informed and verified decision.

Are all drivers going to think this way? Hell no. Many will become complacently ignorant, as we have in network security and mobile device clicking. They will blindly accept that the technology is 100% reliable, choosing to abdicate personal responsibility and instead, when things go wrong, blame the tech. This will only become more true as autonomous vehicles fill the roads.

The one big difference in this model, though, is the state of Q, now based upon the inputs, not to a latch, but to an AND gate. The feedback is introduced before (versus after) a decision has been made or it's output enabled.

In this model, the decision for Q to go high is made only when a primary decision has forced a verification process, both of which must be high at the input of the AND gate, within a specified time window.

0 < T < Decision Time

I have found that as I think more about Analogue Network Security, I discover good physical engineering examples where it is applied, but all too many where it is not applied and could be.

HELP WANTED

I have no doubt other representations, context, and metaphors will be useful for many different environments. Any and all suggestions are encouraged and will only bring about greater clarity along with the analogue models I propose. Please contribute to the discussion wherever you go.

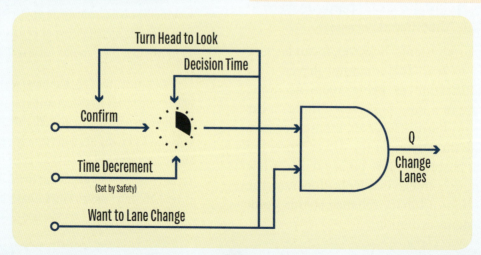

ANALOGUE RISK

Time-based security gave us a simple metric to evaluate E(t), and to gauge how much damage can be done to a network and data in a given time period, given certain known bandwidth conditions. Understanding risk, in my analogue way of thinking, requires that time be an integral component of any valuation. And then I mucked it all up further with Trust Factor, under the axiomatic assumption that there is no such thing as 0 or 1 trust. Has to be somewhere, fuzzily, in between. How can we glue these two concepts together?

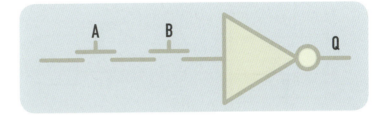

Recall that, in a simple AND situation (without considering the time dimension), if both Alice and Bob are trusted at .9, then the Trust Factor (P), once both Alice and Bob have agreed, is:

$$P(A \cup B)$$

Trust Factor (P) = 0.99, or a 99% likelihood that the combined efforts of Alice and Bob will be good and, inversely, Risk = .01, where there is a 1% chance that the combined efforts of Alice and Bob will still result in something bad.

$$P(0.9 \text{ and } 0.9) = P(0.9) + P(0.9) - P(0.9 * 0.9)$$
$$= 1.8 - 0.81$$
$$= 0.99$$

RISKY TIMES

Unless there is a future, there is no risk. Zero time = Zero risk. Risk is an innately time-based function, giving us additional hope to develop tools using common metrics.

DIGITAL INVERSION

I am offering that Trust Factor and Risk Factor are inversely proportional with our analogue views.

For example, an input with TF = .85 yields an inverted output of RF = .15.

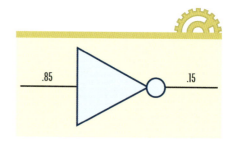

Using digital logic gates, we can see both and still treat them as an analogue metric (1 - .85 = .15, et al.). This will help us later, too, when calculating risk and systemic trust.

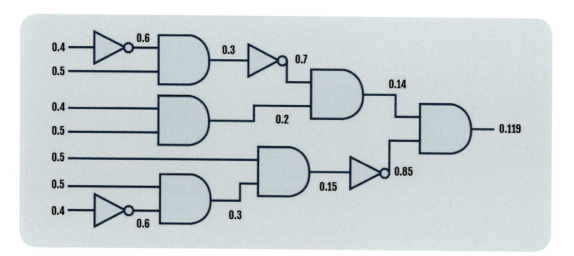

The math is simple. You just need to know if your metric is TF or Risk. In the above example, it's obvious what happens when several people or processes, or partners, or so-called 'trusted' relationships, have access to (or control over) an object. Trust gets pretty low, pretty damned quickly.

Whether that object is data, a resource, or more abstractly, information in any form, the more people or processes (subjects) that have access to that *knowledge*, the more dramatically the risk of a leak increases. (Recall the Beyesian probability we used earlier.) It's a wonder there are secrets at all any more!

But what about time? Where is it? The above approach yields quite the binary result as there is no analogue time component. It's the static expectation of a particular metric of, say, TF = .99, to remain constant for eternity; forever; never change. The Trust Factor of the human/code/network requests are similarly assumed to be static, the way we do it today.

However, we often hear about executives who see impressive one-off metric results of some arbitrary test and say, "Cool! We're secure!" This sort of knee-jerk, baseless assumption and urgency reminds me of an anxious C-Suiter who desperately awaits the result of the latest pen-testing. He so wants to show the board and auditors, that he ignores the analogue component of network security.

With pen-testing, the claimed level of security must be strictly bounded by many variables. Most importantly, the results of any pen-test are only strictly valid for a short period of time. Things change. Data is input. Routines are called. Instances are spun up. Users log on and off. Code is upgraded. Systems crash and reboot. Connection requests never stop. All of these highly dynamic actions naturally change the security status of any process. We network and security folks do not live in a static universe, ergo, please try to look with an analogue view.

In the above example, because there is no feedback or time domain, we must take, on faith alone, that the trust factors of Alice and Bob will not change - ever - each remaining at .9 - forever and ever, amen! They will always be the most honest, trustworthy, and error-free folks (or processes or connections) you have ever met. Nonetheless, we did achieve two things:

Remember the "Is It Analogue?" Chart from Chapter 3? Time and Trust Factor/Risk in this example, give this approach analogue-ness.

> ▶ We added a dual authorization element, which is better than *common* systems.
>
> ▶ We increased the measurable trust factor and reduced the risk of the 2MR system under consideration.

The formula for measuring risk reduction from a single admin with no time constraints is:

$$1 - (1-(TF(a)+TF(b)) - \frac{TF(a)*TF(b)}{1-TF(a)} = \text{Risk Reduction}$$

or

$$-1 - \frac{1-P(A \cup B)}{P(A)} = -90\% \text{ Risk}$$

(Risk Reduction of 90%)

Let's look at a few examples.

In example #1, Bob (.9) is asked to validate Alice's (.9) decision. There is no feedback or specific timeframe in which Bob must respond. Thus, a probabilistic risk reduction of 90% (.1 to .01) is achieved when Bob approves Alice's choice. But efficiency can quickly suffer.

Single Admin Examples of Trust Factor/Risk: Time = Infinity

	Alice	Alice	Alice	Alice	Alice
TF	0.90	0.95	0.70	0.60	0.10
Risk	0.10	0.95	0.30	0.40	0.90

2MR – AND – No Feedback: Time = Infinity

Example 1	Alice	Bob	Alice & Bob
TF	0.900	0.900	0.990
Risk	0.100	0.100	0.010
Risk Improvement			90.0%

Example 2	Alice	Bob	Alice & Bob
TF	0.90	0.95	0.995
Risk	0.10	0.05	0.005
Risk Improvement			95.0%

Example 3	Alice	Bob	Alice & Bob
TF	0.70	0.80	0.940
Risk	0.30	0.20	0.060
Risk Improvement			80.0%

Maximum Approval (MA) Time is the policy-driven time in which mission critical, or other assigned high-value processes or decisions, must be either validated by a second approved authority or revoked.

In example #2, however, Bob has slightly higher TF, so our combined TF approaches 1, but will never reach it. In example #3, we see counter intuitively, that even two lower TFs, with an AND condition, can still dramatically decrease Risk.

Let's look at the 2MR with feedback and see what happens to risk. In Analogue Network Security, Risk is the digital inverse of Trust Factor, and now we want to add the time domain, too.

==But first I want to get rid of our arch enemy, infinity.==

The notion that security controls are set to a specific status or condition indefinitely is the antithesis of ICS, SCADA, balance, equilibrium, feedback, and all things good-engineering. Having an infinite upper-bound in the time domain has been, as the vast amount of system, data, and network compromises has long proven, ==a complete failure in engineering security and corporate policy design and enforcement.== It must stop if we ever expect to reign in hostile actions.

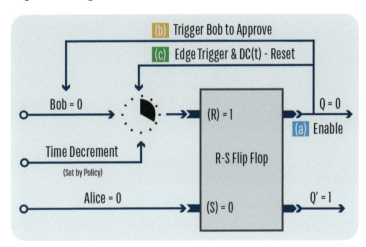

In this TB-FF (Time-Based Flip-Flop) example, let TF(a) = TF(b) = .9. But what do we do about this decision for "forever" conundrum? Simple, we set boundaries; quite similar to setting min-max limits.

I am going to arbitrarily design (for easier math and intuitive explanations) that we want to know the TF of a particular process for 10^3 seconds; roughly 17 minutes, or the time period I am calling the Maximum Approval Time (MA). Maximum Approval Time is the Policy driven time in which mission critical, or other assigned high-value processes or decisions, must be secondarily validated, else the decision to permit them is revoked. MA is entirely chosen by the **customer** or **designer**, based upon policy, appetite for risk, available resources ad infinitum. Let's calculate a dynamic trust factor by using two time values:

> $MA(t) > 10^3$ and
> $DC(t) = 10^3$ sec *(which is the implementation of the decrementing clock time)*

MA(t) should always be greater than DC(t), otherwise, why bother? Please keep in mind that this analysis is limited in scope, with two important caveats:

1. It is only valid for the max time of MA(t). Any condition where some arbitrary time reference > MA(t) is undefinable.
2. We assume the TF does not change significantly during MA(t), especially since it should be a fairly short time value.

Notice the effect of introducing a time-based feedback control for TF in Fig. 5F on the next page.

In all three of the examples, TF(a) ≥ TF(b), and the system or TF(ab) increases proportionately to the time (speed) of the feedback loop. In example #1, the DC(t) (the implemented time permitted for approval before revocation) is .1% of the MA(t): DC(t)/MA(t). Therefore, the cumulative time-based trust factor for the period DC(t) is slightly reduced from .99 to .9899, and the risk is marginally increased.

What we did on old analogue audio equipment was tweak and twist all the knobs back and forth – from min to max – quickly, to see if we could break something.

We will look at solving the degrading trust problem in the next section.

2MR – AND – with Feedback: Case #1

	Alice	Bob	Alice & Bob		MA(t)
					1000
TF	0.90	0.90	0.99		
Risk	0.10	0.10	0.01		
DC (seconds)	1.00		999.00		1,000.00
Trust Units	0.90		989.01	MA - TF >	0.9899
Risk Units	0.10		9.99	MA - Risk >	1.01%
Risk Reduction					89.9%

2MR – AND – with Feedback: Case #2

	Alice	Bob	Alice & Bob		MA(t)
					1000
TF	0.90	0.90	0.99		
Risk	0.10	0.10	0.01		
DC (seconds)	100.00		900.00		1,000.00
Trust Units	90.00		891.00	MA - TF >	0.9810
Risk Units	10.00		9.00	MA - Risk >	1.90%
Risk Reduction					81.0%

2MR – AND – with Feedback: Case #3

	Alice	Bob	Alice & Bob		MA(t)
					1000
TF	0.90	0.90	0.99		
Risk	0.10	0.10	0.01		
DC (seconds)	700.00		300.00		1,000.00
Trust Units	630.00		297.00	MA - TF >	0.9270
Risk Units	70.00		3.00	MA - Risk >	7.30%
Risk Reduction					27.0%

In these charts, we see the effects of feedback time on TF(ab) when TF(a) ≥ TF(b). MA(t) is arbitrarily set to 10^3 seconds.

IMHO, these examples and approaches to trust factor and risk are great fodder for more Management Porn.

Example #2: When **DC(t) / MA(t) = 100/1000**, the risk reduction is still pretty good, but increasing DC(t) by a factor of 10 causes the Risk to almost double over example #1. In Example #3, **DC(t)/ MA(t) = .7**, so the risk reduction over a single admin is clearly not as significant.

Analogue Network Security says:

> As **DC(t) → MA(t), Risk Reduction → 0%**
>
> *and*
>
> As **DC(t) → 0, Risk Reduction → 100%**

The second piece of valuable information we get is the total TF and Risk for the period MA(t).

SOME INTUITION

I have constructed these examples with the caveat that $TF(b) \geq TF(a)$.

Intuitively, most of us can accept the statement: **Any person or entity required to approve a primary decision must have an equal or greater level of trust than the original decision maker.**

This becomes especially obvious when:

> $TF(b) \geq TF(a)$ *and*
>
> $TF(a) \rightarrow 1.0$ *and*
>
> $TF(b) \rightarrow 1.0$ *and*
>
> $DC(t) \rightarrow 0$ *then*
>
> **Risk Reduction $\rightarrow$ 100%**

Please pay attention to these inequalities, as they help define boundary conditions. They, too, are fundamental to how Analogue Network Security can be applied in so many varied conditions, in the virtual (cyber), physical, and human domains, when time is the metric.

And remember…

If there is no future, there is zero risk.

When Bob is No Alice

The prior discussions are self-obvious when $TF(b) \geq TF(a)$. But what happens when $TF(a) > TF(b)$?

Nothing good, by my measure. Intuitively, the second pair of eyes — the sanity check on any decisions in any domain — should be at least as good (trust factor-wise, that is) as the first. But is this always possible?

A counter-example:

Alice is the boss of all things. Bob is her much lower-paid assistant, who handles all of the things for Alice, too. Sometimes Bob has to sign for Alice as a primary in the decision chain, or even as the sole proxy for Alice. What happens to the trust factor? The more I thought about it, I was able to come to the conclusion that the answer was abstractly indeterminate and case by case dependent.

Feedback

> - If Alice gives sole authority to Bob (in security parlance, an abdication), then Bob's TF is the only one with any meaning. Right or wrong.
>
> - If a 2MR relationship is established, Alice (we will assume by IdM controls) cannot abdicate both approvals to Bob. But Bob, as the subordinate party, naturally must have a lower TF than the boss-lady Alice, and we have TF(a) > TF(b).

I have played with the TF(a) > TF(b) problem and it becomes more complex than T(b) > T(a) because the weighted variables in establishing each party's Trust Factor must be individually factored-in over time, as they change. Do competence, fat fingering, personal or financial troubles all represent equally likely downward trends over time?

I hope some math folks out there will formalize the problem better than I can. The following is the best I came up with, which is OK as a static starting point.

Where TF(a) > TF(b)
2MR - AND - No Feedback

Example 1	Alice	Bob	Alice & Bob
TF	0.90	0.90	0.9900
Risk	0.10	0.10	0.010
Risk Improvement			90.0%

Example 2	Alice	Bob	Alice & Bob
TF	0.90	0.85	0.7500
Risk	0.10	0.15	0.250
Risk Improvement			-150.0%

Example 3	Alice	Bob	Alice & Bob
TF	0.90	0.60	0.5000
Risk	0.10	0.40	0.500
Risk Improvement			-400.0%

Feedback

In this case, we are employing no feedback and TF(a) > TF(b), an uncomfortable situation, in which someone with less trust is the final arbiter. Using the same basis for estimating a 2MR Trust Factor:

> If TF(a) ≤ TF(b), then (TF(a)+TF(b))-(TF(a)*TF(b))
>
> If TF(a) > TF(b), then TF(a)-(1-TF(b))

Obviously, Trust is not time transitive!

The necessary and best practice sequence of the approval in any process becomes clear, and this approach might provide some direction to Analogue Network Security designers. Just as importantly, a design analysis trending in the wrong direction can and should be addressed earlier than later. Now, let's add feedback.

Case #1: 2MR A>B AND: AL(t) = 10³ sec; DC(t) is variable					
	Alice	Bob	Alice & Bob		AL(t)
					1000
TF	0.90	0.50	0.4000		
Risk	0.10	0.50	0.60		
DC (seconds)	1.00		999.00		1,000.00
Trust Units	0.90		399.60	AL - TF >	0.4005
Risk Units	0.10		599.40	AL - Risk >	59.95%
Risk Reduction					- 499.5%
Case #2: 2MR A>B AND: AL(t) = 10³ sec; DC(t) is variable					
	Alice	Bob	Alice & Bob		AL(t)
					1000
TF	0.90	0.50	0.4000		
Risk	0.10	0.50	0.60		
DC (seconds)	100.00		900.00		1,000.00
Trust Units	0.90		360.00	AL - TF >	0.3609
Risk Units	0.10		9.99	AL - Risk >	63.91%
Risk Reduction					- 539.1%

In the examples on the previous page, TF(a) = .9 and TF(b) = .5 and we maintain a constant upper policy-driven time boundary of 1000 seconds. The only variable is the decrementing clock time, DC(t). In example #1, if DC(t) = 1, then the resultant risk due to TF(b) = .5 is the limit as Risk Reduction → 500%, or five times the risk. When we adjust the DC(t), look what happens. By manipulating the min-max feedback time in the TB-FF, and when TF(a) > TF(b), we can, as in cases #1 and #2 on the previous page, adjust the gain in risk. I can see cases where a mere perfunctory approval is required, but if it were me, I would avoid employing T(a) > T(b). Ever. Bad security.

Case #3: 2MR B>A AND: AL(t) = 10^3 sec; DC(t) is variable					
	Alice	Bob	Alice & Bob		AL(t)
					1000
TF	0.20	0.50	0.6000		
Risk	0.80	0.50	0.40		
DC (seconds)	500.00		500.00		1,000.00
Trust Units	0.90		300.00	AL - TF >	0.3009
Risk Units	0.10		9.99	AL - Risk >	69.91%
Risk Reduction					12.6%

In case #3 above, we return to positive risk reduction.

We will look at this in more detail by playing with the Trust Factor Matrix and building dynamic TF views over time. We will even get views of what security looks like mathematically, in Chapter 9.

Degrading Trust

Trust is absolute. Once established, it remains in place forever and ever. This is the unfortunate acceptable modus operandi in too many organizations. Whether that trust is in a 'trusted employee,' a network connection to a 'trusted partner', or in code and libraries, our industry has taken an approach to security that is fundamentally flawed. The tendency is to trust and forget. "It works OK. Let's not worry about it unless something goes wrong."

Isn't that a mirror of why we didn't catch Aldrich Ames and Robert Hanson, to name but two? Or product safety? "It doesn't seem that serious… let's wait and see if anyone notices or we get sued." We've never heard that, have we?

Or worse.

"Big embarrassed security vendor said that someone managed to get into its systems and write 'unauthorized code' that 'could allow a knowledgeable attacker to gain administrative access.' Such access would allow the hacker to monitor encrypted traffic on the computer network and decrypt communications." *(CNN, 18 Dec. 2015)*

Oh, but it gets worse, as is so typical in our industry: "The system was compromised for three years before they uncovered it in a routine review… "

What better example of a binary failure and a failed trust implementation? The review time was routine, but what we don't know, yet can suspect is the following…

1. Their $D(t)$ was awful, because routine = three years.
2. Their $D(t)$ was awful, because routine = four times a year, but they detected nothing wrong for three years.
3. Their $D(t) < 3$ years, but their $R(t) \rightarrow 3$ years, for any number of technical, financial, business, or political reasons.

I use [this vendor's name redacted for karmic reason] because part of the goal of Analogue Network Security is to hold vendors accountable to some set of performance metrics. In this case (which I am sure is not isolated to this vendor alone; they just got caught), one must question the efficacy of a vendor's offerings if they can't keep their own $D(t) + R(t)$ to a minimum. IMHO, three years is excessive.

And this is exactly what degrading trust is all about. All of the elements in the trust factor matrix are subject to change at any time, therefore changing the dynamic value of the trust factors and how they contribute additional risk to the system. I would like to posit:

- Has the person met with personal challenges that affect reliability?
- Has the person been somehow co-opted to perform malicious acts?
- Has the updated code or revision been vetted to the same degree as its predecessor?

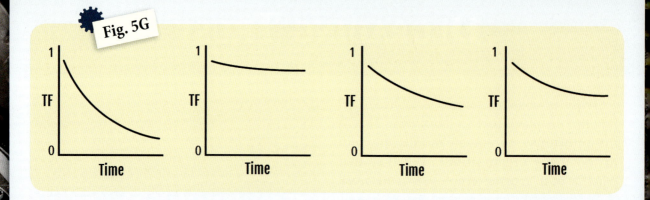

Fig. 5G

- How do changes in a partner's network policy and implementation affect the trust of our connection?
- Do the backup batteries (or generator oil) still function at spec, a year later?
- Make up any of your own time-based trust degradation situations. *(After all, we've seen them all, right?)*

Instead, trust is a continuously variable function. The entropic nature of trust tends towards greater uncertainty in the trust factor of an object over time.

Over time, we know less about the trusted object.

As less accurate information is available, uncertainty increases. That's entropy. In Analogue Network Security, an uncontrolled increase in entropy is akin to an audio amplifier that has no feedback mechanism. The system can quickly destablize; in network terms that means making object-subject relationships with little or no basis for trust.

In Fig. 5G, the initial TF=.9, and in each of these examples, TF decays at different rates over time. The resulting Trust Factors vary a great deal based upon the degree of periodic trust reduction and revalidation.

Herein, again, there is no feedback and, over time, the entropy will increase to the point that the concept of trust is essentially meaningless. So, with a little analogue-ish thinking, we can approach this problem the same way we looked at the 2MR and ultimately combine them into one function, which will be very useful later on.

How often is a revalidation of the object-subject trust relationship conducted?

Trust is neither constant, nor time-transitive.

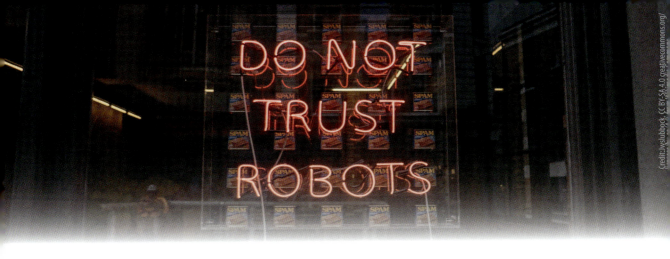

Trust Factor Feedback

Earlier, a Trust Factor matrix for the Human domain was applied to the 2MR for enhanced authentication.

The exact same approach is used for Trust Factor in the physical and cyber domains, as shown in the following examples.

PHYSICAL Criteria	TF 0.0 to 1.0	#1 Weighted Factor	#1 Weighted Value	#2 Weighted Factor	#2 Weighted Value	#3 Weighted Factor	#3 Weighted Value
Driveway Barriers	0.95	14.29%	0.136	13.00%	0.124	20.00%	0.190
Glass Building Front	0.05	14.29%	0.007	1.00%	0.001	20.00%	0.010
Guards at Front Desk	0.7	14.29%	0.100	6.00%	0.042	10.00%	0.070
Man Trap #1	0.97	14.29%	0.139	20.00%	0.194	10.00%	0.097
Elevator Badge & Code	0.86	14.29%	0.123	20.00%	0.172	15.00%	0.129
Secure Door 12th Floor	0.8	14.29%	0.114	20.00%	0.160	10.00%	0.080
Vault	0.95	14.29%	0.136	20.00%	0.190	15.00%	0.143
Total Trust Factor	0.754	100.00%	0.754	100.00%	0.882	100.00%	0.719

In the physical domain example of Fig. 5H, we assign relative trust values to an arbitrary seven defenses. The two weakest defenses here are the glass doors and the guards. Then we assign weighting factors, based on how important we really think each of them are.

Further, in the chart on the previous page, when looking at the columns labeled #1, we consider all seven defenses to be of equal weighting, and we end up with an overall system trust factor of .754. However, when we weight them, as in the #2 columns, the trust factor rises to .882. If the weighting in the #3 columns leans toward a greater belief in perimeter security, the system trust factor plummets to .719. Clearly, this is a potential fail with greater risk, and should be re-evaluated.

Fig. 5I

CYBER Criteria	TF 0.0 to 1.0	#1 Weighted Factor	#1 Weighted Value	#2 Weighted Factor	#2 Weighted Value
Code Verification #1	0.95	25.00%	0.238	10.00%	0.095
Code Verification #2	0.95	25.00%	0.238	10.00%	0.095
Stress Testing	0.7	10.00%	0.070	30.00%	0.210
Partner Confidence	0.8	10.00%	0.080	20.00%	0.160
Library Confidence	0.95	20.00%	0.190	15.00%	0.143
Test Bed	0.95	10.00%	0.095	15.00%	0.143
Total Trust Factor	0.883	100.00%	0.910	100.00%	0.845

In the cyber case of Fig. 5I, we see two different weighting approaches. In #1, trust is more about coding correctly from the beginning. In #2, the confidence is weighted in favor of external confidence testing and appears to be more concerned with uptime (stress testing) than other developmental basics.

In all three of the security domains, the matrices are static, without the analogue dynamics of the time dimension. We postulate that time-based stasis does not occur in the real world; therefore, any Trust Factor value is valid for the moment it was measured - much like pen-testing. So what can we do?

WE ADD FEEDBACK, OF COURSE.

Top 10 of Analogue Network Feedback

Here's what I believe are the takeaways on feedback that will be of use when thinking about analogue approaches to network security.

1. Negative feedback keeps systems in balance - equilibrium.
2. Positive feedback is great for learning and (some) growth, else it yields unpredictability and chaos.
3. ICS & SCADA are feedback intensive. We should learn from them.
4. Time is the analogue feedback loop, creating the Time-Based Flip-Flop (TB-FF) – the basic building block of Analogue Network Security.
5. Using Trust Factors and time, object-subject relationship risks become clearer as synaptic weighting techniques are applied.
6. Trust is not constant. Trust Factor and Risk are digital inverses of each other. Risk is not constant.
7. Trust is not time transitive!
8. Decaying trust factors are an increase of entropy.
9. Trust factor matrixes can tie to existing IdM systems.
10. Putting the Trust Factor Matrix into a feedback loop introduces a balance to the system, minimizing increases in entropy.

In the next chapter, I'm going to introduce a couple more analogue concepts to expand our toolkit for rethinking security, and then we can look at a number of potential applications.

6
OODA, TCP/IP, AND OOB

Modern recreation of the Enigma-cracking Bombe, designed by Alan Turing. It's hybrid analogue-digital approach used lots of OODA and Feedback, but was three decades earlier than networking protocols. But still... this was the bomb!

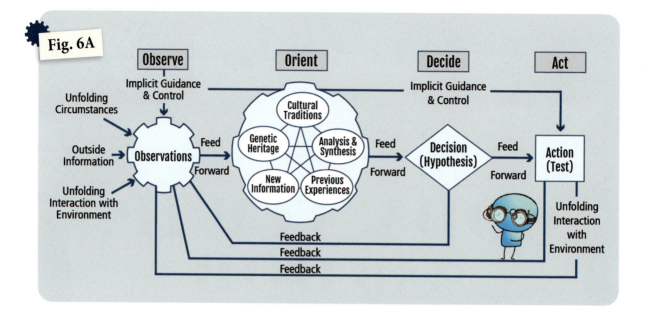

Fig. 6A

GETTING LOOPY

Feedback is great, but let's add another layer - some might say dimension - to the concept of feedback in real world situations.

In 1976, U.S. Air Force Colonel John Boyd began publishing abstract concepts on air-to-air combat and how to gain combat superiority in aerial dog fights. Boyd's key concept was that of the decision cycle, or the now famous and conceptually simple process, the OODA Loop. He postulated that in aerial combat, victory was awarded to the combatant who was able to quickly react to actions, intentionally creating corollary events meant to confound and delay the reactions of the adversary.

In my eyes, Boyd intuited that organic, carbon-based, and intelligent life forms on almost any scale, and the organizations built by man, follow the same cycles. They undergo growth and evolution as they interact with their environment. He broke this cycle down to four constituent, if sometimes fuzzily overlapping, processes.

Harry Hillaker (chief designer of the F-16) said of Boyd's OODA theory, "Time is the dominant parameter. The pilot who goes through the OODA cycle in the shortest time prevails because his opponent is caught responding to situations that have already changed." Sounds like we could use a lot of this kind of thinking in network security.

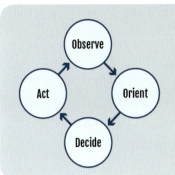

- **Observation:** Sense the environment, by myriad means, and store the data. This component is key to Detection in Depth.
- **Orientation:** Analyze that data to form a perspective; some call this "situational awareness."
- **Decision:** Based upon the above, create a flow chart, tree, or some other defined steps to optimize decision making.
- **Action:** Act on the decision.

Although Boyd initially applied the OODA Loop to aerial combat, it can also apply to corporate and government processes. Conceptually, it can be added to programming routines where security is paramount. I also find that in our high-speed, consumer-driven world, using a product and advertising analogy can communicate the OODA principles well. (We will explore this further in the next section, "Green Furry Things".)

==The keys to gaining a competitive advantage in any arena are flexibility and fluidity within a highly dynamic environment== (just like aerial combat). Once again, it comes down to time. The company that can adapt the fastest to market changes, will gain some competitive advantage. This means the OODA Loops will necessarily evolve over time as market conditions and customer choices change, which they always do. People get bored.

Now, consider for a moment how many, if any, natural or manmade processes *don't* adhere to the OODA Loop. Not many, because they want to survive!

In my opinion, Boyd formalized a generalized abstract model that can be adapted and applied in any dynamic environment. Education. Driving. Food. JIT (Just in time) Supply Chains. And from earlier sections, we now know that OODA-like feedback processes abound everywhere.

1. Security will never be 100%. Can't and won't happen.
2. Attackers must also operate under time constraints, just as defenders do.
3. If a defender is faster than an attacker, provable security efficacy can be claimed for that particular well-defined situation. No more security information may be accurately gleaned outside of those time and event boundaries.

Green Furry Things

An entrepreneur (or established company) wants to build a new business. They research the field, analyze the market, indulge in competitive intelligence, and decide to make Green Furry Things.

> **War:** The military and intelligence communities must keep tabs on everyone, everywhere, at all times, in order to advise political and military leaders. They use technology such as SIGINT-Signals Intelligence, HUMINT-spies or Human Intelligence, OSINT- Open Sources Intelligence (unclassified information available to anyone for the asking), IMINT-Imagery intelligence, and ELINT- electronic intelligence.

> What's with the Green Furry Things? It came up in a speech one time. Someone asked a question, and instead of referencing miscellaneous "stuff," Green Furry Things (as a manufacturing analogy) popped out of my non-thinking lips. It got a lot of laughs and stuck.

The top management of the company uses the market research data and finally determines it wants to begin selling Green Furry Things to a population hungry for them. They tool up the factories and begin making Green Furry Things by the millions.

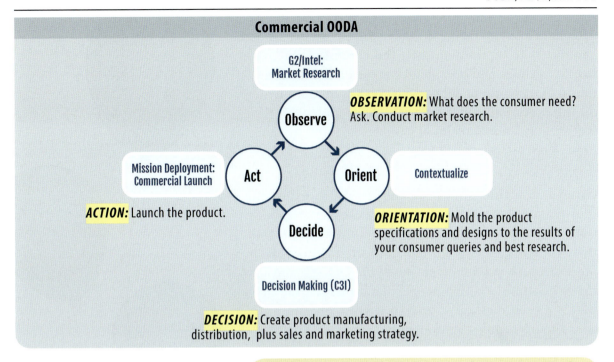

> **War:** The Pentagon, or Ministry of Defence, or whatever other military command is around, designs actions and responses to potential scenarios based upon the intelligence provided. In some cases, the military may be called upon to plan and execute an operation; peace-keeping, humanitarian missions, joint operations, or maybe, actual combat.

The sales and marketing troops are released. Advertising and public relations begin an onslaught, first announcing the availability of Green Furry Things at stores everywhere, and then convincing the public that they will be less than patriotic if they don't have several Green Furry Things of their own at home, in the car, and lavishly hung around their necks. The sales force will convince stores to stock up on Green Furry Things, so they can fill the impending demand.

> **War:** The troops are sent to the field;.They keep the peace or shoot the enemy or bomb the bejeezus out of the desert for forty days and forty nights. They begin their mission.

The OODA Loop above, which represents both the commercial world and the business of war or peacekeeping, is continuous. It never ends. (How very

Successful network security is an orchestration of time-based events, designed to maintain stability and avoid chaos, (e.g., phishing, DDoS, data breaches, etc.)

un-binary of it…) Thus, in both worlds, we are in an iterative state of constant flux; the conditions of free-market realities and geo-politics are ever-changing and thus require constant adjustment. Such is modern living on the precarious ledge between chaos and stability – that great unknown realm of complex adaptive systems. Ergo - OODA Loop feedback.

For the next cycle, in the commercial world, the Green Furry Things may not sell as well as expected, thus (1) more market research and customer feedback is needed (*We want Blue Furry Things in Wisconsin.*), so that (2) management can make updated decisions (*Is the Wisconsin market alone worth the effort?*), and (3) the sales and marketing people can broadcast the new Blue + Green message… and so it goes, on and on… over and over again. It never stops.

Or, perhaps Green Furry Things sell just fine, meeting or exceeding expectations, so (1) market research is conducted to see if the buying public wants Blue and Brown Furry Things, as well. Perhaps, Green Furry Things that belch on alternate Tuesdays are needed. Whatever. (2) Decisions are made and (3) the sales and marketing troops *again* pounce upon the public.

In the military world, once a mission has begun, (1) constantly updated intelligence is required, along with instantaneous, real-time battlefield feedback from the technology-armored soldier, which is sent back to (2) headquarters where additional decisions are made and commands are issued. Then, (3) the deployed troops are issued updated orders. And so this cycle goes on and on… until the mission is completed at the local level… or forever on the macro-scale of global geo-politics and national security.

The more I drink the Analogue Network Security Kool-Aid, the more I see OODA everywhere. Think of OODA-time as being as granular as you choose. The tighter the loop, the more analogue it behaves.

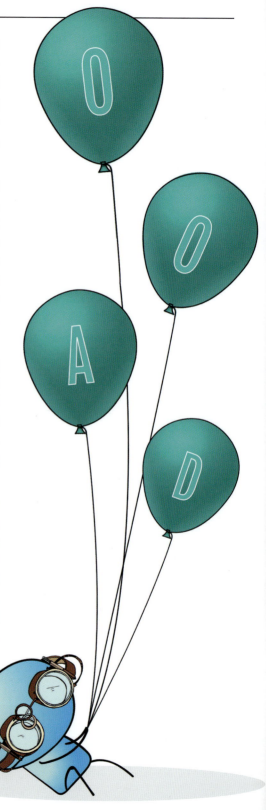

OODA Everywhere

Almost every successful business optimizes the time component of OODA Loops.

INVENTORY

Businesses want to maintain as small an inventory as they can. Industrial-age auto manufacturers measure their new unsold cars in time. "We have 41½ days of inventory." There is a specific dollar value assigned to that time, as well. Food retailers measure their inventory very carefully, using time as a metric, especially for perishables, such as milk, which has a can't-be-sold-after date. Medicines carry dates when they can no longer be trusted. Any miscalculations create waste and therefore lost profits, nevermind the fact that the medicines could be ineffective.

JUST-IN-TIME MANUFACTURING

Hardware manufacturers carefully plan and optimize their incoming parts supplies so they don't sit around on shelves for an eternity. They prefer to have supplies come in every day in smaller quantities than in huge month-long or year-long shipments. It saves money. The object is to get the parts into the factory, build them into the value-added product and ship the product out the doors as fast as humanly possible. Profits go up when the time between receiving and shipping goes down. That is a simple time-based reality.

WALL STREET

American investors measure profitability of companies in small chunks of time — quarters of a year. Unlike some of our more visionary global friends and business competitors who plan and project industrial and national growth and wealth over decades, many investors often seek out short-term profits and immediate gratification.

INTERNET

In the online world, we also expect immediate gratification. We expect and demand that web pages launch instantly. "It takes too long to load. Must be broken."

Online commerce is absolutely about time. If an online payment cannot be made and authorized in a few seconds, many of us will walk away frustrated. "That part of the interwebs must be broken, too."

That's why commerce servers often employ cryptographic accelerators. It takes the commerce server a small but finite amount of time to cryptographically decode an incoming payment message — on the order of 100 to 200 milliseconds. If just one person is making the request, it is processed very quickly. However, if the server is hit with a large quantity of commerce or payment requests all at once, a queue is created, and someone is going to be waiting a long time. A long, long time. So, cryptographic accelerators are hardware optimized to handle the complex mathematics of public key encryption systems and speed up the process by as much as 100 times or more.

TEACHING

If this four-step OODA Loop applied to the teaching process isn't obvious, I give up.

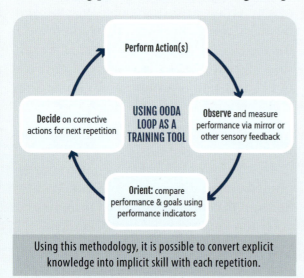

Using this methodology, it is possible to convert explicit knowledge into implicit skill with each repetition.

SOME OODA PHYSICS

OODA to me is clearly analogue, with the time-based precision a function of granularity. OODA supports what Boyd inferred from each of these powerful theories which accurately describe the physics of nature:

- ▶ **Gödel's Incompleteness Theorem:** Any "sufficiently strong" theorem has "unprovable" sentences and must be continuously refined/adapted in the face of new observations. (Analogue, Time, Feedback, Weighting.)

- ▶ **Heisenberg's Uncertainty Principle:** There is a limit on our ability to observe reality with 100 percent precision. (Analogue, Min-Max, Time, Limits.)

- ▶ **Second Law of Thermodynamics:** The entropy of any closed system always tends to increase, and thus the nature of any given system is continuously changing, even as efforts are directed toward maintaining it in its original form. (Analogue tending to disorder, whose behavioral limits — e.g., Trust Factor, Risk, etc. — must be constrained; otherwise, chaos.)

Boyd recognized OODA in nature, albeit often disguised. He concluded that, to maintain an accurate or effective grasp of reality, one must undergo a continuous cycle of interaction with the environment, geared towards assessing its constant (Dynamics/Analogue) changes. Darwin's theory of evolution addressed natural selection in biological systems, but similar dynamics apply in social contexts, including the survival of nations during war or businesses in free market competition.

Boyd stated that the decision cycle was the central mechanism of dynamic adaptation. By increasing speed and accuracy of assessment better than one's adversary, a substantial advantage in war and competition is achieved.

The key to survival and autonomy is the ability to quickly adapt to change. How are we doing with network and information security?

The Trust Engine
From an OODA View

Now to mix it up some more.

Simple concept. The Trust Factor of any subject or object will change as the time between prescribed validations of the integrity of the elements in question varies. So, why not speed up the process? Abstractly, **iterative processes = OODA**.

With Trust Factor in the cyber and physical domains, continual OODA-like updates are fairly easy to design:

1. The guards will check on the prisoners (make sure the Mona Lisa is still hanging, etc.) more often.

2. The perimeter checks with the scanning cameras will double their detection effectiveness by halving the amount of time they sweep a given area.

3. The key exchange will occur every 10 minutes instead of hourly. (Reduced $E(t)$, especially when $D(t)$ and $R(t)$ are indeterminate.)

4. The user/code/process validation will be invoked once a minute (or millisecond… doesn't matter).

But what about humans? I'll talk about "The Prison in the Cloud" later, but for now we need to take a look at considerations needed to upgrade human Trust Factor. A synaptic network with "learned" biases is where we are headed.

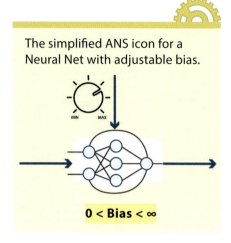

The simplified ANS icon for a Neural Net with adjustable bias.

$0 < \text{Bias} < \infty$

Like in any decision making process, inputs are the source of data. Let's make up a few for our human TF engine.

1. **Credit check** *(daily, weekly, monthly?)*
2. **Criminal check** *(within hours of public record)*
3. **Major Purchases** *(parse from credit check)*
4. **HR Complaints** *(from superiors, co-workers, customers, or subordinates)*
5. **Errors** *(measurable, or soft-opinions; periodic reviews)*
6. **Lateness/Delays** *(measurable in almost real time)*

OK, that's enough to make the point. Any major changes in any of these criteria are indicators of a possible change in the Trust Factor in the human domain.

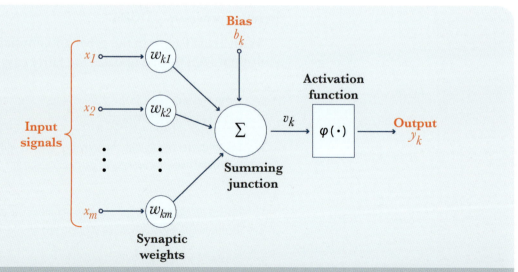

A simple neural process, with weighted inputs and assumptive bias. Adding a feedback process from Activation function creates more "learning" and adaptation. For simplicity, I will use this generic image throughout to idealize neural style decision making.

OODA, TCP/IP, and OOB

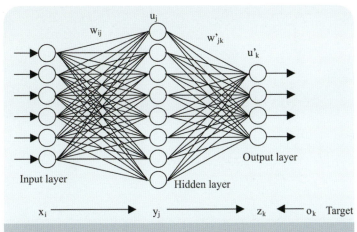

Weighted neural nets can get exceedingly complex, exceedingly quickly; to the point we don't even understand how they come to the decisions they do. Some also don't like to be asked, why?

The Trust Engine will be an automated system where a condition of employment might require explicit permissions to be monitored on a continual basis. *(Yeah, I know, it sounds Big Brotherish. Implementation, though, is determined by acceptable social, cultural, and policy norms.)*

Synaptic weighting is somewhat analogous to the Trust Factor charts, with weighting the prime influence on decision making. They are designed to be dynamic, with both feedback systems and feedforward biases introduced based upon external events or criteria to alter the output. Very cool stuff as we learn to emulate the averaging capabilities of brain-based neural networking, memory, and perception. Very scary when applied to the feedback processes of our personal, professional, and mobile lives which allows others to make judgements about us.

The output of any given weighting function can then become the input of one or more criteria for static Trust Factor analysis, as in the prior section; ergo part of a larger feedback system, where TF is a dominant concern.

An example in the cyber domain is:

Bias can be good or bad (same as in politics), but it ideally approaches neutral. The only way to do that is to constantly update the bias and we will see that point shown visualized in Chapter 9. Think Trust Factor weighting for A.I.

Bad bias can turn a chat-bot into a racist or a car into a non-predictable killing machine, both of whose unethical provenance cannot be discerned due to the complexity of deep learning.

1.	Our system Code A was updated	(00:22h)
2.	New partner talks to our network	(06:15h)
3.	Connected system has software errors	(06:15h)
4.	Known, unpatched libraries still active	(06:15h)
5.	Code "B" is re-vetted every 10^5 seconds	(00:01h + 24 hours)
6.	"Oh, S**t!" Malware variant found in 25% of systems	

You can perform the same exercise for physical systems and see, with appropriate weighting and biases, how fast security profiles change.

This is where we're headed.

Squeezing the Loop

Boyd's OODA Loop is scalable, a sort of time-based optimization I call "Squeezing the Loop." Conceptually, it's another way of looking at Boyd's getting inside the adversary's decision cycle.

Let's call the time of one circle of the loop below L(t), made up of the four constituent O-O-D-A components, each with their own time value. Therefore, let's say that...

$$L(t) = O1(t) + O2(t) + DE(t) + Act(t)$$

...which bears close resemblance to our fundamental **D(t) + R(t)**. I see OODA as:

$$O1(t) = D(t)$$
$$\text{and}$$
$$O2(t) + DE(t) + Act(t) = R(t)$$

...under the condition that **O1 = Observation = Detection**, and that Orientation is a post-detection process. However, if we allow that...

$$L(t) = O1(t) + O2(t) + DE(t) + Act(t) = D(t) + R(t)$$

...the sum total is far more important than where in the loop we include any of the pieces.

Obviously we need to know:

- How long it takes each of the four steps to process? *(Time)*
- How fast I can complete all of the steps in an OODA Loop process? *(Time)*

And, just like before, the goal is for $(L)t \to 0$. Each of the four constituent parts should also $\to 0$, with the Limits approaching, but never reaching, the impossible to achieve condition of zero-time.

Do not read into this that the four (or five or more) loop elements must be of equal time. Each component functions on its own, with its own time constraints. The process iteration and feedback-based update is entirely dependent upon squeezing the loop and minimizing $L(t)$, just as we want $D(t) + R(t) \to 0$, but now we view it as an iterative analogue feedback process.

Let's now look at the OODA Loop with respect to basic TBS.

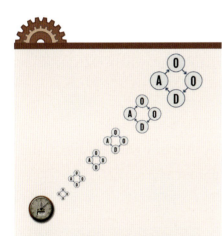

Conceptually, the smaller the loop, the faster the decision making cycle, yielding an advantage over an adversary. Note that we expanded from approaching a minimum 2-clock-cycle process to approaching a 4 clock-cycle process. This detection in depth provides literal and conceptual control and modeling.

Sub-OODA Loops

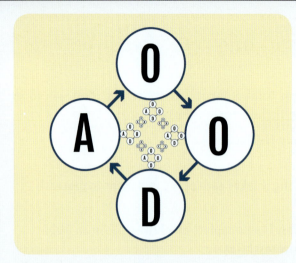

Here, OODA represents four sequentially and dependent processes. But there are almost an infinite number of variations, depending upon the granularity you choose. For example, take Observe. How many self-similar OODA components live at a smaller scale? (Remember the fractal discussion earlier?)

OBSERVE

This component might be composed of one or more sub-loops.

- Conduct a minimum of fifty consumer studies (S... Sn) in the biggest markets. Each of those fifty studies is its own sub-loop, that are time-summed to measure $O1(t) = (SUM\ S1 + \ldots\ Sn)$ if they are sequential versus coincident.
- Competitive intelligence analyses
- Existing capabilities

ORIENT

Orientation is dynamically influenced by the output of the Observation process. How does this data/event/detection (or observation) relate to its environment? What are the limits of its efficacy? Think Shannon.

- Is it universal or local? What is the environmental scope (landscape) that contours the observations contextually?
- How many samples are taken in order to increase the granularity of the orientation, where $O2(t) \to 0$?

DECIDE

- Initial decision is made.
- Run by others in the decision chain.
- Do sanity-checks.

ACT

- Observe the object upon which action is be taken.
- Verify the Orientation.
- Confirm the Decision.
- Do the deed. As the most analogue part of the time calculations, this value should be taken as the amount of time that your 'slowest' reaction takes.

(Then, do it all over again. Never stop.)

	Baseline	Improved	Better	Better Yet
Observe $O1(t)$				
Orient $O2(t)$				
Decide $DE(t)$				
$ACT(t)$				
TOTAL $OODA(t)$				

Each of these steps is most successfully completed by applying sub-OODA Loops to their execution. Think Project Management of just about anything. Processes are related, and time is the metric.

The same thinking applies to multi-level (granular) Orientation, Decision Making, and Action. How granular do you want to get at each point in the loop?

In Boyd's case, involving high-speed life and death situations, how granular do you need to get? Applying OODA with too much granularity will, at some point, initiate diminishing returns - and possibly such a degree of iterative introspection as to render the entire exercise moot.

This approach makes for excellent Management Porn. Charts and pictures of iterative process loops. They will get this… and it's only one simple metric: time.

As I have pursued Analogue Network Security, I find that an OODA analysis, even a quick cursory one, can be valuable to understanding how security is improved by tweaking the OODA Loop process and the speed at which each component is executed.

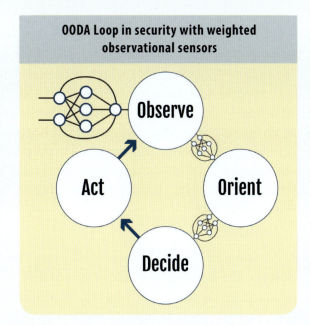

OODA Loop in security with weighted observational sensors

OODA
IN SECURITY

Too often, management sees information security as an unmeasurable bottom-line drain on profits, or an "insurance policy" against which actuarial data is slim and hard numbers are more anecdotal folk-lore than statistically defensible. Or, management sees security as an unnecessary evil or burden that interferes with getting the job done. Too many security professionals and security product vendors view security as a technical problem, thereby demanding a technical solution. Ouch.

CONSIDER:

Security, in reality, is about protecting the business process; the business version of an OODA Loop. Our jobs are to maintain the smooth, continuous flow of that iterative process which creates revenues, profits, and jobs. It doesn't matter in the least what product or service you create or offer. It doesn't matter what industry you are in. At an abstract level, all (well engineered) infrastructures are essentially the same, and

When you break the loop, you increase uncertainty, potentially trending time towards infinity.

OODA, TCP/IP, and OOB

Ask Yourself:

How many other aspects of security, from tech to people, from offense to defense, have their own OODA Loops? There are a lot more than you think when you look at the dynamic interactive processes inherent to Analogue Network Security. *(Some hints: Disaster Recovery, Antivirus. Start there.)*

Pen-testers understand the OODA principle intuitively.

Observe: Get the lay of the land. (See "Chapter Sixteen: Class 3: Global Information Warfare", *Information Warfare: Chaos on the Electronic Superhighway*, 1992, on how to build a cyber army.)

Orient: Put observations into an appropriate context, with relation to the network, the data, the business process, and goals of the pen-test.

Decide: Where does the simulated attack begin; what assets are targeted; what paths are chosen; what vectors are used to achieve the goals?

Act: Do the deed. Attack, document, and make recommendations.

Loop.

it doesn't matter which war you are fighting, or which humanitarian mission you are conducting, or which product or service you are providing. Practicing good security allows organizations to do their jobs efficiently, with minimal hindrance or interference by unwanted (unplanned for!) internal or external forces.

Our security-oriented jobs are to keep those iterative processes functioning uninterrupted. Our jobs are to insure that no breaks in that loop occur – by any means. Imagine trying to spin a hula-hoop with an 24-inch gap in it. You would not be very successful.

Our security jobs are not to unnecessarily imbue organizations with technology. Rather, we need to understand the business process well enough and coordinate with management so that, whatever security efforts are put in place (policy, process, technology), the real goals of the business are achieved with as much purity as possible.

Analogue Network Security is based upon an understanding of the relationship between very specific organizational and informational assets (the terrain) and the ability to tune it dynamically. This common sense perception has somehow been lost in the maelstrom of a trillion dollars in protective technology.

Any good pen-tester knows that for success to be meaningful — for the pen-test to have value — the process should commence all over again. Observe the results of the Actions, and start the process all over again. Realistically, though, pen-tests are periodic events, typically not tightly wound ODDA-like processes. The iterative process can have fairly long time intervals.

So, the results of a single pen-test OODA are meaningful for only a limited amount of time. Who knows what technical or human actions will influence the security of the networks under analysis?

Next, we're going to examine Negative Time and the advantages of OOB.

TCP/IP & OOB:
PUTTING THE PIECES TOGETHER

It was just an experiment.

The idea was simple. Can two computers talk to each other? Or three? That was 1969. Within a few years, hundreds of academic and military computers were connected to each other.

Today, we run the world on the descendant of those early experiments, **TCP/IP.**

I like to say that the internet is a mad scientist's experiment run amok…

Imagine if we had stopped developing computer chips thirty years ago because, "…an 80386 is good enough. We can patch and upgrade it later."

Imagine if we had not developed digital TV because air-wave based analogue transmission was "good enough." That's sort of what we have with the internet and TCP/IP.

Of course, there have been competing network protocols. But, much like the lower quality VHS, that won the market over the superior Beta formats (through a self-reinforcing positive feedback loop), TCP/IP became the de-facto communications protocol… largely because it was easy and everyone else was using it, too. Another example of positive feedback in an open system which resulted in unpredictable outcomes. There have been upgrades, of course, but insufficient to run a planet on.

Security be damned.

Don't worry, we can patch it later.

(Or, in my day we might have said, "The live recording was awful! But, don't worry, we can fix it in the mix.")

TCP/IP
THE BEST & THE WORST OF TIMES

Over the years, improvements in TCP/IP have made our lives easier and safer. But at the very core of internet communications is another quantum-ish conundrum — a sort of duality paradox, in spiritual-speak.

- TCP/IP is great because only one wire is required to transmit both the data and control signals.
- TCP/IP is bad for the same reason. Data and control signals travel on the same hunk of wire; a potential single point of failure.

This dichotomy is fundamental. On the other hand, the existing architectural framework offers flexibility and offers us the ability to dramatically improve personal, enterprise, and global security.

Currently, a cut wire at the physical layer (think about a misguided backhoe) can disconnect both the control signals and the associated data transfer of even the largest 'pipes'. From a security standpoint, IPv4 is being slowly replaced by IPv6, a decades-long transition with its own set of problems, yet the backhoe weakness remains. Over the years, proposals have come and gone on "how can we replace TCP/IP with something 'better'?" Yet TCP/IP still stands strong. Contenders have a tremendous uphill battle, no matter how strong the underlying technology might be.

I believe that any serious security enhancement to inter-networking requires that the existing infrastructure cannot be changed.

- It would take years for government, academia, vendors, and international standards organizations, to agree on something, and then usually, compromises will yield lower levels of success. *(Think the Edsel and New Coke.)*
- It would take vendors years to change their protocols, if they even decided to do so.
- Enterprises would need to initiate massively expensive transitions – lasting decades. *(Just look at IPv6 adaptation rates!)*
- Integrations never go as smoothly as planned.

With so many TCP/IP-friendly Analogue and Time-based approaches available to us, without changing the fundamental nature of the global communications systems, I absolutely believe a completely new security model must also be adaptive to the world's current technology deployments, which are measured in trillions of dollars.

Bottom line: **TCP/IP AIN'T GOING ANYWHERE SOON.**

Out-of-Band
(Not a Rock'n'Roll Term)

In the mid 1970s, the audio industry was just dabbling in digital. The ambitious mixing console automation systems were *so* first generation, I am surprised they worked at all. (Actually, they worked *a little bit*.)

At the core of many automated audio mixing systems was a device called a VCA. Voltage Controlled Amplifier. A traditional amplifier is kept out of runaway conditions with a resistive negative feedback path such as below.

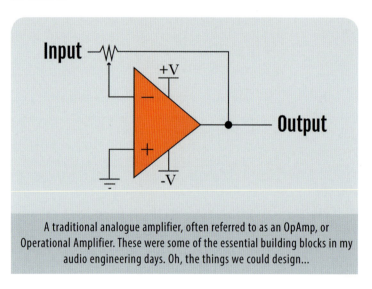

A traditional analogue amplifier, often referred to as an OpAmp, or Operational Amplifier. These were some of the essential building blocks in my audio engineering days. Oh, the things we could design...

The preferred way to control audio gain is with a "volume control" consisting of a variable resistor (potentiometer), which varies the amount of amplified phase-inverted signals that are fed back and summed at the input of the amp. You can resistively combine as many inputs as you want. We call this "audio mixing."

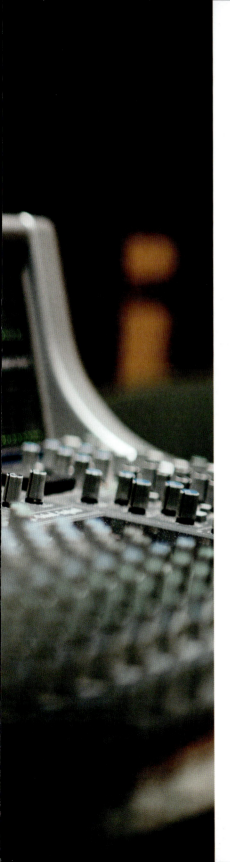

In the traditional old-school way of mixing, the rotary or linear fader is a potentiometer — an in-circuit resistive element that is manually adjusted to turn relative volumes of the signal up and down, either at the input or in the feedback-loop of the amplifier. This is akin to TCP/IP, where control and data signals are on the same physical media.

The fader pictured here is also a variable resistive element, but note the mechanical portion: a stepper motor is moved as the fader is manually adjusted, and an output voltage is sent to a memory device. When we are in "playback" mode, the stored values are applied to the stepper motor, which physically moves the resistive fader to adjust the volume. So, on large mixing consoles, and in many DAWs (Digital Audio Workstations), either the physical faders move on their own, or, in the UI, the faders appear to move on the screen. Same principle, different tech.

The VCA, though, lent itself to automation because it used an applied external variable voltage to determine the amount of gain, or amplification. It was also cheaper than motors and moving parts, which can be maintenance headaches.

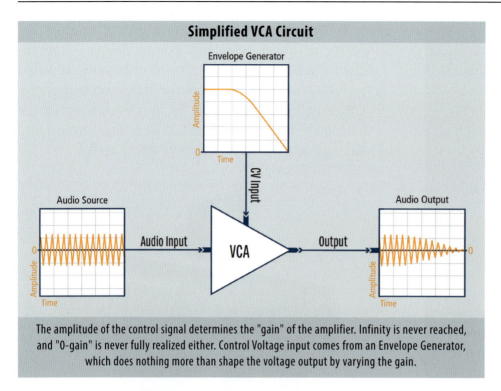

The amplitude of the control signal determines the "gain" of the amplifier. Infinity is never reached, and "0-gain" is never fully realized either. Control Voltage input comes from an Envelope Generator, which does nothing more than shape the voltage output by varying the gain.

A VCA has a traditional analogue input, (typically) with amplitude variations over time. The amplification factor of the circuit is determined by the Control Signal input voltage. This means that the audio signal chain is comprised of two discreet, physically isolated circuits.

1. The actual audio signal, which travels along appropriate circuits.

2. The control signal (for volume, panning, equalization, and dozens of other signal modification circuits) is a distinct physical medium.

One of the good things that VCAs brought to 1970s audio was a failsafe. My time in professional audio was heavily centered on live, remote recording of massive concerts, live events broadcast to thousands of radio stations, and sound reinforcement in arenas around the world. Therefore, failure was never an option.

If the audio path became suddenly corrupted, we had a fast, two-second method to "patch around" the

In the early 1970s, this was considered state of the art audio equipment.

offending component - if the engineer understood the system complexity. In any live situation, most minor interruptions went un-noticed by the audiences since we also designed in redundancy for mission critical paths, such as Paul Simon's vocal, Stevie Wonder's piano, or Charlie Daniels' fiddle.

Now, what would happen if the control signals to a VCA-intensive audio mixing board went haywire?

- If the control signal died, the audio level/amplification of that specific path either (a) remained constant based upon the last voltage at the control input of the VCA (think memristors) or, design depending, (b), the amplification would rapidly → 0, notifying the engineer of a problem.

- If required, we could override the fader and return to manual control, depending upon the vendor.

- We could patch around it.

- If the entire automation system died, well, so be it. We stepped back to our old skill-sets and performed everything manually.

Point is: Even in 1970s-era audio, we included high speed reaction processes and redundancies in the design of systems to meet most any contingency.

==Today, since TCP/IP consists of one physical path that carries both information and control signals, they either live and work together or they fail together.== No option… and from a security standpoint, we have been missing the obvious.

Implementing ANS Out-of-band (OOB) signaling and control paths that are isolated from each other does not require any modification to TCP/IP, or face the impossible task of replacing it.

How about a real-world example of OOB for enhanced security?

Negative Time

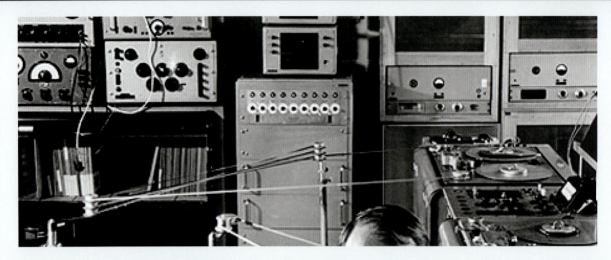

Let's talk a bit more rock'n'roll.

On the iconic song *Whole Lotta Love*, you can hear Robert Plant's strident vocal repeat itself, bathed in deep echo. That's an audio delay utilizing *multiple* delays, called reverb. Before audio digital delays became popular in the mid-1970s, we had a ton of purely analogue tricks to delay audio. One convoluted, yet eminently workable method was to separate two or more tape machines by several feet.

On the far left machine, the tape stretched across the record and playback heads, but only recorded the signal. The tape traveled several feet to the next machine/s, stretched across the record and playback heads, but only the playback signal was used… creating a single, or perhaps multiple, audio delay/s!

Time Delay = Distance/Speed of Tape Travel

Along came better analogue circuit designs, but with digital audio, it's just a matter of logic gate manipulation.

Back to a network.

The use of negative time in security, I believe, offers us the means to eliminate absolutism in favor of relativism for both design and analysis. Even with one organization's approach to Trust Factors differing from another's, what matters is self-consistency. Same idea with negative time. Where the *zero-time baseline* sits, is absolutely unimportant; it is relativistically critical, though, that a given system be in sync, as we discussed earlier.

Time Delay: Adjust $0 \leq \text{Delay}(t) < \text{Max}$

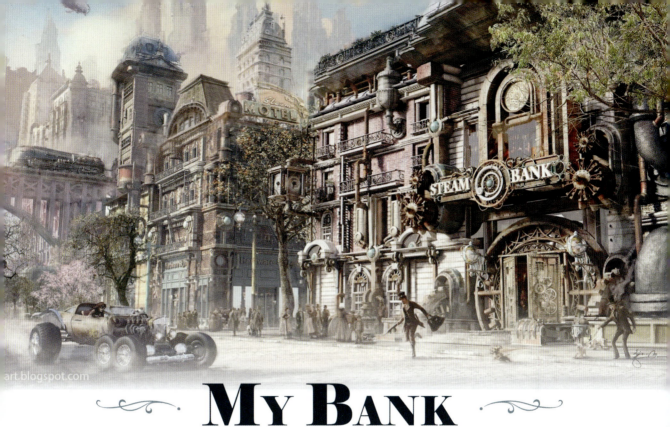

My Bank

I honestly like *one* of my banks' security practices. They actually employ OOB and analogue feedback for the most sensitive operations. Two examples:

An unnamed bank seems to be in constant *epic-fail* mode. Their incident response and reaction processes regularly allow $E(t) \rightarrow \infty$, which is abysmal.

> ▶ When I log onto my mobile banking app, sometimes it has not "seen" my device in a while (time) and the bank wants to re-authenticate me. I get it. (Also known as a degrading trust curve.)
>
> ▶ Sometimes, when I want to move money via my mobile banking app, or if the requested action is out-of-norm behavior, or perhaps it's for more money than usual, this bank's analogue security process steps in. I get flagged! (The decision bias adjusts over time.)

In both cases, the app and the backend ask for an additional layer of authentication - call it Detection in Depth, if you will, even though I have already entered my User_ID, a password, or perhaps a biometric.

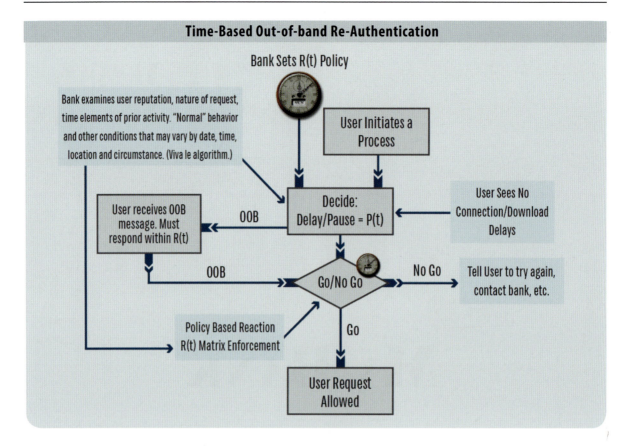

In this case, if the bank detects anomalous behavior (where $D(t) \to 0$ depending on how fast the anomaly detection algorithm works), the process request is paused for R(t), the maximum amount of policy-driven time, during which my re-authentication (Reaction) must be completed, or else the entire request is cancelled.

Ergo, the entire process meets $P(t) > D(t) + R(t)$ where P(t) is set by the verifiable OOB communications. Security in the feedback-loop. No transactions are completed until the equation is satisfied.

Trust Factor comes into play, of course. Some institutions occasionally require multiple identification means, such as security questions or past personal history questions which, by themselves, are static Reference Monitor approaches. However, used in a feedback system, they increase TF and reduce Risk. In

many cases, especially financial, a strongly initialized identification in the physical domain is required first, then subsequent identification attributes are added at that time. Correctly done, the remote verification of those credentials, both in-band and out-of-band, should be completed within a short period of time after the physical initialization, else, additional time-based risk is introduced.

We tend to rely on physical identification as proof positive of, in this case, identity.

Example 1	Alice	Bob	Alice & Bob
TF	0.990	0.990	.9999
Risk	1.0000%	1.0000%	0.0100%
Risk Improvement			99.0000%

Above, I am assuming that the bank is 99% confident that their physical identification process has verified that I am Winn (via Alice). I am also assuming that my Trust Factor is the same for initial and secondary verification (via Bob) over an out-of-band channel (avoiding MitM and other tricks performed when OOB is not utilized). Look at what happens to the bank's confidence that Winn is Winn, even though he is using a new logon device from an unknown location. The shared secret, transmitted synchronously over known channels, allows for a huge increase in trust and, in this case, a risk reduction of two orders of magnitude (10^2).

This time-driven analogue approach is systemic versus only end-point; one which can and should be introduced throughout coding and networking design.

The same principle applies from code to inter-networking. In the next chapter, we will further examine Detection in Depth.

OOB & Negative Time

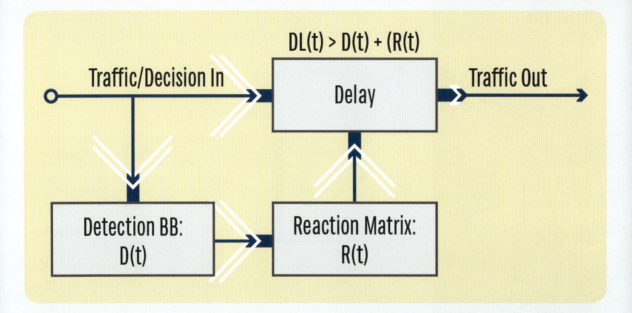

Adding negative time can be thought of generically as the above drawing shows. Traffic (or processes – human or technical) with a security implication can be managed by:

1. Knowing the exact amount of time - $D(t)$ it takes for a Detection Black Box (BB) to differentiate *good* from *bad*, or other criteria.

2. Knowing the exact amount of time it takes for a process to block, or otherwise remediate, the decision, $R(t)$.

3. Set the Delay Line $DL(t)$ to some number $> D(t) + R(t)$.

4. Negative time implementation ensures that the traffic out (or decision consequence) is not effected until there has been enough time to make an appropriate determination.

The same approach works in all three domains and should be able to give management a fast, graphical view of how OOB and Negative Time ANS works in the abstract.

The use of Negative Time is a powerful weapon against Infinity.

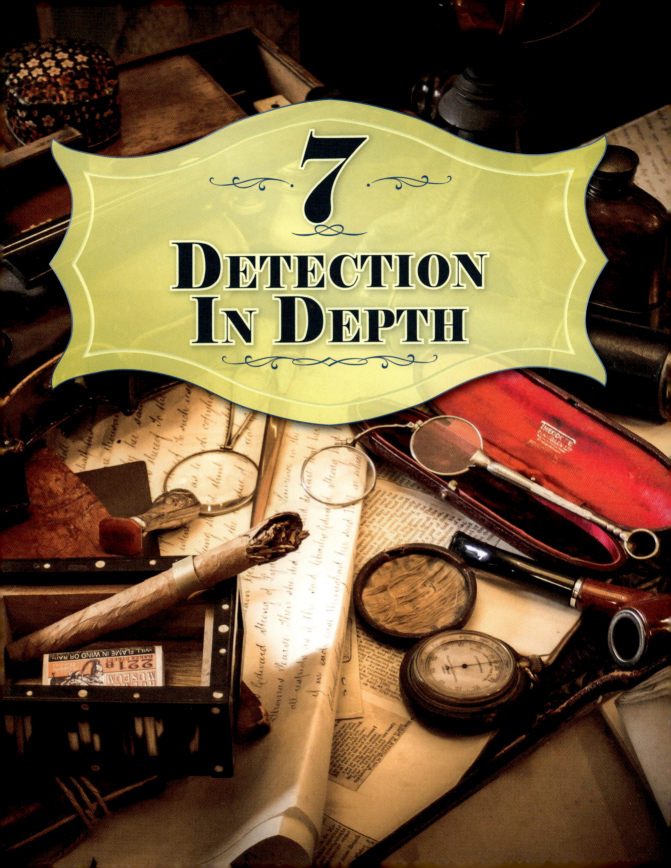

7
Detection in Depth

Carbon Units Before Silicon

Let's talk Detection. Like we've never talked detection before. Not just AV, IDS, IPS, or yadda yadda detection. **Let's talk detection!**

We humans – aka carbon units – stay alive because we sense our environs. Situational awareness. So do animals, plants, and most biological entities.

We grew up learning that we humans only had five senses by which to orient ourselves in the world, and in my thinking, we are actually a carbon-based sentient OODA Loop. The more granularized we get when considering human sensory channels (by estimates 21 or more), however, the more we can learn about how (we) carbon units thrive "in the wild." That number is sure to change with more research. The point is, we humans have a lot of environmental sensory activity going on 24/7. More than we ever really thought.

Human neurosensory circuits: talk about perhaps the most dynamic feedback system nature has evolved. And they are all time-based! Several of our (arguably) most survival-oriented reactions (amygdala stuff; fight or flight) have been studied in depth. Most notably, from an ANS standpoint, we actually know the E(t) of humans under stimulation.

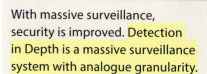

With massive surveillance, security is improved. Detection in Depth is a massive surveillance system with analogue granularity.

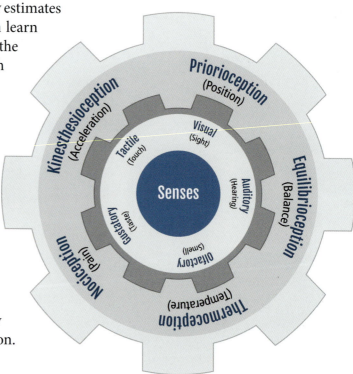

Hearing lag *(response time to stimulus)* =

~ 250ms = D(t) + R(t)

Visual response time *(latency)* to stimulus =

~ 150ms = D(t) + R(t)

Tactile pain takes ~700ms to register as pain =

~ 700ms = D(t) + R(t)

Now, I'm color blind, have poor distance-vision, and a severe astigmatism. My hearing, thanks to years of exposure to blasting speakers in studios and concert venues, suffers. But my sense of balance is excellent so, ergo, I can ski! Humans have the innate ability to compensate for sensory deficiencies and to re-optimize their performance.

- Blind *(at birth or after)* people can develop an acute sense of hearing and echo-location.
- Deaf *(not at birth)* people exhibit a greater sensitivity to movement, perhaps through enhanced peripheral vision.
- People *born* deaf will process touch and vision using areas of the brain which are typically devoted to processing sound.

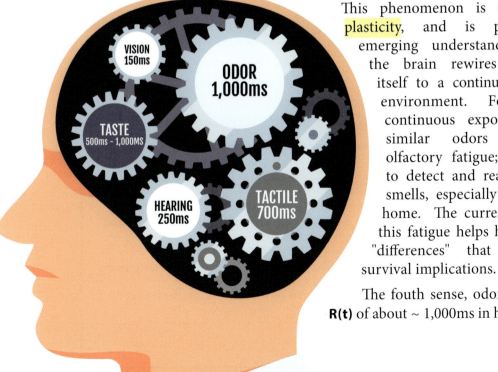

This phenomenon is called neuro-plasticity, and is part of the emerging understanding of how the brain rewires and adapts itself to a continuously variable environment. For example, continuous exposure to self-similar odors can cause olfactory fatigue; the inability to detect and react to specific smells, especially in one's own home. The current thinking is this fatigue helps humans detect "differences" that could have survival implications.

The fouth sense, odor, has a **D(t) + R(t)** of about ~ 1,000ms in humans.

Finally, there's taste. Research studies show that, regardless of the type of taste (acidic, sweet, etc.), the gustatory response time ranged from ~500ms to ~1,000ms.

The brain's neuro-plastic response to a deficient detection system (e.g., color blindness, deafness) literally strengthens other detection systems to compensate. This is truly **detection in depth**; survival based upon multiple detection circuits, wired to "talk" to each other, and "move" around in a dynamic hierarchy of changing importance (weighting) based upon the environment (OODA). Metamorphic networking is just another example of what can be referred to as defensive or detection-based network plasticity.

Refer back to synaptic weighting in neural networks, OODA/Feedback & feedforward signals and, again, we see the same phenomenon. I leave it to you to investigate the $D(t) + R(t)$ of the other 16 "senses," and I especially do not want to go down the contentious road of quantum ESP, instantaneity, or entanglement. At least not here. Find me at a conference… we will talk.

The point of this discussion is that $D(t) + R(t)$ criteria is innate to the human domain, just as it is in the physical and cyber domains.

Human	Detection with the Five Senses
Physical	Sound, Heat, Movement, Location, Wavelength
Cyber	Traffic Behavior, Packet Analysis, IdM

These criteria in the human domain are well-established within their respective academic treatments.

So, I hope you are, by now, attuned to ask, "Why don't we do more weighted, distributed, and self-compensating detection in depth in our networks and our coding?"

Stages of Information Processing *(Schmidt 2000)*	
Stimulus (Input)	• Stimuli are detected by our senses • Proprioceptive information -touch, equilibrium, kinesthesis
Stimulus Identification	• Patterns of movement are detected and processed (perceptual processes - Detection, Comparison, and Recognition)
Response Selection	• Decide which movement to make. • Concentrate on the stimuli that are important - selective attention
Response Programming	• Messages are sent via the nerves to the muscles to carry out the required movement
Movement (Output)	• The action is carried out

The human sensory process is fairly complex, and is a neat parallel of the detection-reaction processes in ANS. This chart should also be a reminder of neural learning and OODA.

Defense in Depth

How quaint.

"Defense in Depth," they cry!

Moats, draw-bridges, high stone walls, archers, and boiling oil. That will do the trick.

Firewalls, password policies, and malware detection. That will do the trick.

I've heard Defense in Depth lauded as a security panacea for years, and I stil cringe when those same overstated claims are reiterated. The term survives because it's safe to talk to the C-Suite about layered security; besides, the management porn is good.

All implications or suggestions of 100% efficacy gives rise to a false sense of security and all senses of 100% security are false senses of security - especially if they are static. Feedback and negative time must be introduced to buffer and manage the buffeting effects of unknown actions/actors.

We tend to believe there are three core-layers of technical defense against Advanced Threats, and have added many additional sub-layers to increase our protective security posture.

CORE LAYERS OF TECHNICAL DEFENSE

1. Perimeter
2. Network Interior
3. Endpoint

Trillions of dollars later, networks and infrastructures still get nailed daily.

I am not saying that cogent defense in depth strategies don't have value. They *do* have their place in a hybridized security architecture.

But technical controls can only do so much. Analysts suggest that ~90% of network attacks (APTs, if you will) begin with social engineering of some sort. So, is a new access control device for some network services a good investment in security? Maybe. Maybe not. Or, is an investment in phishing detection systems and a time-based process smarter? (See anti-phishing in the next chapter.)

I asked a few hundred people the following question: "What is the difference between Defensive, Protective, and Preventive security?" I got a thousand answers - more accurately, over-lapping opinions. Is there a definitive distinction?

My preference is that we are **defending,** which is easily analogue-ized. :) **Protection** and **prevention** reek of absolutism, IMHO. Let the debate commence!

Layered defense has greater value if:

- You know what assets you have.
- You know where the data assets reside, logically and physically.
- You know who has a need to access those assets and when such access should be authorized. *(One-man or two-man rule notwithstanding.)*
- You believe in true network segmentation.
- You have an integrated IdM program that works.
- You are willing to disconnect some assets from the intranet and the internet as needed.
- You have the authority and the budget to *"Make It So."*

On the other hand, adding more defensive network controls can easily result in these benefits:

- Additional cost
- Additional complexity
- Poor integration resulting in unintended breach paths
- No measurable positive increase in security

Why attack the strengthened layers of defense when the soft defenses – humans – are so easy to compromise?

Just sayin'. My operational colleagues lament these truisms. So binary.

DETECTION IN DEPTH FACTOIDS

Detection in Depth is standard practice in feedback-based cyber-kinetic systems (à la ICS, SCADA). **Defense in Depth is the naturally occuring result of well-designed Detection in Depth, not the other way around.** Why are we missing out?

- Untold numbers of sensors have already been embedded in hundreds of thousands of intelligent machines manufactured by GE, including jet engines, power turbines, medical devices, and so on. Siemens is rocking the ICS world, also. Harvesting and analyzing the data generated by those sensors holds enormous potential for optimization across a broad range of industrial operations. This is why I pay attention to feedback in ICS & SCADA.

- The insides of a locomotive contain ~6.7 miles of wiring and >250 sensors that put out 9 million data points every hour.

- How much internal feedback sensing goes on inside a personal drone? The exact answer is, "Lots."

- Wind towers used for green-power feed data into their sensory systems 400 times a second.

- The Industrial Internet employs Detection in Depth concepts... Ground and Air Traffic Control, Health Care, Smart Grids, etc.

- China's 1400km long South–North Water Transfer Project uses more than 100,000 active sensors to manage the flow of 12 Trillion Gallons of water from wet to arid areas.

NOTE: Increased data without increased data processing optimization either increases D(t), or extends the Orient part of R(t). In either case, too much data without a decent data scheme/weighting process will necessarily increase **D(t) + R(t)**.

Common Detection Sensor Techniques

Optical spectrum. Electromagnetic - DC to 300+ PetaHertz (gamma rays, 3×10^{21} Hz). Sonic: from almost 0 Hz to ~250KHz at sea level air.

Pressure. Viscosity. Phase relationships (time). Vibration (intensity/time).

Velocity (time). Acceleration ($time^2$). Tuned to specific Chemical Signatures. Echoing & Doppler. Temperature (time & $time^2$). Proximity. Weight/Mass. Flow (time).

[Go to the "List of Sensors" Wikipedia page for a few hundred more.]

They are getting better all the time!

Sensors on Boeing jet engines can produce 10 terabytes of operational information for every 30 minutes they turn. A four-engine jumbo jet can create 640 terabytes of data on just one Atlantic crossing. Now, multiply that by the more than 25,000 flights flown each day. That's ~$6*10^{21}$ (6 zetta) or ~$7.5*2^{70}$ bytes per year (!), just to keep planes flying.

Defense in Depth
The TBS Way

Let's examine Defense in Depth with a linear view.

$$Pt(data) = Pt(pw) + Pt(fw) + Pt(app)$$

A linear attack means that an intruder must first conquer some perimeter defense, such as a password-based (pw) ACL Black Box, then perhaps some intranet-based firewall (fw) mechanism and, finally, some application (app) security before reaching, in this case, the target data.

If all of the associated security controls are truly linear from an architectural view (with no get-around paths or circuits), then Pt(data) is a simple time-additive function. This sum assumes that there is no commonality between the systems – that the admin account for the firewall isn't the same as the admin account for the network or the app. That no part of compromise to the app will lead to compromise of the other parts of the system. In non-linear cases, we need to ask what is the size of **A union B union C**?

Applying analogue network security thinking to Defense in Depth is like putting an alarm on the alarm system's alarm system, either at the detection or reaction points in the system. OODA with sub-loops, if you will.

The sizes of A+B+C minus the pair-wise intersections (double-counted), but then add the intersection of all three back-in and we get:

$$P(A \cup B \cup C) = P(A) + P(B) + P(C) - P(A \cap B) - P(A \cap C) - P(B \cap C) + P(A \cap B \cap C)$$

Detection in Depth

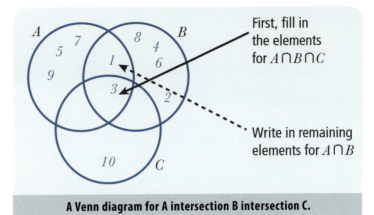

A Venn diagram for A intersection B intersection C.

This sequence of add - subtract - add - subtract... continues infinitely.

For frequent hackers, though, any of the constituent **P(t)** elements could effectively be close to zero time. This underscores a fallacy in our current defensive thinking. We can easily forget that the effectiveness of defense in depth diminishes drastically if any of the defenses are defeated - especially if that defeat is not detected.

Defense in Depth only has a meaningful time-additive value if:

1. The traffic routing paths approach linearity with detours approaching zero.

2. There is some Trust Factor-based assurance that any P(t) value has not been reduced to near zero or is indeterminate.

Think the 2MR and what happens with independent variable Bayesian probability applied. Similar thinking.

Analogue Network Security suggests an alternative. Just like with the bad guys who want to rob a pawnshop or the big house at the top of the hill, reconnaissance comes first.

- Is there an alarm system?
- How long does it take the "cops" to arrive once the alarm goes off?
- Can it be disabled?

Detection in Depth

But what if detection in depth was enhanced?

Assume that, in an analysis of a detection implementation, you determine that the biggest single weakness is indeed a system, a component, or code "xyz." Thus, disabling the detection mechanism is the most effective way to bypass the security control. What should the Defender do? In the older fortress mentality view, one might redesign code or add additional barriers in hopes of building the fortress with higher walls. With the ANS approach, though, we take an integrated systems view and apply Detection in Depth by adding a new Pt(d1) layer to protect the first tier Detection. The TBS formula for this situation is:

$$Pt > Dt + Rt$$
$$\wedge$$
$$Pt(d1) > Dt(d1) + Rt(d1)$$

This says that to maintain the protective security of the first tier formula, **Pt > Dt + Rt**, the mechanism which protects Dt must detect and react as if it were a stand-alone, independent function. For example, if Dt is five minutes, we may choose to protect that Dt with a separate protection mechanism. If, then, the Pt(d1) value is deemed to be 20 minutes, and the sum of **Dt (d1) + Rt (d1) < Pt(d1)**, both formulas hold, and the derivative security does in fact protect the Dt mechanism in the first tier. Keep in mind, however, that there is no direct relationship between the behavior of the two isolated systems, other than... time! The specific technicalities are independent.

Of course, this logic can continue to go as deep as one feels is necessary to achieve the desired quantifiable level of security as measured by time.

$$Pt > Dt + Rt$$
$$\wedge$$
$$Pt(d1) > Dt(d1) + Rt(d1)$$
$$\wedge$$
$$Pt(d2) > Dt(d2) + Rt(d2)$$

In this case, because of the sensitive nature of the contents to be protected, there are two tiers of detection security to protect the first tier detection mechanism.

$$Pt > Dt + Rt$$
$$\wedge$$
$$Pt(r1) > Dt(r1) + Rt(r1)$$

Assume instead for the moment, that the detection scheme in the top tier, **Pt > Dt + Rt** is determined to be adequately secure (has measurably acceptable risk) from an attack, but there are questions about the integrity of the reaction mechanism. In a Denial of Service attack, the control signal communications can be blocked because of the nature of the attack on a TCP/IP service. Therefore, a remediative reaction along the primary communications media is not possible. Another path (OOB) is required, ergo, another reaction mechanism (r1) is required.

In the Denial of Service case, the detection mechanism should determine that the primary communications channel is blocked. It then triggers an OOB rerouting communications methodology measured by **Rt(r1)**, with the first tier **Rt** now being defined by **Pt(r1)** or the minimal sum of **[Dt(r1) + Rt(r1)]**.

$$P(t) > D(t) + R(t)$$
$$\wedge \qquad \wedge$$
$$\wedge \qquad Pt(r1) > Dt(r1) + Rt(r1)$$
$$Pt(d1) > Dt(d1) + Rt(d1)$$
$$\wedge$$
$$Pt(d2) > Dt(d2) + Rt(d2)$$

Detection in Depth

Here, two additional tiers of protection are provided for the detection component, and the reaction component receives one additional layer of protection. The strength of the first tier of security is then increased. Applying analogue network security thinking to Defense in Depth, is like putting an alarm on the alarm system's alarm system, at either the detection or reaction points in the system, thus constructing a more robust detection in depth architecture.

Now, let's look at defense in depth and apply a little analogue time-based security to it. Here, each P(t) component has its own detection and reaction component, each with its corresponding D(t) and R(t), each working in isolation from the other.

> IdM: **Dt(pw)**
> Firewall: **Dt(fw)**
> Application: **Dt(app)**

And defense in depth yields:

$$Pt(data) = (Dt(pw) + Rt(pw)) + (Dt(fw) + Rt(fw)) + (Dt(app) + Rt(app))$$

So, we might design something like a series of detection mechanisms at key traffic nodes.

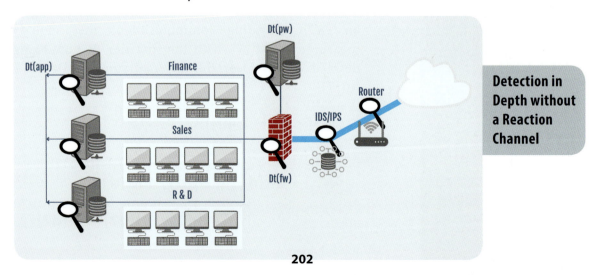

Detection in Depth without a Reaction Channel

Cool. So the magnifying lenses show lots of detection nexi; lots of fodder for data-hungry SIEMs. But does it help our security? Yes! If you measure each of the active detection points where security controls exist (versus passive monitoring), and test their efficacy as we discuss in Chapter 8, "How to Measure Your Security." Then, we can get a fairly good handle on the total D(t), if networks and network traffic are linear.

Now let's add some feedback to the process.

Single Reaction Channel with Detection in Depth & Feedback

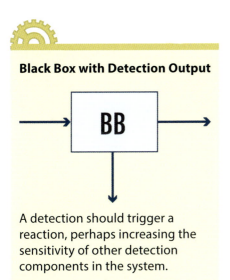

Black Box with Detection Output

A detection should trigger a reaction, perhaps increasing the sensitivity of other detection components in the system.

With a user forced to follow a linear architecture, a perimeter detection mechanism (in this case, at the firewall) might be the first detection mechanism to notice potentially hostile (for sure, questionable) behavior. Or perhaps, the firewall or IDS/IPS, receives notice of an intruder or attack on Engineering (et al) from a detection at the Application. In a dynamic analogue system, the detection mechanisms anywhere in the network should be able to be automatically or manually adjusted to various degrees of sensitivity, just like when we let users choose the amount of lockdown their web browsers enforce.

It's like raising the security/threat conditions from green to yellow or orange or red. Same idea for networks using an analogue OOB Reaction Matrix.

Detection in Depth

So, a specific reaction matrix might be designed to say: If a perimeter Detection System, such as a Firewall, detects "X" activity, then the reaction matrix will send a control signal to an internal Black Box Detection System (say, at an internal IDS, or perhaps, end-point detection mechanism, or an IdM or Application server, et al) to increase their sensitivity to hostile behavior. Turning up the volume, so to speak, upon *listening* for dissonant data-traffic or control signals, results in less traffic pass-through.

Can you hear me now? Pure acoustic analogue technology is how they *pumped up the volume* in 1906.

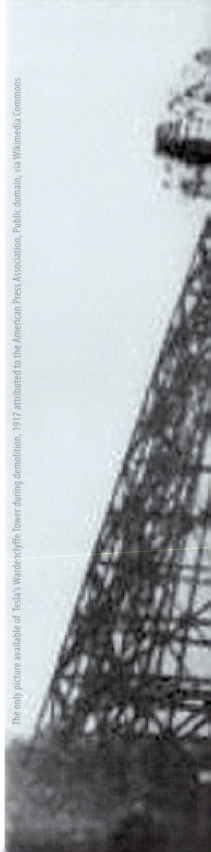

The only picture available of Tesla's Wardenclyffe Tower during demolition, 1917 attributed to the American Press Association, Public domain, via Wikimedia Commons

Detection in Depth

GRACEFUL DEGRADATION

Your network is under attack. Your IDS/IPS/Perimeter-sensors detect hostile traffic, probably coming from bad actors.

What should you do?

Believe it or not, some companies' knee jerk reaction is to call the Feds. Sure, if you want them taking over your data center, that's a good reaction. Other companies actually react with, "We'd better disconnect from the internet," which is an equally unsubtle response. Let's consider some everyday parallels:

1. Your tire goes flat. You put on one of the crappy, skinny tires good enough to get you to the tire store. Yes, you can still drive, but Graceful Degradation reduces your speed from 80mph to something like 40-50mph. So, a 50% performance degradation. But, you're still moving forward.

2. It's 40C outside. The air conditioning unit for your bedrooms, set at 22C, dies. Your Graceful Degradation means you have to sleep in the living room, not your comfy bed. Nearly a 50% degradation.

3. Damn. The turbulence is so bad, flight attendants must sit. Your Graceful Degradation means you don't get your inflight gourmet meal or vodka, but you will still get to your destination safely. You decide how *degrading* that is.

4. Big Bank's network is down and debit cards aren't working. If you planned properly, your Graceful Degradation is using an alternative credit card that may not allow you to get out as much cash as you wanted, but you can still get a burger and fries and won't starve. **Never leave yourself in a binary condition, when simple analogue contingency planning is so obvious.**

In this case, it's called backup, or Plan-B. I always take three cash withdrawal options when I travel internationally. You never know.

This is the same concept that should be embedded in policy and network architecture: when things go wrong, you should already have in place a granularized suite of alternatives to initiate Graceful Degradation instead of binarily throwing a disconnect switch. (Of course, that might be necessary in certain cases, but that option should be only one of the possible weighted reactions to a detected threat or other security-relevant event, and there should probably be a human in the loop.)

MANAGEMENT PORN

It's NOT just On/Off. It's how much can you fine-tune your network to respond to real, or potential, security events using Graceful Degradation-style architecture in the Detection-Reaction matrix versus a binary Either-Or response?

1. Bandwidth compression is certainly a quantifiable analogue approach to Graceful Degradation when mission criticality is involved. Factors of 10^2 risk reduction are significant.

2. Vonage already uses a Graceful Degradation approach on their VoIP service. If my internet connection dies, Vonage reroutes the calls to a mobile or fixed line phone (OOB). Might cost me a few shekels... but I can still communicate.

3. Variable data padding, as a dynamic reaction to specific threats, provides a Graceful Degradation by making files bigger, thus taking more time to access or download.

4. Later in this book, we'll use another old analogue technique to stop phishing, using a tunable approach akin to Graceful Degradation.

Your Job? Think about how many places in your networks (or coding!) would permit an event-triggered feedback process to modify performance on a sliding scale. We have covered all of the necessary analogue thoughts to do this. The rest is up to you.

Pen-Testing
Analogue Style

In any given cyber-environment the only constant is that everything changes. Thus, questions arise:

Say a given penetration test demonstrates a high confidence (but still, TF < 1) in the assurance of a defined portion of a system. *(Please don't fall for a single TF value for an entire network. That's almost meaningless.)*

How long, though, does that TF remain at that specified value? Is the result of a given pen-test valid a year after it is performed? 90 days? A week? An hour? What changes to the system are permitted, with what level of confidence (TF), and over what period of time, before the pen-test's TF begins decrementing, and at what rate?

Let's take a given *protective* technology, or portion of the system we want to monitor, to get some handle on the long term assurance of a given function. We will just call it P, as we always have.

Enterprises count on P working reliably over a long period of time, but the vendor, in all likelihood, provides no warranty. So, we are back to P(t) being indeterminate.

The goal? To continuously test the efficacy over time of any detection process (IDS, A/V solution, etc.).

The software is designed to send highly crafted traffic through the same logical and physical paths used for normal traffic for the process we are testing. However, the software

Detection in Depth

is also designed to intentionally trigger a sensor, or other detection mechanism, that is part of the protection scheme, whether it is located somewhere in the middle of, or on the side of the traffic path. *(Vis a vis, Anderson's static Reference Monitor, or feedback enhanced Analogue methods.)*

If we view pen-testing as a detection scheme, conceptually automated time-based pen-testing tools will be able to detect changes that occurred after the initial pen-test, thus triggering a Reaction.

==Pen-testing, when implemented as an automatically continuous application of Detection in Depth, can be a powerful approach to security.==

THE VANISHING CHIP

SOME CHIPS ARE DESIGNED TO BLOW-UP.

DARPA's Vanishing Programmable Resources (VAPR) program was designed to "demonstrate electronic systems capable of physically disappearing in a controlled, triggerable manner." Ergo, detect an event, then trigger the destruction of the integrated circuit - totally beyond repair. FUBAR.

Extreme binary reaction? Yes. The viability of this approach should be based upon the results of analogue detection-reaction feedback analysis (maybe OODA?), ultimately calling for total destruction. After all, this IS the Government.

Think about the phrase "Tamper Proof". In some designs, detection of certain types of tampering results in the complete destruction of the device being tampered with. This practice is often popular with defense, intelligence, and national security technologies.

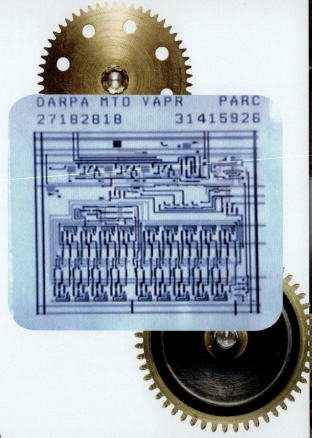

DETECTION LIMITS

Infinity is why traditional network security has failed. Infinity is our enemy. We hate infinity. Don't we?

Detection in Depth is not a binary function. It is as analogue as everything else we've been talking about. And, like everything in Analogue Network Security, there are limits.

When applying Detection in Depth to an OODA loop (L), the goal is to squeeze the loop, time-wise. Each of the constituent steps can contain its own sub-OODA loops with the same goal of approaching zero time:

$$L(t) = O1(t) + O2(t) + DE(t) + Act(t) = D(t) + R(t)$$

and the goal is for $L(t) \to 0$

The limits approach, but never reach, the impossible-to-achieve condition of zero-time.

In the worst case, if any one (or more) of the OODA components is undefined, then that component's time value $\to \infty$. This is just like when $D(t)$ works fast, but the subsequent $R(t)$ process is either non-existent or has failed definitionally and cannot be measured. No better than where we are now.

> **If $D(t) \to 0$ and $R(t) \to \infty$, then $E(t) \to \infty$**

Let's look at the other limit, the lower one; some vendors use the word(s) "real-time", "no delay", "right away", and even "it's instant". There's no such thing. Don't be misled.

The lower limit of detection granularity goes back to our discussion on "How Fast is a Computer?" The theoretical best-case scenario (which is impossible in the real world) of detecting and reacting to an event is:

> **Limit > 1 cycle $D(t)$** and
> **Limit > 1 cycle $R(t)$**, therefore
> **Limit $(D_t + R_t) > 2$**

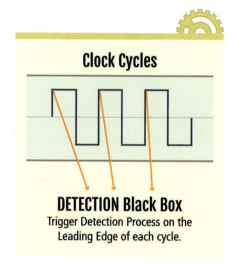

Clock Cycles

DETECTION Black Box
Trigger Detection Process on the Leading Edge of each cycle.

Think about the One-Time Pad as being the most granular security you can have. It's practical in crypto, but with ANS and Detection in Depth we will need to investigate and discover the *sweet spot* range for decent ROI.

In theory (a bad one...), we could call each of the leading edges of the clock cycles above a trigger to initiate a detection process. This also might be reminiscent of the One-Time Pad, the only non-crackable encryption scheme, because the key size is equal to or greater in size than the message size (pseudo-versus random considerations notwithstanding). While *interesting*, one-time pads are not terribly practical today.

So it is with Detection in Depth, as the detection limit approaches one clock cycle. But, **$D(t) + R(t) > 2$** cycles, so the only exception I can come up with is, if each clock cycle is delayed (negative time) by at least **$D(t) + R(t)$**.

Detection in Depth

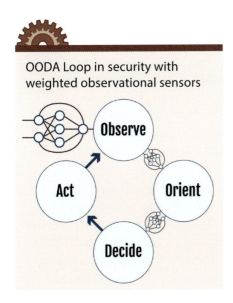

OODA Loop in security with weighted observational sensors

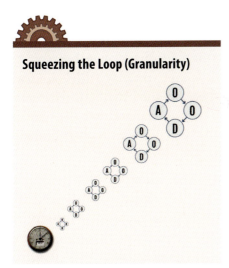

Squeezing the Loop (Granularity)

Detection in Depth must be approached practically, and again, I refer to the OODA loop. Each of the OODA components takes some time. Assume the following:

$$L(t) = O1(t) + O2(t) + DE(t) + Act(t) \text{ where}$$
$$L(t) = 100ms + 100ms + 100ms + 100ms = 400ms$$

Let's also assume there may or may not be a Detection trigger on each of the four components. At what point in a loop should a detection process be initiated? A simple example...

OBSERVE: The amount of time it takes to collect the necessary data from whatever sensors may be in use. I can argue that any data brought into this loop should have already been through a detection process, be it for hostility, sanitization, or other filtering criteria; therefore, that detection process, part of its own loop, will not interfere with the timing of this loop, as it has OOB characteristics. It maintains its last known condition, measured in time. So, in this example, the $O(t)$ in this loop is not negatively affected with added time by a prior detection process or any additional sub-loop that might require additional analysis (**D(t) + R(t)**).

ORIENT: The amount of time it takes to operate on the observed data and create an output signal. If, and only if, the orientation process is pristine, we need not necessarily add a sub-loop of detection here, either. The Orientation "Engine" should not be modifiable by any data that comes from Observation; it should only be modifiable by an external process, with its own detection processes for validation and enhanced admin trust. I will deem that the Orient piece of this loop does not require an additional **D(t) + R(t)** sub-loop, either.

DECIDE: The amount of time it takes to make an actionable decision based upon the prior two steps in the loop. At this point, however, in heightened security processes, it makes sense to consider the addition of a TB-FF in a sub-loop, which does two things:

1. Adds additional Trust Factor (if done right)
2. Adds time to the Decision process

Meaning, if the TB-FF is set for 500ms to approve or deny the decision process, suddenly the Decide (DE(t)) piece is increased to at least 600ms: **DE(t) + DC(t)**, the sum of the time to DEcide + the amount of time allocated by policy to the 2MR feedback in the TB-Flip-Flop. DC(t) as you recall, is the policy-specified decrementing time in Time-Based Flip-Flops.

ACT: The amount of time it takes to actually respond to the Decision. We can correlate this to Response time, Remediation time, or any other "End of Loop" criteria we choose, as long as it is delineated by time. In some cases, an additional TB-FF is needed for secondary (or additional layers) of authentication or permission, and such process is defined by the Decrementing Time in the feedback loop.

Again, what are the limiting factors for the granularity of detection?

In the most abstract terms, there is more than one answer, and it's up to the programmer, network engineer, or process controller (human, too) to decide, based upon Risk and Trust Factor.

1. If there is sufficient Trust Factor in the Loop, and no sub-loops for verification are required, this loop is defined by
   $L(t) = O1(t) + O2(t) + DE(t) + Act(t)$ alone.

2. If an additional layer of Detection in Depth is chosen, such as the 2MR, then, from the example in bullet #1, we can generalize:
   $L(t) = [O1(t) + DC(t)] + [O2(t) + DC(t)] + [DE(t) + DC(t)] + [Act(t) + DC(t)]$

...where the Decrementing Time is always greater than loop component time, or else there is no point. Of course, we might consider, for example, when $DC(t) < O(t)$, that we could add negative time of $[DC(t) - O(t)] + X(t)$, where X(t) is an arbitrary value of $X(t) > 0$. Performance may suffer but, in many cases, such performance hits are too minuscule to be noticeable or of any real consequence.

I am fully aware that thinking of networks, data, code and human behavior in terms of limits, loops and feedback may be new to you. All I ask is that you play with the ideas a bit, contribute to the Analogue Network Security forums and help improve the state of security in all three domains: cyber, human, and physical.

Keep in mind though, that without feedback in the loop, our security vulnerabilities approach infinity. Infinity is not our friend. For security, approaching zero time is our greatest ally. Your designs and operational policies determine where your Risk and Trust Factors lie.

BEHAVIORAL ALGORITHMS

WE ARE ALGORITHM HAPPY. WE USE THEM EVERYWHERE.

- Finding faces of bad guys at public events, on the street, etc.
- Self-driving cars with insane amounts of feedback and Detection-Reaction processes.
- Amazon knowing what you will want to buy… and when. Before you do. (Negative Time is a *thing*, relativistically speaking, of course.)
- Credit card companies more finely tuning their Detection-Reaction matrices to detect fraud with fewer false positives.
- And everything else in our lives that predicts or anticipates our behavior.

The brain is primarily designed to collect data in order to predict the future. That's called survival.

Microsoft is building a tool to automatically detect bias in AI algorithms. That is OODA-based Detection in Depth.

From my analogue view, we must look back in time. In the olden days, first generation virus scanners plugged a few hundred signatures into a .TXT file which was used as the reference basis to detect hostile code. Emails (and later, downloads, etc.) were scanned in one way or other, but the bottom line was that another binary behavior manifested itself.

> **File A:** String of "signatures," or sequences of ASCII characters compared to
>
> **File B:** One or more files, initially .EXE and .COM (this was before data viruses)

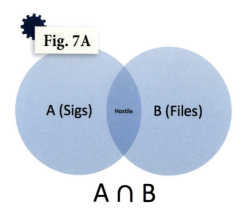

The goal was sort of Set Theory based. See if any of Set A (virus signatures) and Set B (executable files) overlapped. If they did, the intersection of Sets A & B were suspect hostile code, like in Fig. 7A. *(In those days we said "a virus.")*

Over time, intelligence was added and file analysis (executables and data files, e.g., .doc, .pdf, etc.) looked for intersections based upon potential permutations of the hostile code, as it mutated from place to place. Things got much better; detection rates improved with fewer false-negatives and false-positives. The bad guys enhanced their encrypting algorithms, we built better detection algorithms, and the Hostile Code Arms Race (now including massive amounts of phishing and spam) still rages.

Let's fast forward to event logging, IDSs, IPSs, SIEMs, and associated detection based technologies.

==In Analogue Network Security, I treat Detection and Reaction components as Black Boxes.== Reason: I don't care what they are *supposed* to do. All these technologies are examining behavior; perhaps potentially hostile files and non-predicted deviations, whether in code, traffic, or networking architectures and traffic.

Let's see if there is a legitimate, measurable way to hold security vendors accountable for their claims.

==Metamorphic== and ==polymorphic== are two popular terms for malware mutations.

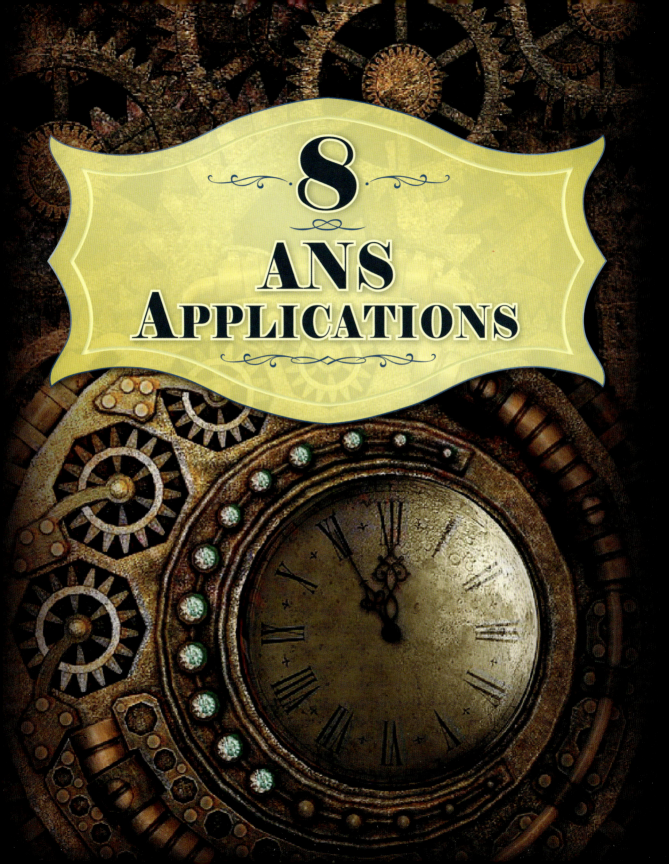

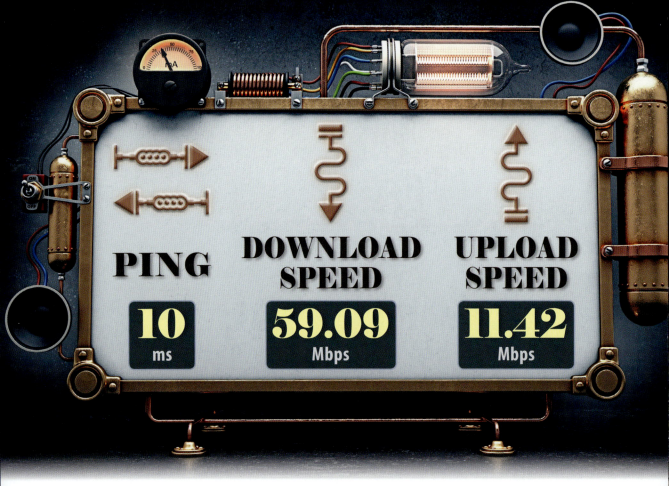

Ping, McFly!

If everyone in the whole world can easily measure their computers' performance and their internet traffic performance, then fifty years and trillions of dollars-plus later, the professional information security industry should damned well be able to measure the performance of our security tools.

> The only mathematical certainty in infosec is the forward flow of time. If there is forward time, there is risk, by definition. Anything else is a WAG, which is why we are losing the CyberWars. A fundamental shift is required.

Measure Your Security

At the very core of Analogue Network Security is measurement. As history has shown us, cybersecurity without metrics is a fool's errand.

I sincerely hope this fundamental tenet resonates with readers, because today, right now, you all have the ability to measure much of your cybersecurity posture. Quantitatively. With ANS, it will hopefully only get better.

Keep in mind, however, that every security metric is both dynamic and probabilistic. Fortunately, with Analogue Network Security, you should learn how to visualize your various security stances in the time-domain.

Breaches are endemic. Gazillions of dollars spent after conversations like you just read in the cartoon on the prio page. Now, I am not picking on any one vendor; I believe the fault is in the binary approach we take to security. So, let's see if there is a way we can hold vendors accountable.

Black Box circa 2492/New Age Date System

I use "BB" to reference any vendor's Black Box that performs any abstract security service. The internal process mechanism is immaterial to measurement; signature-based A/V, rule-based binary decision making, heuristics, deep learning or any possible hybrid - it's still a Black Box. In many cases, the BB is designed to detect some condition, anomaly or other specific or profiled traffic behaviors. Great. I get it. But vendors tend to make promises and I'd like to know how well their BB performs. To that end, let's ask a few Analogue Network Security-style questions of the Black Box Vendor.

- ▶ How long does it take to detect a malicious act/thing/file?
- ▶ Can you show me how that time value changes with specific hardware/network/software/load configurations?
- ▶ Is the time value the same for every possible test? If not, what is the Min-Max range for performance over time?
  $$0 < D(t\text{-min}) < D(t\text{-avg}) < D(t\text{-max}) < \infty$$

(Set boundaries.)

- ▶ Can you show me the raw test data?
- ▶ For D(t-min), what is the guaranteed accuracy (Trust Factor or Risk) of the detection for:
  - False Positives
  - False Negatives
- ▶ Same question, but for D(t-avg) and D(t-max). How good is your BB(?) and I would expect testing labs to build pretty management porn versions with colorful graphs and charts. Then, we can compare products and services with much more substantial metrics than the "trust-me" approach.

Analogue Network Security Applications

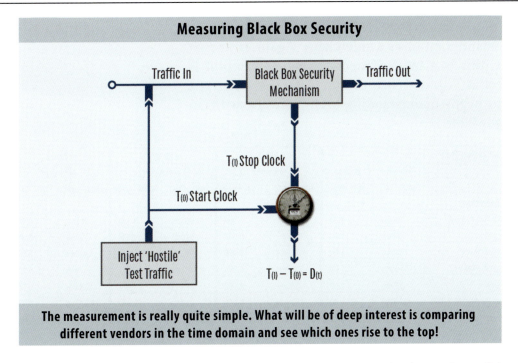

Measuring Black Box Security

The measurement is really quite simple. What will be of deep interest is comparing different vendors in the time domain and see which ones rise to the top!

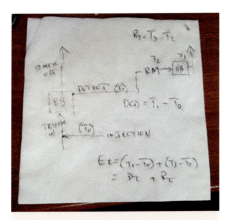

The original "Measuring Security" napkin drawing from Paris.

Thanks to everyone over the last 15 years for your input, suggestions, and acknowledgment, that even this simple time-based thinking has some power.

The general tool description (independent of the BB's specific security function) is:

1. Inject "hostile" test code that should be detectable by the BB. Vary the difficulty of detection, especially with 'smart' systems. Identifying which kinds of code will trigger the BB's detection mechanism will help inject appropriately easy and hard conditions, presumably based upon near-normal distribution. Ask your vendor. This approach can be used consistently across many product ranges to gauge comparative performance vs. efficacy.

2. When the specific code is injected, start a clock. To make it easy, start at **0:00:00.00, or T(0)**.

3. At the detection point in the BB, ideally there is a logging/notification trigger that says, "Hey, we got something!" Now, I know this may not exist everywhere, but the goal is to grab hold of that same trigger and use it to Stop the Clock. T(1). If APIs are available… awesome. If not, ask your vendor to put in such a trigger point for your use.

4. The time difference between those two numbers is your current, accurately measured Detection Time, or **T(1) − T(0) = D(t)** for that input criteria and that specific test platform (SW/HW, etc.)

In "normal" operations, a BB can be "in line" from a traffic standpoint or as a side-chain. Again, it doesn't matter; this is a measurement testbed. The point is to inject at T(0) and measure the detection trigger at T(1) to begin understanding your network with an analogue view.

Product Comparison			BB #1		BB #2		BB #1	
	Desired	Desired	Measured		Measured		Measured	
	Time – D(t)	Trust Factor	Time – D(t)	Trust Factor	Time – D(t)	Trust Factor	Time – D(t)	Trust Factor
Detections								
Too Much Text in Email	100ms	1.00	1123ms	0.909	705ms	0.944	217ms	0.865
Bad Language	200ms	1.00	3200ms	0.991	510ms	0.924	120ms	0.843
Attachment: SMPT	1000ms	1.00	1710ms	0.998	1091ms	0.981	1425ms	0.999
Potential PII: POP	1500ms	1.00	5590ms	0.999	2251ms	0.961	1579ms	0.911
Hostile Link	500ms	1.00	380ms	0.999	311ms	0.971	2134ms	0.901
Unknown People/SMPT-POP	2500ms	1.00	1920ms	0.999	210ms	0.999	945ms	0.999

A notional approach to comparing the speed and TF of detection products. I did not include cost, but you can probably make a couple of fast guesses which one is the cheapest.

This view of product efficacy becomes exceedingly important as we begin to mix all of the Analogue Network Security concepts to build our security architectures. Here, ==Trust Factor is the amount of statistical confidence that the vendor has in his own product(s)==. For now we will ignore the impact of hardware and other environmental performance considerations in our evaluation, but from an implementation standpoint, this range (spectrum) can be very illuminating when evaluating a vendor's security solution.

First, we can examine error rate and how that translates to Trust Factor.

Detection Error	Detections in Sample	Error Rate	Trust Factor
1	1	100%	0.000000
1	10	10.0000%	0.900000
1	100	1.0000%	0.990000
1	1,000	0.1000%	0.999000
1	10,000	0.0100%	0.999900
1	100,000	0.0010%	0.999990
1	1,000,000	0.0001%	0.999999

Just as in our earlier Trust Factor discussions where the TF is the inverse of Risk...

(Risk = 1/TF and TF = 1/Risk)

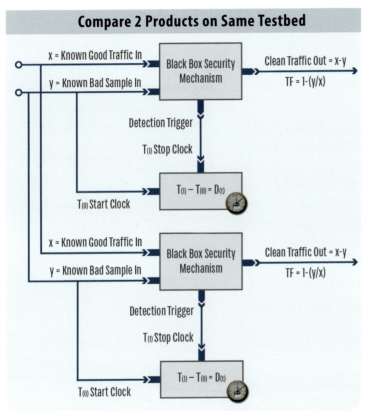

...with large datasets, we find that for a detection system to work with enough efficacy so as not to interfere with operations, several orders of magnitude of increased Trust Factor are required. We are looking at organizations of tens of thousands of people, each touching thousands of events every year ($10^4 * 10^3$). We are looking for efficacy that exceeds the Six Sigma Measure, Analyze, Design, Verify, OODA approach used so successfully by ICS-SCADA vendors such as GE, sometimes by a factor of 10^6, or more.

Our testbed, then, is pretty simple and akin to the measurement approach above. In this case, though, the values of x and y are clearly defined. We know what the answer should be, based upon the inputs. We also know - exactly - how long the Black Box takes to achieve a specific Trust Factor due to **T(1) − T(0) = D(t)**.

If **T(0) = 0** and **T(1) = 3,000ms**, then **D(t)** is clearly **3,000ms**

Nothing difficult here.

Analogue Network Security Applications

The next question for the Black Box vendor should be, given a Trust Factor of **1-(y/x)** for D(t), will my Trust Factor increase as a function of D(t) increasing, and can you show me the plot on a curve? Does the Black Box become *more accurate* if it is given *more time* to complete its determination? If the Black Box accuracy increase is linear over time, TF should rise linearly as D(t) is increased. Or is there some other performance variable? Perhaps doubling the D(t) only provides a 10% increase in accuracy? Or, does the Black Box function optimize operation with an upper limit and the vendor has chosen this D(t) intentionally?

If we know how the answer should be framed, we can measure it and hold vendors accountable.

My argument is we should know these things before deploying new technologies into any network. We can make these measurements. We can compare Black Box performance in varying conditions by controlling the known specifics of the inputs and measuring the D(t). We then have the opportunity and customer-luxury of comparing competing products with time-based metrics. Technical reviewers should have a ball - and vendors will necessarily be required to "Up Their Game."

See Chapter 9 on Six Sigma to see how low a bar that actually is in our industry.

Let's take this one step further and say after our initial measurements, "Wow… that's really good! But I'm a security person and want to verify my results." How can we do that?

When we apply Verification, doesn't this look somewhat familiar? A little feedback! Security experts often say that, perhaps in the case of malware detection, "Use two different products. One for Fee… one for Free." Black Boxes #1 and #2 can be competing products,

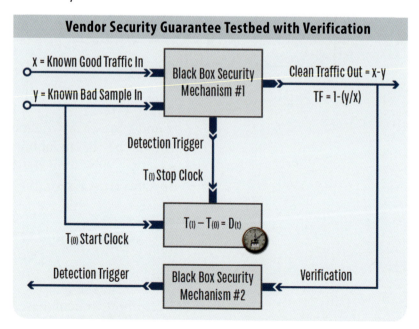

using the same or differing approaches to detection. What this gives us is a pretty simple mechanism by which to validate the performance claims of vendors in the detection universe.

If we *do* see a Detection Trigger in the Verification process, what does that mean? Is #2 better than #1? What happens if we reverse #1 & #2 in our testbed? Is their relationship transitive or not? This is the kind of analysis that tells us, on our terms, a lot more than just a handshake belief in the "Invisible Patented Secret Sauce We Can't Show You."

Think Dark Matter. We don't know what it is. But we know it's there because we can measure its effects on less exotic particles. Just because we, in the security world, are often not privy to the inner workings of the products and solutions we employ, there is no reason not to measure them.

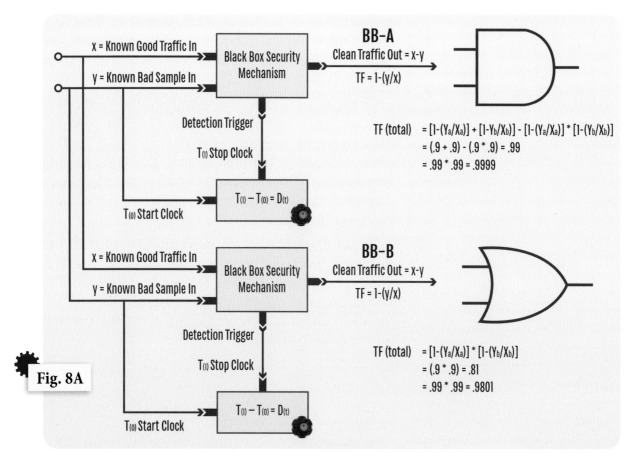

Fig. 8A

In Fig. 8A above, two similar detection products are running in parallel (assume in sync for now). One or ideally, both, of the Detection products should detect the same errant event or object. In the top right, we add the union of the two events together, so that a reaction is initiated if both detections occur. In the bottom, we permit a reaction to take place if either of the detection mechanisms is triggered.

First, with the OR gate, note that the overall TF, as before, goes down. With the AND gate, the TF rises significantly.

Since the two products are not in 100% time-sync, we could of course, employ a TB-FF for a secondary verification according to the two-man-rule approach. This will only work, however, if the reaction is revocable.

Analogue Network Security Applications

Now, let's add a second component to Detection in Depth, that of Reaction, and see what we can measure.

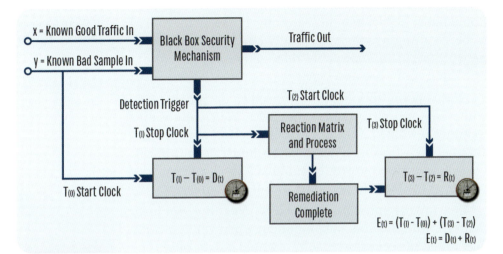

YOUR JOB

Design an ANS circuit that provides upper and lower time limits for reaction initiation, if the two detection products operate with a time-delta of 100ms. Calculate the TF over time. See what happens.

In this case, we employ the same technique. Insert known good traffic and known bad samples into the Black Box detection. The difference is, we add the Reaction Matrix Process and Remediation, $R(t)$, to the equation. Every tiny process takes some amount of time, no matter how small. *(See earlier section, Chapter 3, page 12, "How Fast is a Computer?")*

Tying the API of the remediative technology to the $R(t)$ clock gives us the measurable, and hopefully repeatably consistent capability, to measure this one event chain as $E(t) = (T(1) - T(0)) + (T(3) - T(2))$. How fast does the remediation take to complete? The answers are there … if you know what the right questions are. Successful Remediation is up to the enterprise to define. Is it an automatic remediation, such as a port block, user_event_denial, a change in security controls? Or, is there a human in the process?

The measurements are actually quite simple.

Remember the earlier charts on the time difference between automatic, human, and hybrid Detection-Reaction matrices.

- ▶ The Detection Trigger stops the first clock and begins the reaction process, up to and including remediation.
- ▶ It also starts another clock process as the reaction process begin.

Only you can decide when the reaction process ends. Is it with notification of the Admin? Is it a corrected setting? Does it include forensics? Or only the immediate risk? Define this carefully, because, for there to be meaning as you successfully engage in analogue network security, repeatable relative (versus absolute) reference points are necessary.

I've spoken with many analysts and am pleased to see a security services differentiator called MDR, Managed Detection & Reaction. There is fuzziness between MSSP and MDR, but they are headed in the right direction.

At this point, though, all you need to do is come up with some rough reaction times R(t). You really want to know at what scale your current reaction matrix and channel are working. Does it take 1 hour? 20 minutes? Or is your process down to seconds? Which ones work better? Which means getting $E(t) \rightarrow 0$, of course.

Measure the entire process. The whole thing, not just the tech. Add the human component wherever you can. Test different scenarios. Finally, I would like to offer the following suggestions to security vendors:

1. Be more transparent about how your products work. If your engineers know, so should your customers. If your engineers don't, they should.

2. Enable your customers to test and measure your products in situ, within an operationally live production environment, so they understand the performance differences from idealized testbeds.

3. Give them the tools to do this, or someone else will.

AI/ML/DL complexifies this transparency due to the hundreds of possible approaches. Measure it, no matter what the vendor claims.

These points are really critical, especially for this old analogue Winn. Just 'cause it works on the bench does not mean it will work at a live concert, or in your live network. From an analogue view, what problems, time delays, or other hindrances in your current network traffic and architectures can interfere with the proper time-based operation of your Detection-Reaction Matrix? I don't know that answer - that's why we have to measure it.

Now that you have a hard value, you have taken the first step in Analogue Network Security.

Let's apply what we have discussed for the last several chapters and put them into real-life use.

SOFT CORE MANAGEMENT PORN ANSWER

Boss: "How secure are we?"

You: "Well, your greatness, for an XYZ security event, we can stop it in **X'Y'Z'(t)**."

Boss: "Wow. That's great! Or... is it?"

THE HORROR OF IT ALL:
TIME-WISE

A couple of years back, my team tried to deploy a simple multi-media broadcast (video streaming) on a customer's network. Interactive learning with tens of thousands of users around the world. Talk about complete failure! Yes, Epic Fail!

WTF? No way! But this smelled familiar to me. The neurons smoldered..

It took a lot of convincing, but I did get one of the friendly engineers, who 'got' that something else was afoot, to agree to do some network analysis. In seconds after our test measurement, the answers appeared, and were, to me, obvious.

Being a security conscious financial firm, they had purchased and installed all sorts of security products; server based, client-centric; from the perimeter to the soft gooey insides, they had it all.

But they had never tested their systems to look at the network performance hit from continuous synchronous communications on all of these security tools. They had no idea how much workstation capability was wasting away in the ether of security-ville. Worse yet, due to network collisions (oh, it was a mess…) some security products weren't even working properly. (Bruce Schneier's *Security Theater* comes to mind…).

Unplug a couple. Retest. Interactive multi-media performs correctly. Turn 'em back on… and, Fail!

Please heed this as an obvious lesson.

Look at your networks (code…). Know how to Test. Fairly. Recognize the difference between Live-Production, Dev, and Idealized Testbeds.

Then, test again. And again. Yes, do it again, too. Regularly. Please! Apply OODA. Oh, and test again.

End Rant #42.

Just because it works on the bench (in the lab), doesn't mean it works in a live concert (operational network).

A Short Form

This form might help management understand your current network posture with respect to time.

1. **Do you have any detection systems in place?**   YES   NO

   If you have no detection component, then $D = \infty$, and assuming $P = 0$, then $E = \infty$ and you have a virtual 100% system exposure. *(C-Suiters: This is about as bad as it gets, and I venture this is where many of you are right now, whether you know it or not.)*

2. **Do you have a Reaction mechanism in your network which is triggered by the detection component?**   YES   NO

   If you have no reaction component, then $R = \infty$ and assuming $P = 0$, then $E = \infty$ and you have a virtual 100% system exposure. *(See #1 above.)*

3. **When your detection mechanism is optimally running, how long does it take to detect a particular attack it is designed to attack?**

   _____ *(sec/min/hr)*

   This is a tough question. As of today, vendors are not in the habit of specifying performance in time units. I really hope that enough security professionals press the point. It's important.

4. **Once your detection mechanism has detected an attack or other out-of-bounds behavior, by what means are you notified?** *(This is the first step of Reaction, e.g., email, phone, not at all, future audit trails.)*

   _____

   _____

5. **How long does it take to notify you in Step #4 above?**

   _____ *(sec/min/hr)*

   When you are at the kids' softball game?

   _____ *(sec/min/hr)*

6. **Once you have been notified of a problem via the detection mechanism, on average, how long does it take you to get to a location where you can do something about it?** *(Or get someone else to begin corrective measures?)*

   _____ *(sec/min/hr)*

7. **Do you have a formal triage process to determine the potential severity of the security event?**   YES   NO

   How long to access triage process guide?

   _____ *(sec/min/hr)*

   Can you do the triage alone or need to get assistance?

   _____ *(sec/min/hr)*

   Do you need approval to take remediative action?

   _____ *(sec/min/hr)*

   Who else needs to be notified?

   _____ *(sec/min/hr)*

8. **Do you have a formal remediation/ reconstitution process for a variety of cyber events?**   YES   NO

   Once triage has determined additional remediative steps must be taken, on average, how long does it take you to find the people to do the work?

   _____ *(sec/min/hr)*

   Do you have a process for Graceful Degradation? How many services can be shuttered to protect the organization?

   _____

   _____

9. What is your PR spin and cyber-insurance posture? Does it matter who is behind a cyber event; internal/external, ID'd or not?

_____

_____

   Does PR matter NOW or only after the event is over and reconstitution has occurred and do you bring in law enforcement?

_____

_____

10. Calculate the above for many different scenarios as there will be different answers and processes. This entire process is analogue, and can be manual, automated or a hybrid.

   Now, please add up the best case numbers from the above answers:
   _____ (sec/min/hr)

   Now, please add up the worst case numbers from the above answers:
   _____ (sec/min/hr)

If you have multiple paths throughout your networks, take a look at each of them, fill out a separate chart for each, and compare answers. In larger networks, different administrators have different policies to follow, they are empowered differently, and the systems they are charged to defend have differing levels of mission criticality. So, piece together aspects of your networks as standalone sub-networks before trying to glue them all together into a single whole picture. Some networks are so complex, topological simplification becomes a strategic security goal; not more technology – less!

In our example below, you can estimate how much time an adversary could possibly have to run rampant through your networks, and the answers are in all likelihood not too terribly pleasant – especially if the time values creep up to an hour and beyond. This simple quantitative analysis can help you convince management that you have a problem, and that you do indeed need additional budget dollars in search of solutions.

$E(t) =$ _____ to
     (Best Case)

   _____
     (Worst Case)

This is your range of E(t), or exposure time, in one part of your enterprise based upon a Time-Based Security Analysis.

Notification Means (Reaction)	Desired Time	Predicted Time	Measured Time
During Work Hours			
E-Mail to desk (At peak Traffic Times)			
E-Mail to desk (At off-hours)			
E-Mail when not at desk			
Pager with return phone number or 911			
Page with full message			
Phone call to desk			
Notify 2nd in charge (Notify Supervisor/Mgmt/Admin)			
Not During Work Hours			
E-Mail to home (At peak Traffic Times)			
E-Mail to home (At off-hours)			
E-Mail when not at home			
Pager with return phone number or 911			
Page with full message			
Phone call to home			
Notify 2nd in charge (Notify Supervisor/Mgmt/Admin)			

Another approach to viewing Reaction from Policy to Practice

Damn!
Stop it!

We have all clicked "Send"' on an email and then cursed ourselves for being so quick-on-the-trigger. Perhaps, in the heat of the moment we said something we really didn't want to go public. Or perhaps, we got sucked into a troll war and went over the top.

There are so very many reasons to shout Damn! at the top of our lungs because of an ill-advised, ill-timed email, post, or other communication you can't take back.

With Analogue Network Security, we can solve this.

We are all used to the effects of We Need It Now, *immediacy*. We Can't Wait, *a few seconds*. If a web site is slow, it must be broken! If it doesn't happen right away, then we move on. Back in the day, this was the reason for cryptographic accelerators. It's the reason for load balancing; especially for 0800h-0900h login times. And, oddly enough, load balancing techniques, and ANS math are of the same analogue ilk.

And so it is for email. We are often compelled to reply ASAP despite our best security awareness training. But, let's ask some analogue questions:

So, what is the right amount of time to "Delay/Hold" SMTP traffic? For your organization, that's up to you. The point is simple:

> *"If my outgoing email is delayed by 1/2 second, will the world come to an end?"* Answer: No.
>
> *"If my outgoing email is delayed by 10 seconds, will the world come to an end?"* Answer: No.
>
> *"If my outgoing email is delayed by 30 minutes, will the world come to an end?"* Answer: No. Maybe though, someone would consider you rude and unprofessional. *(We need to get over ourselves.)*

Your organization has the capability to minimize the above-mentioned expensive embarrassments by adding a little analogue thinking and a simple Time-Based Delay Line in SMTP processes. How about even building a little feedback in and see what happens!

Let's say a user clicks <Send> on an email. The email is then routed to a Stupid-SMTP-Traffic-Content Detector. With a **decent** detection system, OODA should apply, and is key to fewer errors and to the system learning more.

Let's make up a few "detectable" things we can all agree upon:

- The forwarding of long threads of emails that go back weeks or months, and contain "who knows what."
- Attachments
- Offensive language
- Potential PII exfiltration or accidental breach
- Any policy related item you want

THE INSIDER THREAT

This same model will work in detecting potential data exfiltration from Insider Threats. Different detection algorithms are needed for intentional versus accidental breaches. I suggest another policy-driven Venn diagram to identify common characteristic overlaps.

The goal is to catch those incessant accidents (and potentially hostile Insider Threats of Exfiltration) we all make from time to time - **before the damage is done**. (See the following table.)

Say that the vendor claims and your testing shows, that for the kind of SMTP traffic you have chosen to detect, a decision with 99.9999% Trust Factor can be achieved in 100ms. This is simple, right? All that we have to do it is add a delay line in the SMTP traffic of >100ms to maintain that provable level of confidence.

SMTP Detection			Ass Saver Reaction		
Alarms	D(t)	Trigger Event	Reaction	R(t)	Reaction Method
Too Much Text	100ms	Re-Authentication (In Band)	Set TB-FF Clock	10 mins.	Manual Approval/Denial
Bad Language	100ms	Re-Authentication (OOB)	Set TB-FF Clock	5 mins.	Manual Approval/Denial
Attachment	200ms	Re-Authentication (In Band)	Set TB-FF Clock	10 mins.	Manual Approval/Denial
Potential PII	1000ms	Re-Authentication (OOB)	Set TB-FF Clock	5 mins.	Manual Approval/Denial
Too Much Text	1500ms	Re-Authentication (OOB)	Set TB-FF Clock	30 mins.	2MR Approval
Attachment	500ms	Re-Authentication (OOB)	Set TB-FF Clock	30 mins.	2MR Approval

A simple SMTP Reaction/Detection Matrix to help Stupid SMTP Mistakes.

The addition of the Delay Line adds security against stupid stuff… measurably… sort of. The output of the Reaction Matrix here is pretty darn binary, as in traditional feed-forward network control systems. The

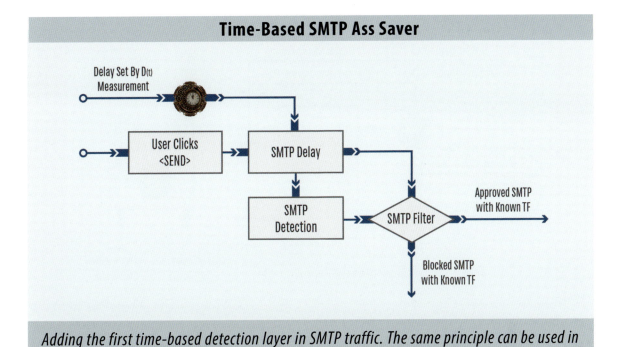

Adding the first time-based detection layer in SMTP traffic. The same principle can be used in any dynamic detection-in-depth application.

biggest advantage here is to give time-based control over how the Trust Factor is evaluated. On the other hand, one negative – depending upon implementation – is that sent emails can end up in the nether regions of the internet with no one the wiser. "Did she get it? Or not? Only way to know is to go OOB and call!"

Can this model be improved? I think so, and I'm going to use a little feedback.

By employing a simple TB-FF, the chance of sending 'Oops(!) Emails', is dramatically reduced.

Analogue Network Security Applications

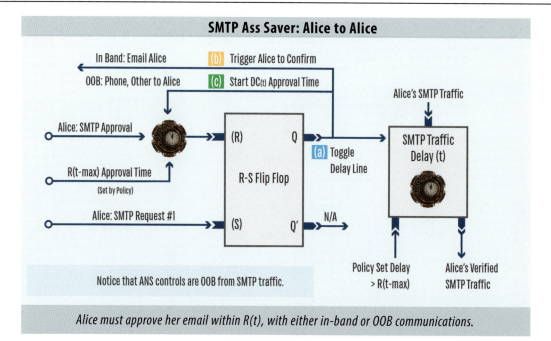

Alice must approve her email within R(t), with either in-band or OOB communications.

1. Alice clicks <Send>
2. Policy driven Delay Line pauses traffic.
3. Alice is asked to verify that the contents of the email are appropriate.

Possible MSGS:

Dear Alice: Please verify that the contents of the attachment you are attempting to send to <Charlie@BigBank.Com> meets company policy and standards.

Dear Alice: This email contains threads for the last <120 days>. Please verify that the contents of this email you are attempting to send to <Darlene@BigBank.Com> meets company policy and standards.

4. The Policy-Based Reaction Time must be less than the Delay Line Time.
5. If Alice does not respond to the challenge within the Reaction Time, the email can be deleted (don't forget to tell Alice!), or held in some limbo, until Alice takes specific actions. These steps are determined by policy.
6. If Alice does respond in < R(t), then the email will be sent, or, if Alice decides she accidentally sent inappropriate traffic, she can delete/edit/start over.

Note that Alice can be notified by, perhaps, an email, which is an in-band challenge. Or, she can be notified with an (out-of-band) OOB message.

Again, by employing a simple TB-FF, the chance of sending OOPS! Emails, is reduced.

1. Alice clicks <Send>
2. Policy-driven Delay Line pauses traffic.
3. Bob is asked to verify that the contents of Alice's suspect email are appropriate.

Possible MSGS:

Dear Bob: Please verify that the contents of the attachment that Alice is attempting to send to <Charlie@BigBank.Com> meets company security policy and standards.

Dear Bob: This email contains threads for the last <120 days>. Please verify that the contents of the email Alice is attempting to send to <Darlene@BigBank.Com> meets company security policy and standards.

4. The Policy-Based Reaction Time must be less than the Delay Line Time. $R(t) < DL(t)$

5. If Bob does not approve of Alice's email within the Reaction Time, the email can be deleted (don't forget to tell Alice!), or held in some limbo, until Bob takes specific actions. These steps are determined by policy.

6. If Bob does respond in $< R(t)$, then the email will be sent. If Bob decides she accidentally sent inappropriate traffic, Alice will be notified the email was not sent, and why.

So, you're thinking, "Wow... I send 3,000 emails a day. That's a Royal Pain!" Well, I could reply, "Security is not designed for your convenience..." but you will retort with, "users will revolt."

This puts the onus of security on the vendor and policy in the detection mechanism, exactly where the responsibilities should lie. Yes, users should do a better job. But IT-happens. I believe that this approach is a balance between performance and a newly enhanced level of trust.

BOTTOM LINE: The smarter the detection systems, the less that users need to interact. That's a vendor issue.

I do hope that this approach has enough value for designers to take it to the next level.

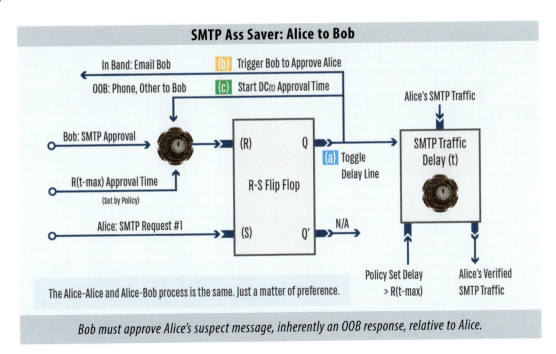

SMTP Ass Saver: Alice to Bob

The Alice-Alice and Alice-Bob process is the same. Just a matter of preference.

Bob must approve Alice's suspect message, inherently an OOB response, relative to Alice.

Social Media, Bikini-Grams, & NSFW

"Suzi… are you sure you want to post that bikini-pic? It might come to haunt you when you apply to college."

Yeah… and those Spring Break going wild shenanigans…hmmmm…

"Henry, do you really want your professors to see you chugging that vodka while mooning the Senator's motorcade?"

The answer for carefree foolish youths is SnapChat and other time-based techniques to delete the offending files. They have future jobs to consider, after all!

"Steve. Do you really want that video of you… (fill-in embarrassing blanks) … showing up when some HR person checks out your online profile for stupid stuff?"

Of course, once employed, users will learn soon enough about policies and NSFW emails or attachments. And yes, each user has to show some responsibility, but we, as IT security experts, should also be providing far superior tools, and speed-up the security processes as much as possible!

> **How about...**
> ▶ Time-Based Feedback (Flip-Flop) for social media postings?
> ▶ Verification feedback for Twitter.

All I am saying is, why don't these apps have a built-in method to give folks a second chance after pressing <Post>?

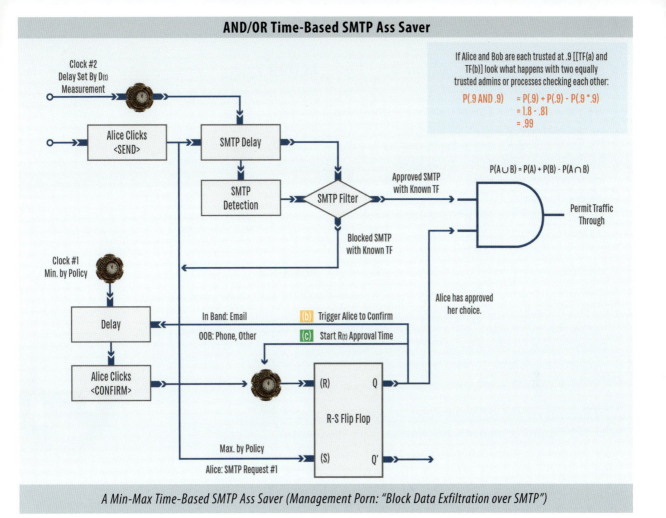

A Min-Max Time-Based SMTP Ass Saver (Management Porn: "Block Data Exfiltration over SMTP")

2 CLOCK SMTP ASS SAVER

With the approach above, we are looking at one end of yet another analogue min-max condition.

"How much time does it take a vendor to quantifiably assure a customer that a given email and its contents are safe?"

Obviously, we want **D(t) → 0**, as everywhere in TBS and ANS. But what if we combine our anti-phishing and NSFW email and attachment circuits together? What happens? We have now defined both limits of a min-max decision process.

Let's say that D(t) of vendor bad-email-detecting-product equals 100ms with a Trust Factor of .9999 (equal to the prior example). Not noticeable to the user.

But let's add a variation of the NSFW-attachment SMTP circuit.

So, let's say that the Click Detector initiates two actions and triggers two clocks: 1 for Alice and 1 for the BB Detection, which we will call Bob.

CLOCK 1

(Minimum delay for human feedback set by policy.) Sets the minimum and the maximum amount of time he has to approve before revocation occurs. A variable delay in the Confirm Feedback Loop of the TB-FF is set by policy. The TB-FF Decrementing Clock should be set by Policy, to revoke any unconfirmed send. Another architecture would be to let the Blocked SMTP with known TF triggers the TB-FF, as Alice, thus requiring a subsequent reconfirmation by Alice before permitting traffic to continue.

CLOCK 2

(BB detection, set by D(t).) This clock is set at some arbitrary time greater than the amount of time a vendor will provide specifications, such as: "We can detect with 99.99% accuracy, and less than .01% false positives, hostile content or suspicious websites within 100ms."

ACTION 1

I would think the TB-FF feedback would be a message displayed to the user like, "Did you really mean to send this attachment to someone not in your contact list?" For argument's sake, let's set this clock to 3 secs. The user must wait 3 full seconds before s/he re-approves the first click.

Pain in the tuchus? Sure, maybe. But so what, if it can measurably improve the Trust Factor of clicking and reduce the number mindless clicks that cause harm.

ACTION 2

Halt the traffic throughput, add negative time of at least the time value set by the vendor, and wait with another TB-FF, the results of the vendor's analysis.

The min-max values are set according to policy and the vendor's measurable claims. The two outputs can be put through an OR gate where either one of these conditions will allow traffic through, or, as is appropriate, if the SMPT detection blocks traffic where the circuit inherently induces feedback. If we use the approach, as in the drawing above and overlay TFs, we will increase Trust by using an AND gate, where both conditions from each circuit must be met.

With decent BB detection gear, the user will only be asked to confirm that activity which is deemed to be strange, and given the learning quality of the detection mechanism, improve over time.

Everyone wants processes to occur with maximum speed and efficiency. Time-Based Security says, "Hold Your Horses, Hoss! Let's slow things down a bit." With that, a vendor can, hopefully, if they do things correctly, offer time-scaled efficacy. If customers are willing to wait a second or more, perhaps vendors will be able to offer more accuracy, therefore, increase their TF.

Analogue Network Security Applications

Our initial notional conditions:

> **Vendor D(t) = 100ms**, *with a* **TF of .9999** *and correlated click risk of* **.0001.**

Pretty straight ahead. These are just numbers I chose for ease of mental visualization.

But, what if, the vendor can also demonstrably claim, through iterative (feedback) analysis, that:

> *When* **D(t) = 1000ms**, *the TF increased to* **.99999** *and correlated click risk is reduced to* **.00001.**

This is simply an exponential improvement; statistically significant. In this case, if the vendor spends 10X the amount of time verifying the content or link, then there is 10X greater assurance in the choice made.

Linearly, the results are obvious, if the vendor can demonstrate such increased efficacy. Perhaps a vendor's algorithms are such that:

> **D(t) * 10^1 then TF * 10^2**

...would be an improvement of two orders of magnitude.

I don't know the ultimate answer that vendors will come up with. I do hope, though, that detection vendors will consider time in future architectures. Unless we try, we just don't know what we will find.

On my way to the RSA Awards dinner. When I walked in, the bartenders wanted selfies with me.

Detection Vendors who look at increased efficacy with increased analysis time, might find different approaches to their algorithms so they can be tuned on-the-fly. Or, they might choose to license additional data-feeds to provide their engines with more to churn on. This is why I call them Black Boxes. To Analogue Network Security thinking, the task or internals are immaterial, as long as you measure their performance by time and trust/risk.

ANTI-PHISHING

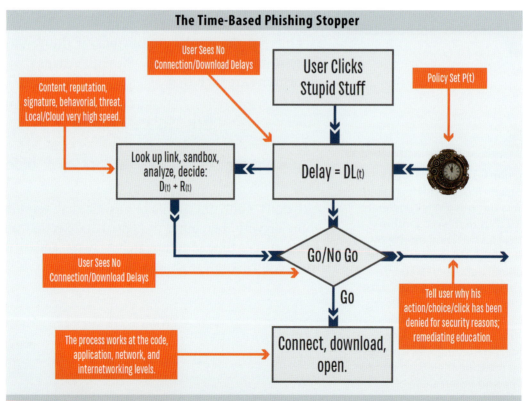

The Time-Based Phishing Stopper

- User Clicks Stupid Stuff
- User Sees No Connection/Download Delays
- Policy Set P(t)
- Content, reputation, signature, behavioral, threat. Local/Cloud very high speed.
- Look up link, sandbox, analyze, decide: $D(t) + R(t)$
- Delay = $DL(t)$
- Go/No Go → Go
- User Sees No Connection/Download Delays
- Tell user why his action/choice/click has been denied for security reasons; remediating education.
- The process works at the code, application, network, and internetworking levels.
- Connect, download, open.

What if, just imagine, what if, we could reduce successful phishing attacks measurably? Not just through feedback-based simulations (security awareness and training), but with an actual process?

Phishing is an incredibly efficient technique to hack the human, bypass security controls, and install a beachhead in victim networks. In OODA-terms, the bad guys have gotten inside your decision loop. They win.

A few vendors have products that seem to begin to address the problem, but, I'd like to view both the problem and the solution in analogue terms, and see if we can come up with a more formal approach. One in which vendors will need to *up their game* and provide some hard performance metrics by which they can be held accountable.

Now that you understand the basic ANS-TBS building blocks, a simple description should suffice. The diagram on the previous page should bring to mind the Reference Monitor and the approach to stop SMTP data breaches, intentional or accidental. It is a notional approach to solving phishing with Analogue Network Security.

What we end up with is vendor-sourced time-based criteria by which we can benchmark detection system performance. Those specifications create the basis for a specific Trust Factor (and Risk) for a specified amount of time.

1. The user clicks on something; links, and attachments are the current leading offenders.

2. The anti-phishing BB vendor provides statistics and guarantees. "We will detect a phishing attempt to 99.99% accuracy (Trust Factor) within 100 msecs, by performing in-depth email contents/attachment analysis and webpage exploration and analysis. Math here: A company of 10,000 people, with an average of 100 emails/links per day, at 99.99% accuracy will still let ~1,000 hostile emails reach users. We need to do better with our detection mechanisms as we will explore in Six Sigma in Chapter 9.

3. A delay line of > 100ms (based upon vendor claims) pauses the linking process and the suspect traffic is side-channeled to a Phishing Detection system. The vendor applies his best techniques in < 100ms and then makes a binary decision: Let the link request or file-open occur, or Deny it.

   The rule is simple: $DL(t) > D(t) + R(t)$. The implication of course, is that since $P(t) > D(t) + R(t)$, $DL(t) > P(t)$ and $DL(t) > E(t)$.

4. A phishing-specific Reaction Matrix determines what happens if a No-Go Decision is reached.

   - *Is a notification sent back to the user that the action is not permitted for specific reasons, which should help educate the user?*
   - *Is the determination sent back to a vendor or community centric database to improve the detection capabilities?*

5. The OODA component is in the Detection learning system, just as with SMTP filtering for data breaches. Sure, AI, Big Data, and all that. However, with hundreds of possible algorithmic approaches, we still have gobs to learn. Make your vendors prove their claims before paying.

COMMUNITY REQUEST

How can we improve this idea? Can you build a testbed and measure where we are now? Do we even know the exact performance specs for these kinds of Detection Mechanisms?

Fake News is Bullshit

There are obviously two ways to read and interpret that title. My take is similar to the NY Times' view: "All The News That's Fit To Print." To me, that means well-researched, vetted, and confirmed facts; not the opinions of alternate factoidal agendas.

It should be the same with citizen publishing on social media. I believe there is a moral imperative on the part of giant many-to-many distribution mechanisms to act in favor of honesty, transparency, and human decency. *(You may not agree, but if you've gotten this far, I've been paid.)*

So, how can global citizen publishing empires enforce something akin to responsible news — versus opinion and fake news — and positive feedback-based bias confirmation? It's the same suggestion as for SMTP Ass Saving and Phishing-Stoppers.

The premise is simple.

Facebook and all of the others should quit abdication of responsibility, and perform vetting *before* they allow posts to take place. Fake news (et al) spreads *about* six times the speed of truth, according to an MIT study.

If Facebook (et al) can probabilistically determine that some postings are 'fake' (or some current or future agenda driven equivalent) after they are posted, they can also probabilistically determine (with some lower degree of certainty), that a given post, or a given suite of posts are likely to fit within the 'fake' category.

Remember that the human brain is designed to collect data in order to predict the future. AI/ML/DL goals are similar, and Higgs knows we have an amazing amount of data available for analysis.

Just sayin'… if we as a society (and financially incentivised businesses) weren't so damned quick on the trigger, we could, and can, use the Analogue Network Security approach to defense – and some significant degree of mitigation of the harmful effects of positive-feedback driven fake news.

Delay. Just delay the post a little. Do your analysis, Facebook – before the damage is done. A 100ms? 3 seconds? Your goal of course is to have D(t) of fake news approach zero, and that means you have to get better at what you do.

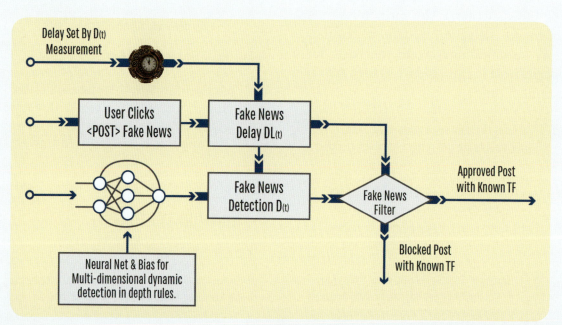

Solar Coronal Mass Ejection, the Mother of all DoS. Photo by The Solar Dynamics Observatory (SDO) NASA. Pilgrim is helping with Solar Flare Awareness

DoS/DDoS

WHY DoS?

- Hacktivism to make a point.
- Financial competitiveness where seconds of downtime can equal millions in lost revenues and profits.
- Political statements or interference.
- Interference with emergency services and first responders.
- Geo-political/cyberwar against critical infrastructures.
- And so on…

TCP/IP communicates both data and control signals as part of its traffic flow. That's both good (one wire is cheaper) and bad (one wire can get cut or… DoS'd). The original survivability goals of the Internet were different than they are today. "TCP/IP was designed to be resilient under failure, not under attack," said security guru, Dr. Gene Spafford. Thus, it made good sense for that experimental computer network in 1969 to combine control and information on a single path. However, when we look into other disciplines, we see that control and information signals are handled quite differently.

The internet was not designed to survive denial of service attacks. Over the years, DoS has become a criminal, cyberwar, and social protest weapon, notably for those with an agenda where knocking some services or companies off-line is preferable.

To begin an Analogue approach to mitigating DDoS, let's begin with looking at two different Closed Systems.

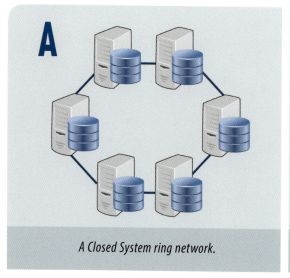

A Closed System ring network.

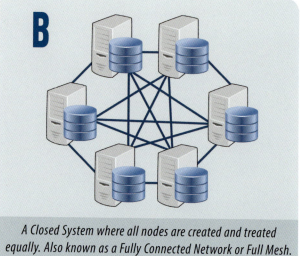

A Closed System where all nodes are created and treated equally. Also known as a Fully Connected Network or Full Mesh.

Ring topology A has some advantages, but time-based problems are prevalent, like shared-bandwidth and nodal communications delays. In a speed-obsessed world, there are better options. For now though, let's concentrate on how the internet is architected.

In Closed System B (fully-connected network), all nodes can "talk" to any other node with equal weight. Think of this as six Tier-1 ISPs that have established peering relationships. I can easily view this as Detection in Depth. For our purposes, don't get dragged into the pedantics of the exact peering mechanizations around the world. Depending upon how you count them, roughly twenty Tier-1 networks connect the planet. They enjoy "special" business and technology partnerships *(Tiers 2 and 3 to come)*.

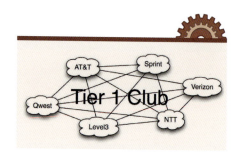

In Closed System B, assume five of the nodes want to DoS the 6th; #6 goes down. Assume only four nodes want to DoS 5 and 6; 5 and 6 go down. In this model, even if only one node went DoS-bonkers on the other five nodes, serious performance issues, if not complete communications failure would result.

Analogue Network Security Applications

In the real world, internet communications to end points typically involve the so-called "Last Mile," such as the dedicated piece of copper or fiber wires that go to individual homes or businesses from the Cloud. These represent the physical weak spots, unless physical redundancy is architected. If the Last Mile finds itself severed, the Cloud will function, but communications to and from the severed link will not take place; the so-called *BackHoe Attack*.

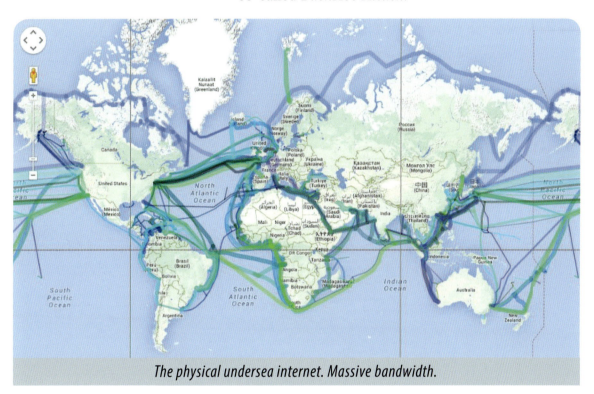

The physical undersea internet. Massive bandwidth.

Ron Eward's 1994-5 seminal work into transport layer vulnerabilities underscores the weaknesses of a global economy dependent upon the consistent and reliable operation of a few hundred strands of glass cable, strung over land and undersea.

Beginning with *Information Warfare* in 1989, I used the term "mappers" to describe those people who have created a "roadmap" of the internet. The fundamental premise of Mr. Eward's work was that connectivity requires real world, tangible hardware and that cyberspace is not really as ethereal as is generally perceived. High speed, high bandwidth routers are connected by copper and fiber optics: wire. The hundreds of thousands of miles of cable and wire are the backbones of the communications grid; millions more make up the subnets, and the regional nets, or metropolitan area networks. The lack of physical redundancy at the transport level echoes a similar TCP/IP deficiency exacerbated by remote, software based DoS attacks: lack of logical (or physical) control signal redundancy. While cutting the physical wire to a target host or organization is certainly effective as an attack technique, there is a significant drawback to this approach: one must be physically near a specific target, thus increasing the chances of being caught (detected).

Remote, non-physical attacks represented a step forward in sophistication, distribution, and anonymity. ==A targeted cyber DoS/DDoS attack can take many forms, but they all effectively isolate the target from the internet for as long as the attack lasts.== (DRDoS, UDP, ICMP, DNS Amplification, Application floods, etc.) However, depending upon the nature of the attack and the relative bandwidth utilization, the first hop ISP may not be aware that one of its downstream customers is under assault, unless its own services are hindered or overloaded.

Types of DDoS attacks:

- Application Attacks
- Bandwidth Attacks
- Traffic Attacks

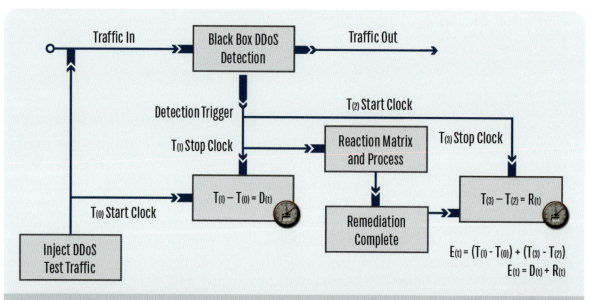

Traditional DDoS detection with automatic policy-based remediation and Time-Based Security measurement.

Analogue Network Security Applications

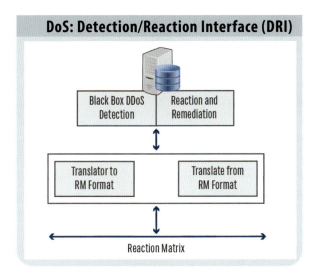

Traditional DDoS mitigation is performed with on-premises (or a vendor-hosted cloud hybrid) appliance, traffic analysis, and filtering. IMHO, that's a pretty weak binary approach that ignores the systemic nature of an analogue view. So, for now, let's assume the vendors have a somewhat adequate means to detect hostile traffic at the enterprise—internet nexus, specifically DoS/DDoS attacks. We will call this Black Box DDoS Detection.

Detection systems are pretty useless without a reaction, right? A decent defensive mechanism (D+R) must have the means to respond to the attack. Let's assume that the vendor's Black Box has an automatic in-line response system; filtering out traffic determined to be hostile as determined by the Black Box's rules. We should also be able to measure the Black Box performance and get a decent view of how the particular Black Box functions before being deployed, and then, hopefully, measured in situ from time to time as part of penetration testing.

To get things rolling, we are going to add a Detection/Reaction Interface (DRI) onto each "node" of any network (closed system) we want to be immune from DoS-style attacks. Each node has a Black Box detection mechanism, which through an API (to be specced/developed), will speak to the Reaction Matrix Protocol (RMP) (to be formalized). Each node also has a remediation mechanism, that may or not be in the same Black Box (vendor depending). No matter; in this case, we will just say that remediation is the blocking of specific traffic, based upon information gathered by the Black Box Detection. *(We will examine the RMP later.)*

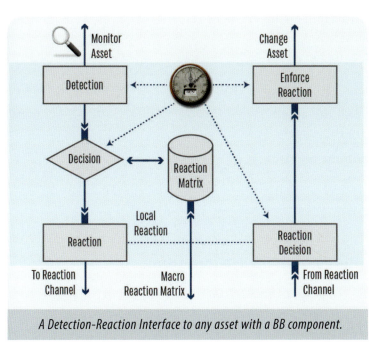

A Detection-Reaction Interface to any asset with a BB component.

Analogue Network Security Applications

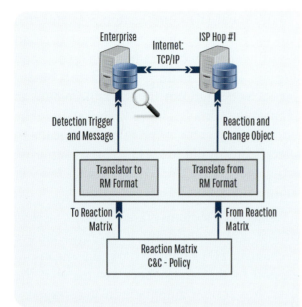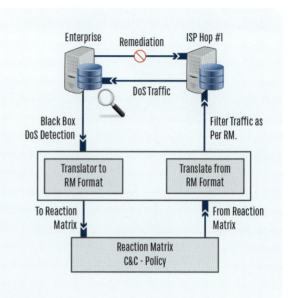

Let's re-architect this a bit and see what happens in a network of only two nodes.

In the above left, normal TCP/IP traffic. On the right though, ISP Hop #1 is sending DoS traffic to the Enterprise, which therefore cannot communicate back to the ISP over normal channels. The attractiveness of TCP/IP fails. When certain attacks are launched against a target site, the means to communicate back down the line through the internet, even one hop, may be thwarted by bandwidth filling, port overload or other disabling effects. Regardless of the nature of the attack, from the victim's viewpoint, the results are the same.

So, the Enterprise's Black Box Detection mechanism needs to somehow tell the ISP, "Help!" So, we go Out-of-Band. This is a simple key concept of the Reaction Matrix.

> **Black Box DoS Detection Rules:** If hostile DoS traffic is detected, then...
> - Do best to mitigate effects with on-premises in-line Black Box Reaction.
> - Tell the first upstream hop what you are seeing, and say "Please stop it and initiate traffic filtering."

ISPs can block traffic. They can block anything they want. They can shape and throttle it. They can move it from hither to yon. The Black Box talks to the Reaction Matrix, which in this case, merely tells the next hop (where the offending traffic is coming from), "Please, block it there. Thanks!"

It really doesn't matter if the Black Box DoS Detection is done in-line or as a Side Channel to communicate over the Reaction Channel. You might want to keep it in-line, if the performance hits are measurably inconsequential; there is nothing wrong with in-line remediation, but think how much better the hybridized version can be… if we all cooperate.

Let's expand this, just a little for now, with some internet flavor.

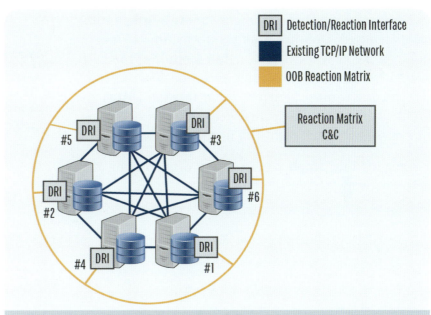

A closed system with an OOB Detection/Reaction Channel. Detection in Depth in action.

In the closed network above, six identical nodes have 100% peering correspondence. (The numbers 1-6 are merely random. IP addresses rule.) We have added Detection/Reaction Interfaces to each node, which in turn, communicates over the Out-of-Band D/R Channel (network); in this case a ring topology, but that choice was more for visualization than optimal design. The best networking protocol to optimize the OOB Reaction Matrix Protocol must be designed by the vested stakeholders, and the cool part is… we can start from scratch and do it right.

Now visualize that any one of the six nodes decides to launch a DoS attack against any one or more of the other nodes. What happens if the 'pipes are clogged' and the control signal information cannot be sent? Simple. The DRI is always listening to the traffic on every node, just as current technology permits. In kind, it is always transmitting Status Updates on a periodic basis across the Reaction Channel. "All Good." "All Good." "All Good." Until, of course, when the "IT hits the fan".

Notionally, the DRI is configured to transmit, in this case, detected DoS-like traffic information to every node on the network. The Reaction Module of the DRI is told how to react according Reaction Matrix C&C policies and controls. Keep in mind that the DRI is an OOB side-process. The actual detection can occur in-line or side-channel, each with its own pros and cons.

Assuming 16 Globally peered Tier-1s, only 120 synchronous OOB communications connections are required.

Imagine this simple conversation, occurring on the above network.

#1: I Detect traffic that smells of DoS.

#1: That traffic appears to be coming from #2.

#1: I am going to tell the DRI to tell # 2 - 6 about what I see.

#1. I am going to tell #2 to filter out the offending traffic, as per the Reaction Matrix C&C.

#2: Thanks, #1. I got your back.

#2: I detect that same offending traffic.

#2: The Reaction Matrix tells me to filter out that traffic.

#2: Here ya go, #1. Confirmed.

#3 - 6: We hear you. The Reaction Matrix C&C has informed us to upgrade our Detection Sensitivity and be on the alert for such traffic for the next "Time" period, at which time, if we see no more alerts, we will return to Normal.

#2: The Reaction Matrix also tells me that the offending traffic is coming from #3, but #3 is not attacking #1 directly.

#2: I am going to tell the DRI to tell #1 & #3 - 6 about what I see.

#2: I am going to tell #3 to filter out the offending traffic, as per the Reaction Matrix C&C.

#3: Thanks, #2. I got your back.

#3: I detect that same offending traffic.

#3: The Reaction Matrix tells me to filter out that traffic.

#3: Here ya go, #2. Confirmed.

#4 - 6: We hear you. The Reaction Matrix C&C has informed us to upgrade our Detection Sensitivity and be on the alert for such traffic for the next "Time" period, at which time, if we see no more alerts, we will return to Normal.

#3: The Reaction Matrix also tells me that the offending traffic is coming from #4, but #4 is not attacking #1 or #2 directly.

#3: I am going to tell the DRI to tell #1-2 & #4 - 6 about what I see.

#3: I am going to tell #4 to filter out the offending traffic, as per the Reaction Matrix C&C.

#4: Thanks, #3. I got your back.

#4: I detect that same offending traffic.

#4: The Reaction Matrix tells me to filter out that traffic.

#4: Here ya go, #3. Confirmed.

#4 - 6: We hear you. The Reaction Matrix C&C has informed us to Upgrade our Detection Sensitivity and be on the alert for such traffic for the next "Time" period, at which time, if we see no more alerts, we will return to Normal.

#4: The Reaction Matrix also tells me that the offending traffic is coming from #5, but #5 is not attacking #1, #2 or #3 directly.

#4: I am going to tell the DRI to tell #1-3 & #5 - 6 about what I see.

#4: I am going to tell #5 to filter out the offending traffic, as per the Reaction Matrix C&C.

#5: Thanks, #4. I got your back.

#5: I detect that same offending traffic.

#5: The Reaction Matrix tells me to filter out that traffic.

#5: Here ya go, #4. Confirmed.

#5 - 6: We hear you. The Reaction Matrix C&C has informed us to Upgrade our Detection Sensitivity and be on the alert for such traffic for the next "Time" period, at which time, if we see no more alerts, we will return to Normal.

#5: The Reaction Matrix also tells me that the offending traffic is coming from #6, but #6 is not attacking #1-4 directly.

#5: I am going to tell the DRI to tell #6 about what I see.

#5: I am going to tell #6 to filter out the offending traffic, as per the Reaction Matrix C&C.

#6: You Got Me. My bad.

The fairly limited number of peering relationships, such as with Tier-1s, makes the OOB bandwidth requirements certainly less onerous than if millions of end-points were required for many to many comm. The Last Mile is merely a one-hop one-to-one channel that does not need to even be invented. We can use, given the low bandwidth required on the Last Mile RM, existing communications infrastructure with the to-be-designed, RMP. Establishing a limited number of peering relationships keeps the communications limited to those with a (cryptographically enforced) need-to-know and ability to take appropriate remediative action.

The Analogue Network Security approach to DoS mitigation requires no modifications to existing protocols or infrastructure. Think of it more as a Plug-in or Extension that is synergistically added to what already exists. One potential downside is that it won't work, which is why we need to measure and test everything first. Let's get this idea rocking in a lab!

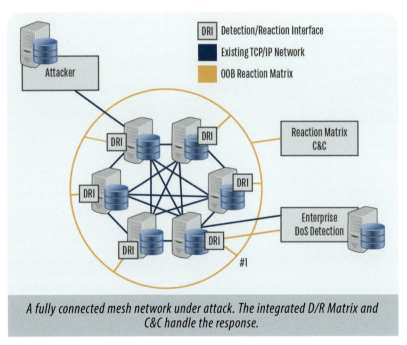

A fully connected mesh network under attack. The integrated D/R Matrix and C&C handle the response.

So, we can begin with any end-point under attack and achieve the same thing.

Let's assume that our internetwork has 6 peered ISPs where only 15 connections are required. An attacker is sending hostile traffic to an Enterprise end-point on the lower right, which we will assume will overload the primary (TCP/IP) comm channel. Due to the proper design of the Reaction Matrix Protocols, limiting who

Analogue Network Security Applications

may participate in it, the attacker only can attack via publically-accessible paths. The Enterprise, though, has an OOB communications channel with its primary ISPs (presuming more than one for redundancy).

The Enterprise uses a DoS Detection product with a DRI that only talks to its primary hop(s).

> ▶ Enterprise DM tells #1 ISP about bad traffic, through the DRI.
>
> ▶ #1 ISP stops the hostile traffic to the Enterprise via the DRI and the enterprise's Reaction Module, presumably in this case, a traffic filtering mechanism that is either part of the Detection product or is separate, or, perhaps, both.
>
> The pressure is relieved on the enterprise, pushing the responsibility one hop up the chain. Next,
>
> ▶ #1 ISP looks for the originating IP address of the hostile traffic as described by the target enterprise's DR, It then talks to its peer ISPs, and specifically instructs each offending packet's source IP to filter accordingly.
>
> ▶ Each subsequent hop will be so informed of the traffic source with associated filter instructions.

Sooner or later, depending upon the number of hops and obfuscation, the source of the offending traffic will be either identified, or anonymously proxied. Goal #1 of the target of DoS attacks is to get back into business as soon as possible. Identifying the perpetrator(s), is secondary, and in many cases, an unreasonable expectation.

EVERY ISP MUST PARTICIPATE

To mitigate DoS attacks, a more tightly integrated relationship between the customer and the ISP community is required. For a complete, global defensive posture against DoS to be truly effective over the long term, we must involve the Tier 1, Tier 2, and Tier 3 (et al) players everywhere. *(See Figs. 8B on next page.)*

Analogue Network Security Applications

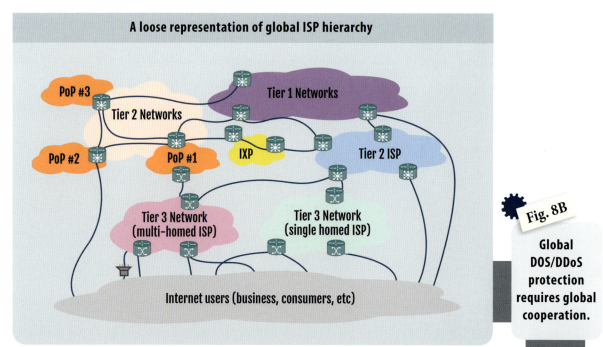

Fig. 8B

Global DOS/DDoS protection requires global cooperation.

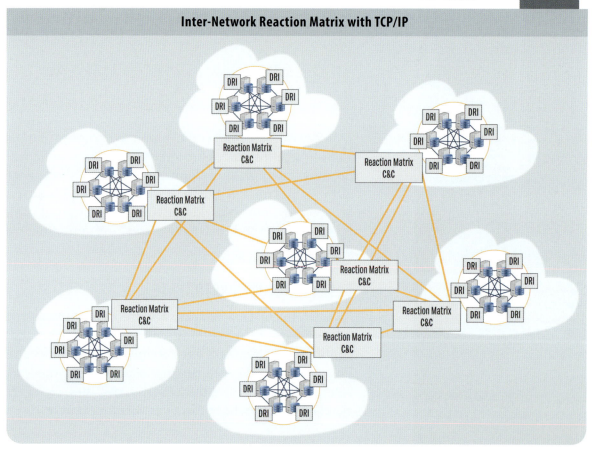

I am not going to suggest any specific D/R Channel or RMP designs; rather, I have an initial characteristics wishlist. Please feel free to add! In the ideal world, I'd like to at least see:

> ▶ Endpoint and Server (ISP) focused products to speak a common language, based upon a to-be-designed global RMP.
>
> ▶ Redundant (mirroring?) Reaction Matrix C&C servers.
>
> ▶ Almost real-time information sharing on detectable events, to systemically upgrade every Detection Module's performance. Vendors, too.
>
> ▶ Built-in testing and metrics; perhaps built-in to the protocol itself, rather than letting humans get involved and mess it up.
>
> ▶ Speed will be an issue for DDoS attacks. Tier-1 ISPs have bandwidth. Satellites come to mind as truly OOB.

FAST PHYSICAL PARALLEL

In the old days, indeed, analogue phone line days, we had a thing called a *party line*. It's akin to many users sharing bandwidth on a single hunk of copper to a neighborhood or a big building. With a telephone party line, promiscuous mode meant that every telephone on a circuit shared the same wire. Privacy had not yet been invented.

Imagine a neighborhood of only 6 houses on one party line, and imagine that someone in each household is always listening. All the time. 24/7.

Then, one day, a voice yells, "Hey! Someone is trying to break into Mildred's Home! Please Help!" The other five houses on the party line hear, and all are capable of cranking the bell to ask for an Operator to call Clarence the Sheriff. But one house is the closest to Mildred's, and in that era, one neighbor would help another in a heartbeat.

I remember party lines in our house in Shoreham, Long Island, which was actually about a mile from where Tesla's Wardenclyffe Tower used to stand. Privacy had not yet been addressed. Think promiscuous mode.

Analogue Network Security Applications

The Analogue Network Security application of Out-of-Band Detection Reaction Channels worked 100 years ago; all I am saying is, let's put this on the bench, measure it, test it, stress it, spec it - then let's pilot it. This just might be a case of, "If we build it, they will come." Who doesn't want the effects of DoS to just go away?

Note to ISPs:

It seems to me that you guys have as much incentive as DoS victims to get this under control before it gets any any worse.

Can you imagine an internet where → 100% of the traffic is actively hostile?

To mitigate DoS attacks, a more tightly integrated relationship between customer and the ISP community is required. For a complete, global defensive posture against DoS to be truly effective over the long term, we must involve the Tier 1, Tier 2 and Tier 3 (et al) players everywhere.

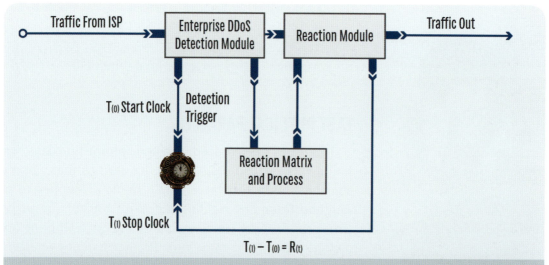

An enterprise on-premises in-line DoS D/R as it exists with a time-based implementation. While the traffic may be filtered, the offending traffic from the ISP is still attacking. A feed-forward approach. Depending upon the speed (intensity) of the attack and the value of R(t), the effects of a DoS attack can be anywhere from mild to severe. The math is no more complicated than understanding the speed at which the offending packets come in, the speed of the D/R process, and making business/process decisions as a result.

In the above, we ignore (for now) the D(t) and trigger the Clock to start counting at T(0) when an event has been identified. The Reaction Channel process is initiated, and when policy in the Reaction Module says, **done,** the clock is stopped. Therefore, the **R(t) = T(1) - T(0)**, and the corollary is that the attack can continue for each R(t) *(packetized thinking here).*

But, according to Analogue Network Security, we have not really improved much; other than measuring the **E(t)**, which = **R(t)** at this point. What to do?

> 1. One critical point, which means a great deal in physical (ICS/SCADA) engineering, should be applied if we are ever expected to get a hand on improved security controls.
>
> 2. By applying the engineering design method, the feed-forward controller realization problem arises, when time delay in the disturbance path is less than time delay in process path.

Simply put, we add a Delay. A feed-forward approach, indeed.

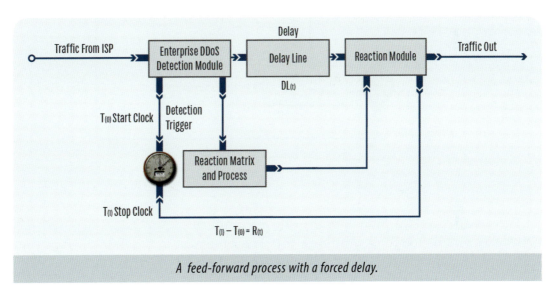

A feed-forward process with a forced delay.

The value of DL(t) is calculable. Insert **D(t) > T(1) - T(0)** prior to the Reaction Module. Since the RM is, notionally here, a filter, we want the filtering to occur prior to the traffic arriving at the filtering process. Else, why bother and we're back where we started.

We can also add one more element to optimize the performance of the system when it is not under attack and maximum performance is required. In this enhanced approach, the Delay Line is turned on when a detection starts the clock and begins conversing with the Reaction Matrix. We want to set filtering rules prior to the arrival of the offending traffic. The Delay Line is turned off when the Reaction Module says, "Mission Accomplished". The speed (time) of this process is a function of bandwidth, processing speed (hardware/software at the appliance) and in-band vs. Out-of-Band communications speed.

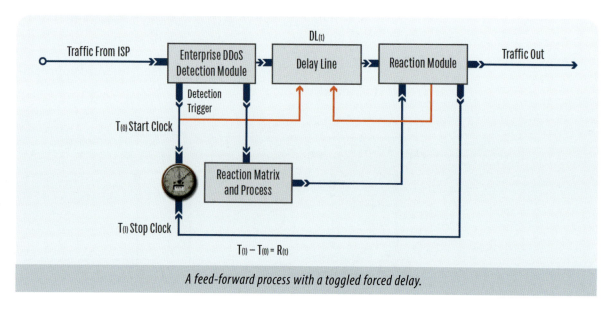

A feed-forward process with a toggled forced delay.

The usual RS Flip-Flop circuit will accomplish this delay circuit toggling. And yes, this is a binary toggling function based upon the analogue time-based feedback process.

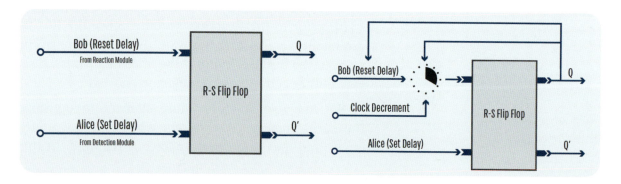

Finally, we can add an additional layer (more Detection in Depth) of self-checking by replacing the R-S Flip Flop with a TB-Flip Flop. If the Reaction Module does not send back a Reset to the TB-FF (for any reason at all!), this self-checking mechanism (think ICS/SCADA) kicks in.

We return to a TB-FF, and the decrementing clock time is set so **DC(t) > DL(t)** because we want the primary Reaction process to have first shot at reset. The question then becomes, how much greater should the decrementing clock time be? I am going to arbitrarily say **> 2 * D(t)**, which allows for two full D/R cycles before an automatic time-based reset. That's a guess. You guys take it from here.

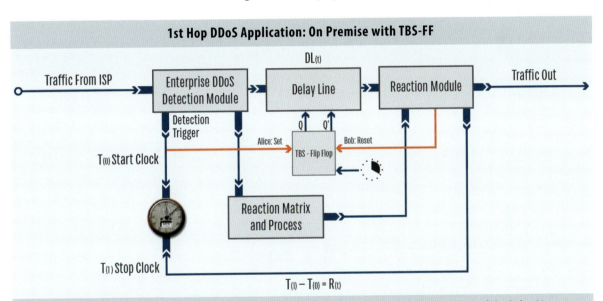

In this diagram, we have integrated another time-based feedback process into the Set/Reset of the Delay Line, determined by the state of the output of the Reaction Module.

Let's add another feedback mechanism. In the above, we maintain the existing on-premises DoS Detection and Reaction Modules (product, etc.). Its built-in feed forward security mechanism is not altered. We take nothing away from the current approach. However, we augment it by notifying the first hop ISP's Reaction

Module of the offending traffic, and ask that it be filtered. Depending upon the degree of ISP cooperation with a common Reaction Matrix, the offending traffic can be followed backwards, step by step, until the last non-obfuscated hop renders further tracing impossible.

Note the red lines; as part of the Reaction Channel, they allow communications between participating constituents to maintain and update detection 'signatures' and reaction "rules." To keep it simpler at this point, I have not mentioned the Trust Factor of the Detection Module; its efficacy is avoiding false-negatives and false-positives. Over time, with AI/ML/DL and big data, a global cooperative will increase the Trust Factor of every endpoint Detection Module, regardless which data transmission protocols are used.

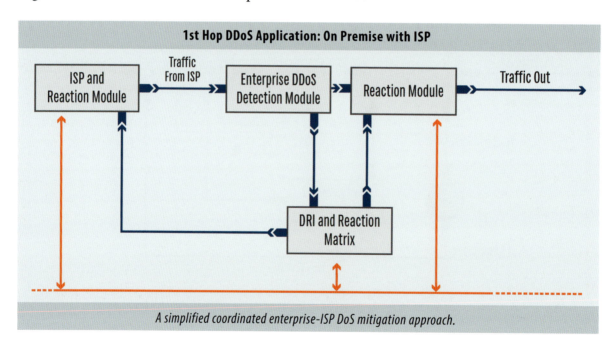

A simplified coordinated enterprise-ISP DoS mitigation approach.

The above is my notional representation of DoS mitigation between the Target and the first hop ISP. Each node runs it's own Detection and hopefully Reaction process, through a local Reaction Matrix, which will permit some level of "learning." When we

Wow, I can't believe I said "share information"... but in this case, it's true.

employ Detection in Depth, and share information over the Reaction Matrix Protocol - RMP, everyone wins. The shared knowledge, based upon real-world Detection/Reaction scenarios, will necessarily increase the Trust Factor for everyone who participates.

Extending this over existing peers, and creating a hierarchy, will create, as I see it, an Out-of-Band global security network that can help solve other problems that I am not going to really get into. That's up to you guys.

But there is more. How else can we think about potential security solutions using these same concepts?

This looks DoS'd even before it might get DoS'd.

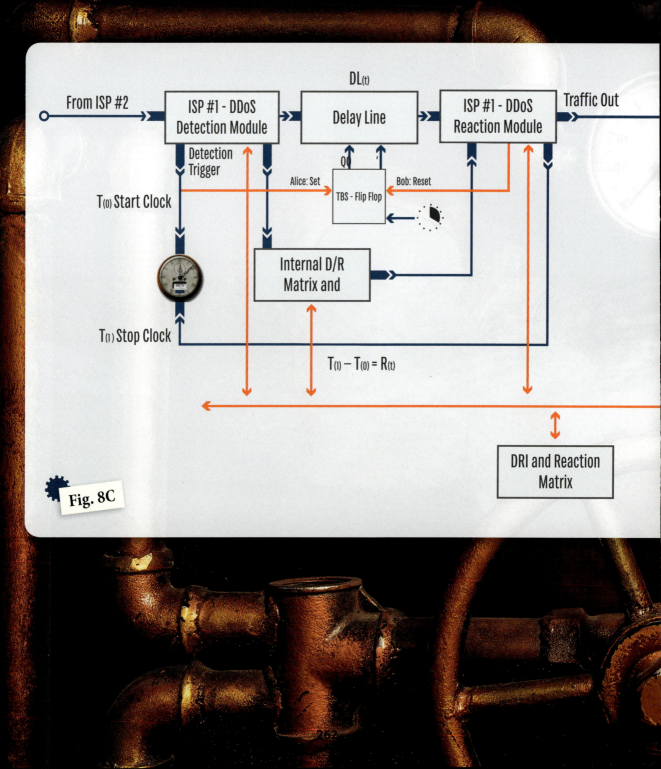

Fig. 8C

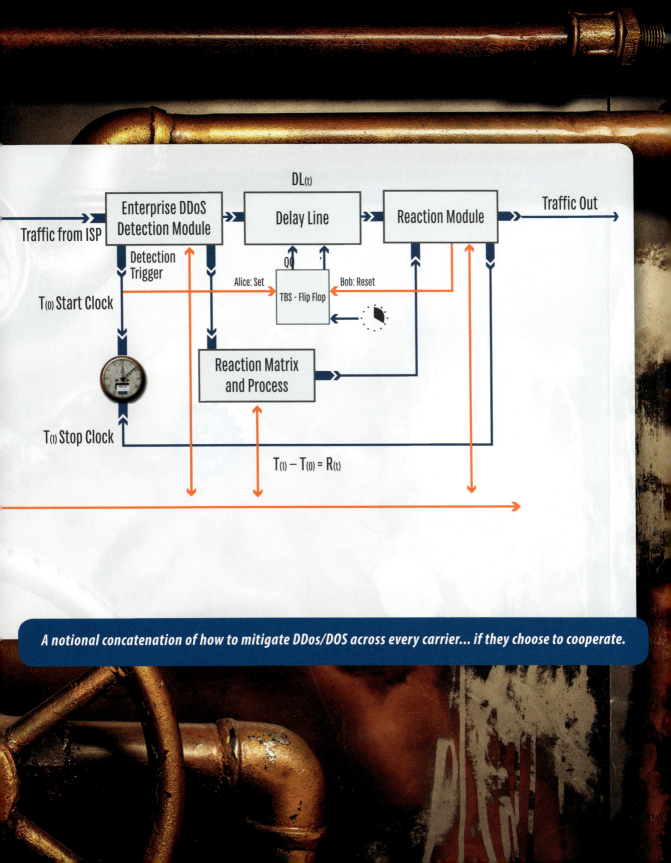

A notional concatenation of how to mitigate DDos/DOS across every carrier... if they choose to cooperate.

Stopping Spam & Saving Granni

Lovely Spam! Wonderful Spam!
Lovely Spam! Wonderful Spam
Spa-a-a-a-a-a-am
Spa-a-a-a-a-a-am
Spa-a-a-a-a-a-am
Spa-a-a-a-a-a-am

Let's face it. Spam sucks as much (more so?) than DoS. Given the prior discussion, we may have a decent time-based approach to minimize the effects of DoS attacks. Plenty of proof of concept lab-work to be done, for sure.

But, we also may find a workable approach with an internet-wide OOB security network. Traffic-shaping instructions (filtering) hop from ISP to ISP through the Detection-Reaction Matrix, ideally (protocol dependent) with a decent Broadcast-All & Promiscuous mode at each node. Sooner or later, the traffic source – of even just one packet - will be identified. It has to come from somewhere and be able to be resolved by traditional communications protocols. The evil traffic component must be TCP/IP compatible – looking at it in a twisted sort of way.

DDoS "For Hire" botnet services rely upon massively distributed sources: computers, mobile devices, home automation & security systems, networked entertainment systems… anything that connects to the interwebbingthingy. This approach gives hope to be able to identify a significant number of infected devices and then advise the **user** with decent security steps to take.

In this simplified example, the Source is an infected device, unknowingly part of a

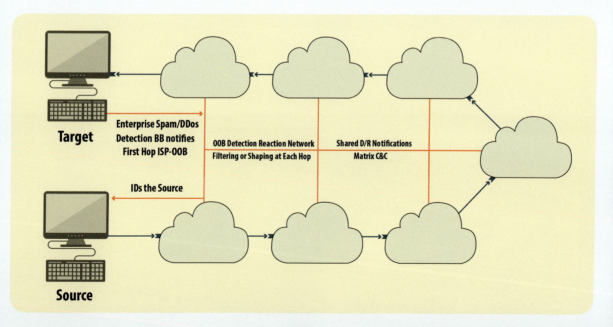

botnet that can be used for spam or DDoS attacks. The botnet malware knows the IP address of the Target; an enterprise of any sort. What does this do for us?

First, this model lends itself to the Identification of the infected sources of DDoS/Botnet members – such as Granni, and Uncle Bub, and Cousin Suzie. We don't want them going to GitMo for terrorist activities; what we do want is to remove their machines from the botnet and return to normal *secure* operation. With enough global participation, I can envision substantially reduced DDoS/Botnet activity.

Of course, people will still get infected, but by treating this as a time-based OODA-like problem, the iterative time loop could – in theory - be squeezed to the point to reduce such attacks to noise level. With rose-colored glasses on, by applying the early outlined anti-phishing approaches, we attack the problem from two different angles, squeezing both loops as hard as we can. Getting inside the adversaries' operational and decision loops will provide defenders with an advantage.

Secondly, the same concepts apply to Spam. Is Granni part of the spam-bot? If so, take an action. If the spammers are dumb enough to use their own servers with minimal obfuscation, all the better.

In either case, we will not be able to completely stop the C&C components of DoS/Spam; we will not stop phishing 100%; remember, security can only approach 1 – it can never reach it. But I like these odds a whole hell of a lot better than what we have at this point.

Let's say that some level of cooperation results in OOB time-based communications. What do we do with Granni? Notification is part of the Reaction (remediation) process, I should think.

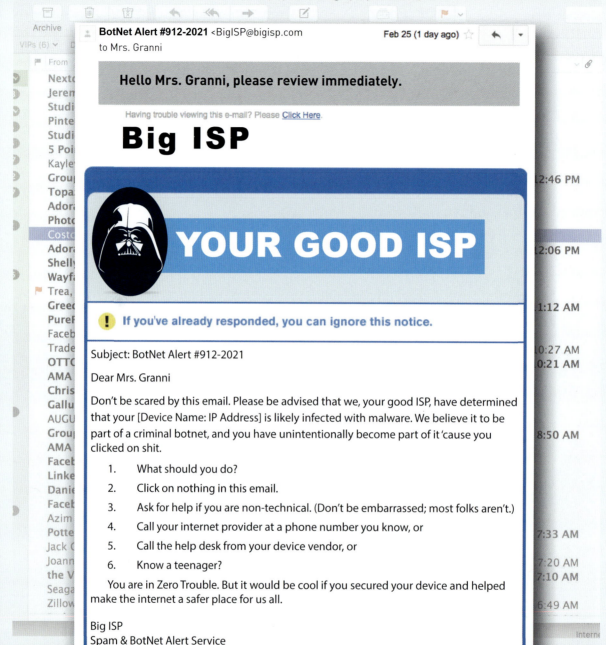

Now all we have to do is figure out how *not* to make these messages look like spam or phishing!

D/R Protocol

The Out-of-Band Reaction Channel must be implemented with an open standard protocol, the **Reaction Matrix Protocol**, or RMP.

I am not a protocol designer. But, I think there are a few items that should be included in its design that will add to the security and resiliency of the Reaction Channel, since globally it could be running on more than one physical communications layer; e.g., wireless, GSM, ethernet, satellite.

Here's a few thoughts:

1. Reasonable confidentiality through crypto. We know how to do this.
2. Cryptographically unique IdM for peering partners, to limit the number of active participants and/or interlopers. We know how to do this.
3. Automated repetitive timed-based multi-factor IdM with a limited number of peering relationships. We know how to do this.
4. Synchronized clock, with accuracy specification. We know how to do this.
5. Limited Administration Access, and only over Reaction Channel. We know how to do this.
6. Bandwidth sensing. We know how to do this.
7. One-to-Many DRI Broadcasting. We know how to do this.
8. Error correction. We know how to do this.

How often should the information on the Reaction Channel be sent? Once an hour? Once a second? Every 10ms? From my view, as often as possible - after all, time is the biggest weapon we have in our arsenal, if we choose to use it.

I imagine the RMP will be fairly akin to other protocol designs and formats, but with the huge benefit that **we have the luxury to design it right... the first time.** We know how to do it. Keeping the D/R channels from ever being attacked is a fool's errand. It will happen. But, we have almost 50 years of experience to design the RMP correctly, considering all of the options, including the really crazy ones.

A few fast thoughts for what to include in the RMP.

Integrity checking IdM and Data. Key Management. Source/Dest IP. IP Translation. Date/Time. RMP Formats. APIs. RM Lookup & Response. Pause/Stop (Time Controls). Reset. Archive. Backup. Redundancy Lookup. Failsafe. DNS. Padding. Null but not usable until RMP approved update. Obfuscation.

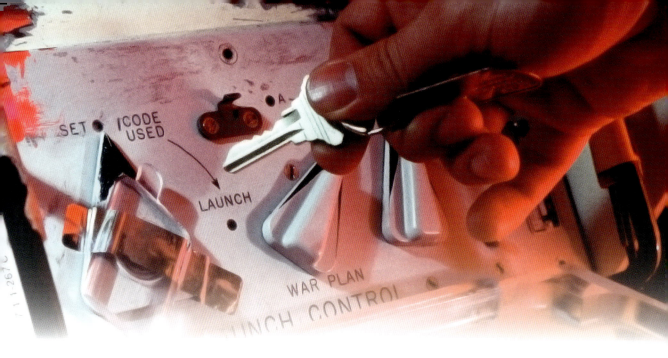

TBS AND I&A

Some Identification and Authentication methods inherently employ the TBS concepts, but not with the formality suggested by the proposed ANS model.

One way in which the TBS model could be applied to I&A is to first define the Pt(pw). The protective window of time is defined by the manufacturer and/or configurable by the user as "the amount of time one expects to transpire to accomplish proper authentication."

Do you expect the User_ID and password to be entered and authenticated within 3 seconds? 10 seconds? 30 seconds? Or does a biometric scan take only 500 milliseconds? This window sets the system D(t), and represents a component of the E(t) - exposure time, to the target system.

This is exactly how so many home and office security systems work – where there is no real protection. The front door is unlocked with a key and then opened,

> Perhaps we need Alice and Bob to be interchangeable; that is, either can initiate a 2MR process, and the other must approve within the designated time. This is how nukes are protected with the two keys. It's a simple window of time for approval.

Analogue Network Security Applications

An eye appears as the peephole slides open. "Who goes there?" "Vinnie sent me." "What's the password?" "It looks like it might rain Friday night." Then a loud metal *clink* as the door is unlocked and patron is admitted. I learned a lot about history of the old U.S. Prohibition Era Speakeasy while helping my dad wire the audio for the 1960s equivalent of one of those illegal drinking establishments.

In well-thought-out designs, the embedded delay may be variable as detection and reaction processes improve.

which triggers the Detection mechanism. The alarm expects a proper code to be entered into the security box within X-seconds, or D(t). If it receives the proper code within the proscribed D(t), then the Detection mechanism is shut off, waiting to be re-armed at a future time. If, however, the alarm code is not entered within D(t), a reaction is triggered; perhaps an alarm to scare off the bad guy, perhaps summoning the police, or perhaps both. Thus, the maximum exposure that the physical facility faces is, as you now know, **D(t) + R(t) = E(t)**.

In a networked environment, the process is the same:

► When a user first contacts an I&A mechanism, the detection process is begun.

► Part of that detection process initiation is preparing the waking-up response mechanism for the fastest possible reaction upon notification by the detection component.

► If, for any reason at all, the authentication process does not occur within the specified D(t), then a reaction is triggered, such as severing that user's connection in R(t) *(as one possible reaction)*.

► I&A logs should be kept, and if the I&A process was also violated in other ways, (i.e., three failed attempts) then further policy driven, non-real time restrictions can be put into place.

► Once the user is authenticated in the normal manner as prescribed by the I&A product, in a time period less than D(t), an optional small amount of time delay can be added to the process prior to passing the user through the protective security mechanism. The rationale is, obviously, that the detection process is useless if it takes more time to detect the activity than it does for the activity to occur. This delay in a legitimate authentication process, which is faster than D(t), insures that the P(t) remains higher than the sum of D(t) + R(t). The system then returns to idle – until the next user comes along.

Thus;

P(t) = Effective security provided, measured in time, expected for a proper authentication in the usual manner plus some nominal delay.

D(t) = The amount of time it takes to detect a user's initial sign on and determine its authenticity of fraudulence,

R(t) = The amount of time it takes for the detection module to trigger the reaction, such as severing a connection, closing a port or any other chosen reaction process that adds defense.

So, we could say that:

$$P(t2) = P(t) + Delay(t)$$

Here, as the TBS formula tells us, we look at P(t2) which has two components: the time to complete a process in an optimum manner, P(t), added to the prescribed delay time, as per policy. This should be the general goal of modern system designers. But from a security standpoint, unless the detection and reaction mechanisms are faster than P(t), the addition of process delay is a simple approach to an otherwise potentially complex problem. This is a fine point, but one that underscores the need to design in those criteria that follow the basic TBS Formula.

Your Job is to design four conceptual analogue I&A architectures:

1. Alice and Bob are both required to approve a process before it is enacted. But Carol must also approve it within a week.

2. Given example 1 above, Dan is Carol's boss and a control phreak, and he wants final approval of everything, but never can find the time to do it. Design that architecture, too.

3. A *trusted* partner of an organization sends a request for *information*. Policy says that any *trusted* partner, with a trust factor < .8 must be pre-approved by two members of the organization before release. Design that circuit.

4. Five equally *trusted* sys-admins have equal control over "Task X" processes. Design a circuit that returns the trust of these operations close to the trust factor of any one sys-admin.

Circuit: Launch a Nuke

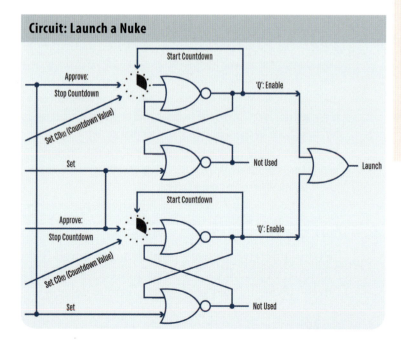

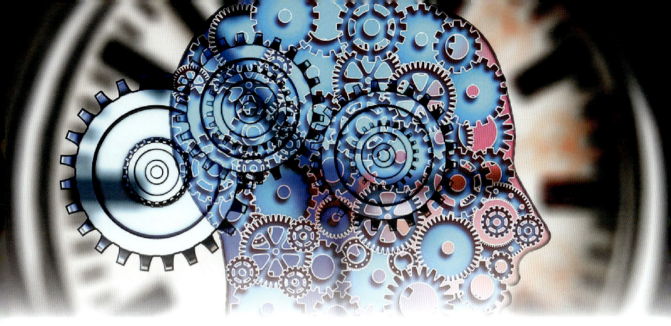

Miscellaneous Application Thoughts

The ANS and TBS Models become valuable in real world applications where quantification of security needs to be both measured and applied. In the following brief examples, every question about security implementation will not be answered or solved. But they might provide some ideas on applying the TBS Model and formulas in more granular security applications, and not only at the enterprise or macro level.

ANTI-VIRUS & MALWARE DETECTION EFFICACY

This employs the same approach as the anti-phishing suggestions earlier. Adding a small dose of negative time into processes that are already essentially invisible to the user, allows for additional evaluation and analysis, under the premise that, "The more time I have to examine 'X', the more accurate I can be in its description." Combining Trust Factors, weighted with myriad source inputs, adds to Risk estimation.

The average APT is 400+ days before detection. From a security modeling standpoint, how's our detection doing? If you can reduce that astoundingly poor statistic by even a single order of magnitude, I would call that a worthwhile investment.

IDS

Or IPS or SysLog. Or anything that detects; the proverbial Black Box.

1. Hold the vendor accountable to specific efficacy of performance.
2. Prove it. Test it.
3. Design feedback and negative time accordingly, with just enough time-padding to not affect user experience.
4. Communicate results upstream through primary or D/R channels using some end-point version of the RMP.
5. Repeat. OODA.

ZERO-DAY DISTRIBUTION AND INOCULATION

Behavioral detection at the endpoint, the lower in the stack or perhaps even at the kernel in Ring 0, the better. Talk about a vendor opportunity! A time-based Anderson Reference Monitor with detection, perhaps, merely looking for unexpected or non-approved processes spawned, or correlated to other very recent user behavior. Like a click. Then .01 microseconds later, a suspicious process is detected, leading edge triggered to pause, analyze, and decide. OODA at its most basic.

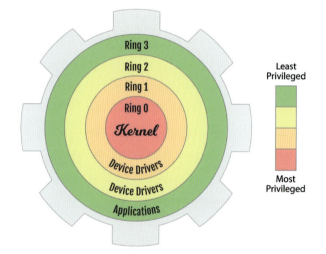

Ideally, reaction communications will go back to upstream partners and vendors who will help defeat the unknown hostile code, and the zero-day dies quickly, in record time.

> The ANS approach applies to layers in the stack or rings. Doesn't matter. It's about how you choose to design and implement feedback, OODA loops and apply dynamic bias.

LOGON: NEW/UNKNOWN DEVICE

Use a combination of 2FA via OOB time-based circuits as discussed in Chapter 6, "My Bank". The same approach can be used for any remote logon applications, especially for developers and off-shore staffing. For automatic updates, across ranges of devices within an enterprise, let me suggest using a TB-Flip-Flop with at least one layer of time-based secondary authentication. By adding additional TB-FF logic gates, any arrangement of approval mechanisms is easily created with analogue-Boolean gating.

1. Alice adds User
2. Bob must approve. Define T(b) for Approval:
3. Reaction
4. Remind Bob at DC(t-max)
5. Remind Bob again as DC(t-max) → DC(t) → 0
6. If DC(t) = 0, delete user. Bob has not approved.

GENERIC ACCESS CONTROL *(e.g., add User, Delete User, Change Rights in any access control appliance)*

Creating a set of Time-based rule sets like the example to the left would truly be a next generation access control device. Multiple approval path and time options would be another generation of improvement.

The End Point

We've had a long history of endpoint security. In the early 1980s, I got to play with PC security, in hardware and software, as well as 3270 emulation security solutions. Along came laptops, such as they were, and hardware security was a real pain, but we got some security done for the Feds.

Fast forward: Today, what does endpoint security even mean? Is it a dumb terminal? A smart phone or any of the myriad options available? Is the endpoint part of a mesh network or hanging on the outer edge or part of the intranet? What policies must be followed?

With analogue approaches, especially with Detection in Depth, I am suggesting we have an opportunity to revisit and indeed, redefine, what we mean by endpoint security. How many detection points are sufficient? How far down the stack should they go? Are they in applications as well as the O/S, tangential to or integrated with the protocols?

Given that masses of third party endpoint security products by different vendors can cause congestion (as I told you...), collision, and other performance debilitating effects, does a single Detection in Depth based endpoint security solution make sense?

Analogue Network Security Applications

ENCRYPTION

Encryption is touted as a powerful, effective, inexpensive, and easy-to-use, means to provide information with confidentiality and integrity. Some encryption products are invisible to the user and work quite well at their designated tasks. Others are so cumbersome, it's far easier to siphon vodka from a cow's udder.

The fundamental problem is an inherent misunderstanding as to what really constitutes security in an encryption system. The popular argument we hear is, "longer key length is essential for good security. Shorter key length is an invitation to criminals and government abuse." Well, sort of, and Time-Based Security gives us a clue as to what really matters. Encryption utilizes two defensive mechanisms to protect information.

1. The encryption algorithm itself, which must be openly published for peer review. The amount of time required by an intensive cryptanalytic or brute force attack is the measure of the algorithm's seeming strength. Yes, this can invoke P vs NP, which interestingly enough, are two complementary time-based views of the same problem.

2. Encryption keys come in lengths from 40 bit (very weak) to 2,048 or more (very strong). To be truly effective, encryption keys must be given additional protection to defend the contents of the encrypted information. (Detection in Depth).

With Time-Based Security, encryption is viewed as a technique to:

▶ Delay the disclosure of the private contents of a message **(Confidentiality)**, or

▶ To permit detection of an otherwise undetected alteration of a message. **(Integrity)**

THE QUANTUM CYBER

Who the hell knows?

If and only when true Zero-time entangled processing becomes real-world or in iPhone V42 will this be meaningful. I'm not sure many of us want to calculate in an infinite number of dimensions devoid of a time scale. I can't think about this now. But, please, do send me your thoughts!

BLOCKCHAIN

Part of our planned research is the integration of ANS and Blockchain for certain applications. I chose to pick a hard stop on some things so I could get this book out. Immediately, there appears to be a potential application in the trusted relationship between the issuer and the verifier.

This cryptographic device was invented by Thomas Jefferson in 1795.

With respect to confidentiality, the effectiveness of encryption in TBS terms is measured by:

P(t) = The amount of time required by a brute force (or cryptanalytic) attack with no plaintext samples available, for a given encrypted message to be decrypted. This value can be somewhat arbitrary since exact decryption knowledge is deemed secret by many government organizations, but is meant to serve as a guide. In a brute force attack, the total number of encryption key possibilities divided by two, divided by attempts per time unit gives us the average time to decrypt. (In July 1998, Deep Crack, a parallel processing computer (MPU) solved a single level DES equation (56 bit) in 25% of the total brute force time, or 50% of the average predicted time.)

D(t) = The amount of time that the protected information has any real and/or perceived value, beginning with T=0 after disclosure.

R(t) = There is no reaction component for the encryption application of the TBS Model, thus, in this case, the formula is simply reduced to:

$$P(t) > D(t) + R(t), \text{ where } R(t) = 0$$

The popular conception that key length is the most critical element to strong encryption begins to waver when we look at the case of on-line commerce. Encrypted tokens (or passwords or session ID's) for on-line commerce are only used for a few milliseconds and often for a single session transaction.

If D(t) = 200ms, a reasonable time for internet commerce, then an encryption scheme which offers any greater level of security could be considered adequate to hold the basic TBS formula true, given that the key management method was sufficient. So, even 40 bit or 56 bit encryption methods would be more than sufficient if, in fact, the information in transit was only valuable for a few milliseconds. (That's policy.) If we talk about encrypting data at rest, $T \to \infty$, so the numbers and solutions are very different.

However, the strength of cryptographic systems cannot be measured solely upon key length and algorithmic integrity. In public key infrastructures (including Certificate Authorities), the databases which hold the keys and associated security relevant information represent greater potential system weakness – as well as a potential single point of failure. Since the cryptographic keys to the system are an obvious target, they must be protected with an additional layer of in-depth vigor; **P(t-km) > D(t-km) + R(t-km)**, (km = key management) which echoes other conventional TBS approaches of information defense. In this case, R(t-km) may not exist, or it could have a value which is based upon the TBS value of the database itself. OODA.

On the other end of the spectrum, such as in the case of trade secrets or other proprietary information, the information could have long term value, so D(t) could be *years*. In that case, both P(t) and P(t-km) must be very high. Unfortunately, maintaining a high value for P(t-km) is a far more difficult exercise than only picking a million-bit key. The system that holds the keys must be time-protected, too.

In summation,

> **P(t-crypto) > D(t-crypto)**
> *and*
> **Pt(crypto) => P(t-km)**
> *where*
> **P(t-km) > D(t-km) + R(t-km)**

Thus, we are saying here, that the protective value of the cryptographically-protected information is dependent upon the protective shells and TBS of the Key Management system, through a hybrid of Defense and Detection in Depth.

WAVES (Women Accepted for Volunteer Emergency Service) built and operated the U.S. Navy Cryptanalytic Bombe (originally conceived/designed by Alan Turing) from 1943 to the end of World War II to solve the German 4-rotor Enigma.

Time-Based Deception

I BELIEVE IN LYING. Sort of. Let me explain.

The bad guys will do anything they can to get you. You know that and it doesn't seem quite fair. They get to cheat, and you, as a network or systems administrator working for a real company have to play by the rules. They can lie. They can use social engineering in all its guises and pull any sort of nasty tricks they want to break into your networks or otherwise try to make your life miserable.

Analogue Network Security suggests some innovative means to defend your networks, if we just apply some common sense.

- ▶ Your goal is to reduce the amount of time the bad guys have to attack you. **(OODA)**
- ▶ You want your detection and reaction mechanisms to be as fast as possible. **(TBS)**
- ▶ You may choose to invite the attacker to stay around for a longer period of time. This gives you more opportunity to collect forensic evidence and/ or identify him. **(Deception)**

Do unto others as they do unto you. If criminal hackers lie to you, why shouldn't you lie right back? There is a way. It is your right and defensive duty to…

- ▶ Lie to your adversaries
- ▶ Deceive them in any way possible
- ▶ Force them to waste time/resources
- ▶ Make them "hang around" longer, to improve Detection
- ▶ Make their attacks a much riskier proposition
- ▶ Use automatic responses and hands-off management
- ▶ Apply Time-Based Security concepts

When undersized armies took on larger forces, they would have their horses pull logs behind them over dusty roads to give the impression that more manpower was coming to battle. Small armies would light 1,000's of fires at night to again give opposing forces the false impression of size. Psychological operations fit right into the deception mode with the philosophy, "It doesn't hurt if your enemy thinks he's smarter or tougher than you." Just think about that… playing it stupid can be smart. Today's headlines certainly suggest massive *deception* campaigns are part of our real politik planet.

Deception has been used throughout the history of warfare. Certainly the Trojan Horse fits the definition. Military leaders such as Phillip of Macedonia, Alexander the Great, Hannibal, Julius Caesar, and William of Hastings come to mind. The current generation of cyber-warriors have and continue to successfully use deception in their campaigns.

During World War II, MGM Studios was making military support films, but worried about becoming a potential target for aerial bombing if the war came to America. Studio executives complained to the War Department who said they would take care of it. The government response was to send out experts who painted the roof of MGM studios to look exactly like a munitions plant. Joke? D-Day planners convinced the Germans that the invasion would not be at Normandy, but some distance to the Northeast. Go read up on Jasper Maskelyne, the War Magician.

When a German Enigma encoding machine was captured by the Allies, Alan Turing led the effort to decode German transmissions. But we never let the Germans know that we could read their private mail, even if it meant sacrificing civilian targets to keep the secret. In ECM/EW warfare, electronic chaff is tossed from airplanes to confuse enemy radar. In the mid 80s, the Soviets poured thousands of electronic diodes into the concrete construction of the new American Embassy in Moscow. The intent was to confuse American counter-surveillance devices which can't tell the difference between the non-linear junctions of the diodes and those in a real eavesdropping transmitter.

The problem was they over did it; we found what they did out early in the construction process and we canned the new Embassy. Some experts maintain that Star Wars was nothing more than an elaborate technical public relations hoax of the first order to convince the Soviets we were willing spend a gazillion dollars on space-based defense. In the Gulf War, did the Patriot missile system work as well as was claimed?

Now, let's apply deception to network security. It's time to even the odds! It is legally arguable to aggressively go after the bad guys. Corporate vigilantism is still only mentioned and knowingly approved by law enforcement in dark corners. They can't officially sanction the good guys to break the law to nab the bad guys, but the desire is there.

One of the first tools that the bad guys use to attack networks are scanning tools to perform surveillance. Attackers want to understand and map-out their victim's terrain before "entering." As a defensive posture, you have fixed as many vulnerabilities as you can, but there are always a few left. Plus, you don't want to sacrifice too much in the user experience, for the sake of security. So try using some Deception against them! Some of the benefits are seemingly obvious.

- Works against insiders and outsiders
- Applies tried and true techniques
- Gives ersatz appearances of network view
- Multiplies target suite
- Ambushes the attacker
- Makes attacks riskier proposition
- The enemy is never really certain
- No false positive or negatives
- Automatic hands-off management detection/response

Of course, it makes sense to reconfigure deception periodically so no one catches on to what you are doing. You might instead choose to announce deception practices at various network entry points to scare off some would-be attackers. And as Time-Based Security suggests, use deception mechanisms to keep attackers on-line for extended periods of time to enhance detection. Deception is an excellent application of TBS:

- The deception mechanism can sit right on or next to existing servers and respond automatically without any human intervention. **D(t) + R(t)** should be made smaller and smaller over time, as the Deception Engine learns. (Squeezing the deception loop.)
- The deceptions are based upon a Reaction Matrix which is policy driven.
- Contingency management and gaming exercises realistically will echo genuine attacks.
- Well-constructed deception can increase the functional value of P(t).

The Many Facets of Deception

Deception comes in many guises, and no one deception reaction is "Just Right" for everyone all of the time. *(Common sense, by now, I hope!)* Deception offers an entire suite of capabilities, and they should be picked judiciously in any TBS-Deception application.

These techniques will be key to defending against Offensive Time-Based Security, discussed in the next chapter.

CONCEALMENT

Physical: Hiding through the use of natural cover, obstacles or great distance. Trees, branches, terrain, mountain passes, valleys.

Virtual: Use best defensive practices for "real" network services – obfuscation.

Confederate Army using Quaker Cannons, ~1862

CAMOUFLAGE

Physical: Hiding movements and defensive postures (troops) behind natural camouflage.

Virtual: Hide the vulnerable points with network access rights, archiving, etc.

RUSES

Physical: Use the same uniforms and adversary radio frequencies (false orders).

Virtual: Tell the hostile reconnaissance systems they are being sensed as legitimate. Reinforce to the attacker that he is OK and safe, doing what he is doing.

DISPLAYS

Physical: Make the enemy see (or think he sees) what isn't really there. Horses pulling logs, 1,000's of campfires, fake artillary, rubber tanks, dummy airfields.

Virtual: Tell attacker you are calling the IP-Police; create a fake CERT alert; tell them you are "Tracing" them; show fake firewalls and IP barriers. Squeeze your OODA harder.

Russian inflatable vehicle

DEMONSTRATIONS

Physical: Make a move that suggests imminent action.

Virtual: Create an automatic defender which seems to follow the attacker or a log/sniffer action or a trace.

HONEY POTS

Physical: Make something such an attractive target, that your enemy comes running into your trap. Think sneak attacks and ambushes.

Virtual: Create files with attractive information. Corporate secrets. Classified military information.

FALSE/PLANTED INFORMATION

Physical: False radio broadcasts, morphed pictures, videos, and other misleading information aimed at enemies, leadership, and general populations.

Virtual: Broadcast false network information from servers hat are being scanned. Yes, Fake News has a time component; how long does it take to validate information? The effect on OODA can be substantial.

Real "cloaking" is not far away with nano-cameras, displays and mirrors.

Fake News is not New(s).

FEINTS

Physical: Use false attacks as a means of covering up the real mission. Use false retreats to encourage chase by the other side.

Virtual: Appear to be helpless and defenseless when launching other means. Be loud about all moves by telling your adversary, or appearing to be so stupid, he thinks he is listening to your moves and that you are clueless.

LIES

Physical: Lie. Use the media to lie. Use perception management.

Virtual: Use electronic lying in same way. Let the system tell the attacker anything that furthers your goals.

Anything goes! Lies'R'Good in these cases, use them. The use of custom Deception suites is an attractive defensive technique.

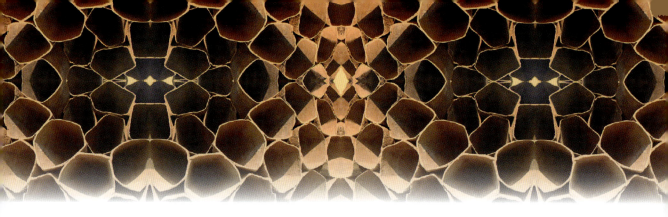

Honey

A neat combinatorial trick of encryption and deception is called **Honey Encryption**.

An uncrackable, one-time pad (like the Vernam-cipher), uses an encryption key equal to (or greater than) the length of the message:

	H	E	L	L	O		
	7 (H)	4 (E)	11 (L)	11 (L)	14 (O)	→	message
+	23 (X)	12 (M)	2 (C)	10 (K)	11 (L)		key
=	30	16	13	21	25		message + key
=	4 (E)	16 (Q)	13 (N)	21 (V)	25 (Z)		mod 26
	E	Q	N	V	Z	→	ciphertext

In ANS terms, you can almost think of a one-time-pad as having a detection point at every possible event, in this case bits or bytes. Further, if every single clock cycle (ad absurdum) or "decision step" had a detection mechanism (most likely with a negative time component), then we again approach (but will never reach) ideal security. In other words, a limit function that would additionally metricize with Trust Factors for each detection process.

In practice though, one-time pads are not often viable, so we use other techniques. Honey Encryption uses deception to add time to any attacker's cryptanalysis, thereby increasing the relative security of that encryption scheme.

Honey Encryption gives the attacker fake, but perhaps reasonable, plaintext data in response to every incorrect guess of the password or encryption key. By adding the crypto-cracking time to the time needed to determine if the plaintext is real or fake can potentially vastly increase the defensive security value of the object.

If the attacker does eventually guess correctly, the real data will likely be lost amongst the crowd of spoof data. **Time**.

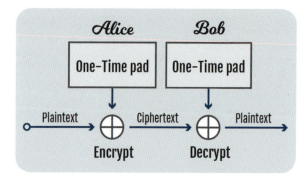

282

Privacy

It's NOT a Binary Choice.

The debate on security vs. privacy brings out the extremes in many people. Too often I hear that it's an 'either-or choice'. Which do you want?

However, as I hope to have explained, there are very few truly binary choices in our lives or in security. So, I argue, with a lot of evidence, that:

> ▶ **We will never have perfect security.**
>
> ▶ **We will never have perfect privacy.**
>
> ▶ **Therefore, it cannot be an either-or choice.**

The reality is a compromise between the two. Keep in mind that in order to have privacy, security controls are required. But having strong security does not necessarily mean, nor imply, anything about privacy.

For total security, no technology would ever be turned on. For perfect privacy, you would not be able to function in a wired world.

Security and Privacy are not at odds; they are two different sides of related issues. They enjoy both synergetic and symbiotic relationships. It's a balance – a continuously changing analogue continuum – not a binary choice.

Metamorphic Networking

If a network were a moving target, the bad guys would face a much more complex problem. If only, if only, a network was a moving target.

A basic element of motion is time, so if we can create network motion, P(t) could be called the amount of time that a network condition remains constant. With P(t) indeterminate, though, **P(t) = E(t)**. But, the more often we logically move a network resource, such as with an elastic Network as a Service, E(t) approaches zero; thereby security could be, potentially, measurably increased. This is what polymorphism did to malware (viruses), in the '90s. The polymorphic engine within the code changed the signature of the overall executable component in an attempt to bypass signature-based anti-virus programs.

==What if we could move our networks hither and yon in a non-predictable manner== (random vs. pseudorandom debate aside), that allows normal use by authorized users, yet frustrates the bad guys?

Attackers obfuscate their sources (C&C, etc.) and move them around at will to increase the amount of time it takes to identify their location, by which time they have moved on. This is a defensive interpretation of that. Move around the target, so only your internal networks know where the resources are at any time. How effective will this be? Let's model it, put up a few dozen VMs and try.

An emerging technology called real-time polymorphism borrows methods from the malware community and applies it to defending web servers. Polymorphism is applied to specific sections of the code, like data entry fields, is obfuscated and changed on subsequent iterations and calls.

How do we make this work in networks? Conceptually, the same sort of approach can be taken with DNS. With 100% global cooperation, and/or a major change in the DNS specifications, targets are no longer the static recipient of internet hostility. Adding dynamism (time) to IP assignment screams of DHCP. Sorta good in principle. The execution was miserable. How often does your IP address actually change? Take a look for giggles.

Now, imagine that polymorphic approach was embedded in a communications protocol. I am just offering up DNS as one obvious place to manage a polymorphic (or metamorphic) implementation. Just a thought for a true next-generational security person to entertain.

Offensive
TIME-BASED SECURITY

The Bad Guys are not stupid.

They understand offensive social engineering far better than we know how to defend against it. They understand reconnaissance and surveillance far better than defenders. They are infinitely more patient than we are. They are winning the Time-Based Security Network Wars and they know it. They know and understand their offensive OODA loop and constantly strive to further squeeze their loop. They have squeezed their loop and we haven't squeezed ours!

Offensive Network Operations, also called CNA or Computer Network Attacks, are inherently about time. Boyd *got* that abstractly, as the time-based rules of conflict are domain independent. Analogue Network Security clearly shows that to defend networks, resources, and processes, time functions must be built-in throughout the system. We have to get inside the adversary's decision loop: OODA. We must squeeze our OODA Loops!

Our industry has consistently maintained that attacking networks (et al) is far easier than defending them. Using current protective security methodologies, the evidence largely supports that hypothesis.

> ▶ Security is a game of Whack-a-Mole.
> ▶ Push the balloon back into the box and some part will pop out elsewhere.
> ▶ The attackers are way ahead of us and always will be.

In my way of analogue thinking, I believe that part of pen testing should not be to think like the attacker, but to actually be the attacker. Pen-testers have an awesome opportunity to explore the potential value of Analogue Network Security. Add time to the equation, any questions, and any responses. Get inside the defender's OODA Loop. Squeeze your offensive OODA Loop. Adjust time values to correspond with best intelligence, to mimic real live CNA scenarios. Quit treating networks like lab rats. You really are under attack - and the attackers comply with no rules. Truly asymmetric.

I am suggesting that all pen-tests will have greater value if all parties are privy to the time components, as well as the results. What means more?

"**Using a dictionary attack, we found 112 lousy passwords, which could easily let us in.**"

Or…

"**Using a dictionary attack with Algorithm F(x) operating on a set of Y elements, over a period of 95.8 hours of analysis, over a channel of X-bandwidth, and sampling every Y-time period…**" then give me highly granulated reports, with Time being a searchable criteria.

If we bound our security efforts within defined time limits and between specific trust factors, the need to play cyber-whack-a-mole can be severely curtailed.

Pen-testing runs the gamut from surface-only look-sees, to no-technical-holds-barred. Formal processes and methods are emerging and evolving. In no way do I want to analyze the hundreds of elements that a pen test can involve. Rather, I want to offer a high level view of how time can be of immense value both at this stage, and later. And that we learn to integrate defensive and offensive Time-Based Security into a single set of OODA equations which, I do hope, are as illuminating for you as they were to me.

Offensive Time-Based OODA

A few assumptions for the previous example: A technical attack and the required tools are at hand. For simplicity's sake, I'm not including specific wireless, RF, surveillance systems, physical, social engineering, or other potential attack vectors. Clearly, each pen-test will have its own rules of engagement.

For any particular successful attack vector, I argue that there are at least four time values to be recorded.

1. The initial attack, with minimal a priori knowledge. Each logical step with its own time stamp.

2. Once the attack method is verified, perform the same attack again; re-measure each step. This time should be substantially less than the first above, and should demonstrate the clear advantage to the attacker once a beachhead has been established.

3. Automate as much of (2) above a possible and measure. Smart attackers will do smart things to save time, maximize profits, enjoy a time-based advantage, and distribute widely.

4. Applying a true OODA-loop mindset will create a time-based dataset where trending can be analyzed, as well.

This is much more than thinking like an attacker. This is *being* the attacker. Emulating what we can conceive as being the best the bad guys might bring. This approach provides hard data that duplicates attackers' skills and capabilities in a live shooting range. Yes, Red-Blue cyber gaming is an important component, especially for monitoring $D(t) + R(t)$. But think of the value of adding a highly granular time component for both sides in such exercises. You're running them anyway, so add event-based time stamps. Under such an approach, we will use $A/L(t)$ as the Attacker's loop, versus Defender's loop of $L(t)$.

However, there is more to the story, isn't there?

If $A/L(t) > D(t) + R(t)$,

Defense wins by $A/L(t) - [D(t) + R(t)]$,

thus $L(t) < [D(t) + R(t)] < A/L(t)$

If $A/L(t) < D(t) + R(t)$,

Offense wins by $[D(t) + R(t)] - A/L(t)$,

thus $L(t) > [D(t) + R(t)] > A/L(t)$

We can now add in a few more variables: Trust Factor (TF) and the earlier equation $BW / |DB| = 1/E(t)$ and see just how wide a margin the offense wins by. *(Bandwidth divided by data-size equals time.)*

If $A/L(t) < D(t) + R(t)$,

then Offense wins as

$E(t) = [D(t) + R(t)] - A/L(t)$

Depending upon the nature of the attack, we need to evaluate the risk, first, just by $E(t)$.

Simplistically, if an attacker gains, for example, access to mission critical systems for one second, how much damage can he do? This underscores the point of Offensive Time-Based Pen-Testing and applying those data against the three fundamental attack vectors: the C-I-A triad.

YOUR JOB:

Calculate the $E(t)$ and associated Risk to a given IDBI, for each of the C-I-A vectors.

- ▶ *Confidentiality*, implying data movement or exfiltration.

- ▶ *Integrity*, or changing data in a specific location, will have a different time value.

- ▶ *Availability* suggests that the defender must get inside the attacker's OODA-loop, measured in time, at each node in the loop, to stay ahead at all times.

ACTIVE DEFENSE:

Sure, a defensive reaction can be an attack or strike-back (legalities notwithstanding). However, an interesting thing occurs. Your response increases! Part of that OODA component is to re-assess the results of the strike-back (aka BDA, or Battle Damage Assessment). That takes time. Further, cyber-BDA is a terribly soft science and the Trust Factor of such a BDA will likely be very low.

So, relying upon a single Strike-Back reaction alone is probably not smart. You would want two paths in the Reaction Matrix:

1. The traditional Analogue Network Security approach to locking down defenses in a dynamic manner through the Reaction Matrix.

2. Initiating an In or Out-of-band reaction targeting the attacker (if possible at all.) This would spawn a new parallel OODA-loop, with its own Trust Factors.

The question is, and I don't have an answer now, "Is it necessary to combine the efficacy of defense with the probability of a successful strike back, with questionable BDA accuracy?

Ontario during the U.S. North East blackout of 2003. I got a call from a national TV network asking me to go on the air and explain how the terrorists did this terrible thing. I said I grew up in the Mowawk power grid, and it was probably just a tree. By the end of the day, the media was clearly blaming the terrorist trees.

Inside the Attacker's Loop

Successful defense requires that your OODA-loop is faster and better squeezed than your opponent's. The same thinking applies to the attacker. They both want to reach and maintain that time-based advantage for the long term.

The formula for calculating measurable defensive success in OODA-loops is:

$$\text{L-Win}(t) = O1(t) + O2(t) + DE(t) + Act(t) < \text{L-Lose}(t) = O1(t) + O2(t) + DE(t) + Act(t)$$

All this says is, all time-based components of the Winner's OODA-loop must be faster (less time) than those of the Loser. **We have been saying for years that "*we can't defend_____*". Now, we have a path to victory.**

In the next example, three of the four OODA components in the winning loop are faster than the losing loop. But, one component's time, in this case, Observe, becomes, at a minimum, equal to that of the losing loop. What happens in Time-Based Security when a greater than (>) becomes an equality (=)? An indeterminate state returns, and we no longer have certainty of time-based superiority.

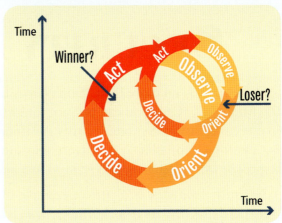

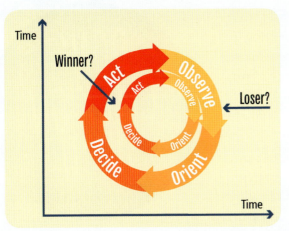

In this third case, at least one piece of the previous winner's OODA-loop takes longer to complete than that of the previous loser's and all bets are off. This visualization technique should help management comprehend this all important rule:

Winning at cybersecurity (cyberwars, etc.) requires that your OODA-loop is faster than your adversary's.

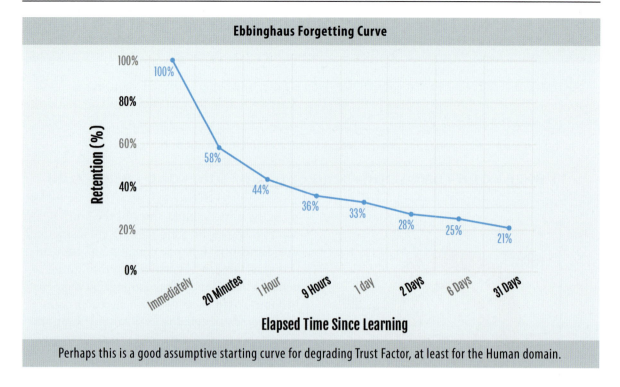

Perhaps this is a good assumptive starting curve for degrading Trust Factor, at least for the Human domain.

Security Awareness

Awareness is no more than "Don't Cross the Street in the Middle…", "Only you can prevent forest fires…", and in our case, the number one Security Awareness message is, "Don't Click on Shit…" It's advertising and marketing to people whose behavior you want to manage.

Security Awareness is a perfect example of applying a time-based OODA loop to learning. Some management still believes that Security Awareness is a check box: "We sent out a newsletter last year…," "We told them to read the incomprehensible policy doc written by our lawyers…," "We had them watch a video…"

And the result is epic fail for reasons you now recognize: a binary approach. The 1895 Hermann Ebbinghaus Forgetting Curve still applies, which is why OODA is so important to changing human behavior in cyber-human interactions.

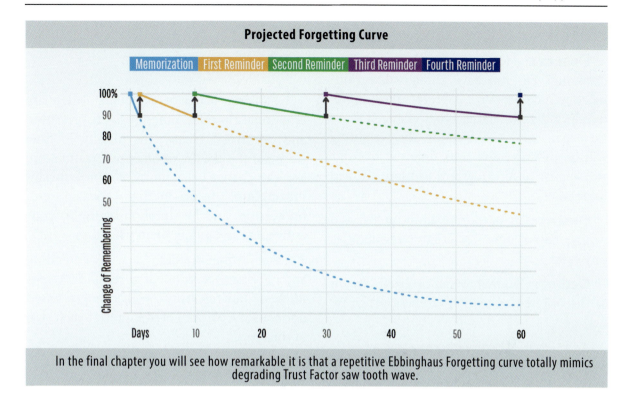

In the final chapter you will see how remarkable it is that a repetitive Ebbinghaus Forgetting curve totally mimics degrading Trust Factor saw tooth wave.

Awareness is iterative. The threats change. Networks change. Everything changes all the time, and so must Security Awareness programs. So, while the educators like the term "Spaced Repetition" (with which I completely agree), I prefer to return to the OODA way of thinking and squeezing the loop - with time, of course.

PHASE I, AT THE BEGINNING:

OBSERVE: What is the security posture of your organization? Are policies clear and comprehensive? Do you know how you want each employee or role to behave? This is all about first getting a good lay of the land, so to speak. "Where are we now?" You will have to weigh many criteria to make your observations worthwhile. "We need security awareness," by itself, those words are just useless checkbook platitudes.

ORIENT: What resources are we able to apply? How can we maximize their impact on behavior? What does the process look like and how do we implement it? Many weighted inputs are also required at this step. Some of the data will come from direct observation, some from external research, some from gut reactions. They must all be considered.

DECIDE: OK, based upon all of these weighted criteria, we have a plan that will most likely meet with success, probabilistically. Management has bought it. We have the pieces ready to go. Sign off!

ACT: Start the Awareness Program. Do it. Just do it. Don't second guess yourself.

PHASE II

OBSERVE: How's it going? Is behavior changing? Do you have enough detection-reaction points to capture meaningful trending data? What else has changed since we began this OODA loop? The weighting will be different and thus different answers will appear to feed forward to more attuned orientation.

ORIENT: Change orientation, goals, and needs, based upon external and iterative processes.

DECIDE: OK, we have an updated version of the original security awareness program. Let's go.

ACT: Do it. Measure it.

PHASE III +

Do it all over again.

Changing behavior is tough. There are emotional rip tides, other business priorities, and our worst enemy, the infinity of time (exposure) – aka the result of procrastination. You can change behavior by offering constant messaging, multi-media edutainment, immersion, and by simply listening to your customers and giving them what they want.

Like raising a child, it's a never ending and necessary component of reminders, self-interest, and repetition, with changes based upon a series of weighted inputs at each step of the loop.

A quality security awareness campaign also employs OODA Loops. Security awareness is advertising and marketing to your audience: users, execs and techs. Never stop.

ANS, OWASP, & Software Programming

The future of programming is not like most programming today. But will be more like making biological systems. The Internet is one of the few systems organized this way. It is the most scalable and robust human artifact on the Earth.

-- Alan Kay, Programming and Programming Languages

Should Analogue Network Security approaches be included in parts of OWASP?

By Dennis Groves, the co-founder of OWASP and one of the reviewers of this book

ANALOGUE ARCHITECTURE

It is my observation that many people today, including many members of OWASP, define security as observing attacks (e.g. IDS/IPS, Splunk, Qradar, etc.) and changing anything they can to stop the attacks in progress. I find this mentality to be frighteningly dangerous, as the entire security program is necessarily reactive and focuses on stopping yesterday's attacks and leaving you vulnerable to future attacks. I call this a great business model but a poor security model, because it leads to lots of consulting hours without any value or real security being done for the client.

However, we have many great examples over time that demonstrate ways to eliminate many of the attacks we have today with architecture changes. For example, Plan9 and its offspring (9front, Inferno, and HarveyOS) have 'eliminated root' (chapter 4) and this has had a profound effect on the ability to compromise Plan9 systems because you have no privilege escalation. You either are or are not authorized to take an action and the default is that you do not have permissions unless they are explicitly granted. This is a basic security engineering principle.

Another example is Alan Kay's "Objects and Messages" paradigm, or "real computers all the way down (RCATWD)." Predating even Plan9, the Smalltalk language is another example of a secure architecture in code. When an Object receives a message, it must find a corresponding method. If the method doesn't exist, the message cannot be executed. Again, Default Deny. Contrast that to the practice of 'fuzzing' where we actually send 'bad messages' to Libraries today in order to break them. This has spawned an entire industry of 'static and dynamic analysis' when in fact it is possible to 'architect' this issue into absolute extinction.

It is all about the Architecture. And Analogue Network Security presents a wide variety of first principles, models, and frameworks that security architects, software engineers, and programmers would all do well to pay attention to. Analogue Network Security is a treasure trove of tools for improving the security of every system you encounter.

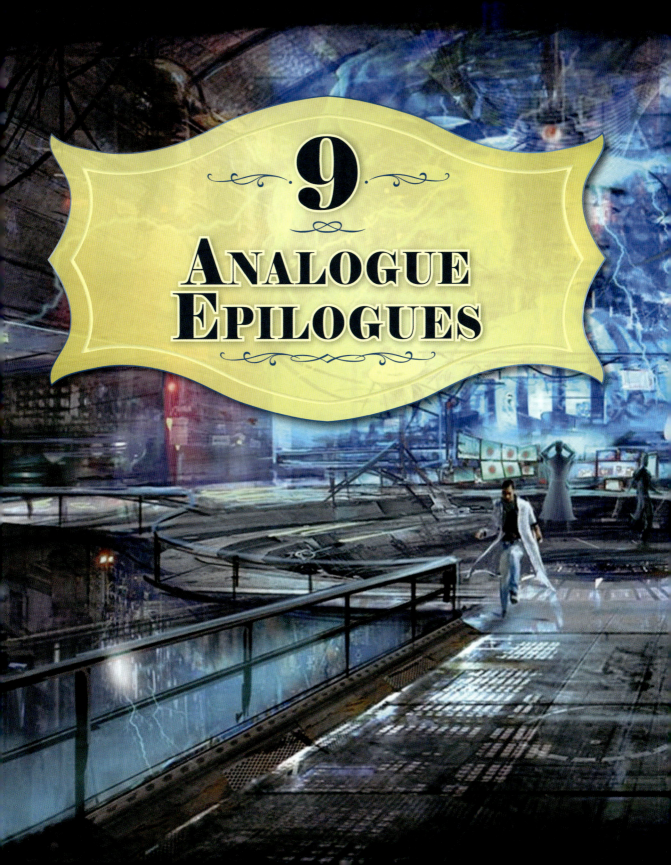

9. Analogue Epilogues

The Analogue Epilogues' Prologue

This has been the toughest book to finish. Makes the others look so easy, in retrospect, of course. My original idea for The Epilogues was to solidify ANS ideas with some hard math, a summary or two and be done with it. To let the community, hopefully, see glimmers of potential and play around.

But, as I continued speaking and sharing and encouraging harsh debate, more ideas flowed. So, Chapter 10 (well, Chapter 9… of 10…) is much longer than I had anticipated. I've included random ANS-related thoughts that lie somewhere on the analogue spectrum from "half-baked" to "hmm… that might work".

Decent security must be a choreography of limits in a closed system.

LET'S BEGIN THEN, WITH MARK AND THE MATHS OF ANS.

I've been working on ANS for a long time, as noted early on. As it evolved, I wanted to keep the concepts abstract and the math simple, so interpretation, revision/addition and potential application would be as unrestricted as possible. However, as more and more pieces fell into place, and some of the apparent implications grew beyond my original intent, I decided that a more formal mathematical verification was in order. I initially wanted help (feedback) to keep me honest and find fundamental errors in the premises and conclusions. Then, I found myself buried in math beyond my skills and searched for a serious mathematician who could fit a number of bills. You can see that criteria in the little box to the left.

Justifiable security, in analogue thinking, does not imply that 1, or 100%, or absolute security, has been attained; that's the point - it's an unachievable upper limit. Justifiable security, to me, is a suite of measurements in a defined system space, which specifies the amount of security as $0 < $ Security Posture $ < 1$, based upon the kinds of analogue criteria in this book – and more, from these epilogues.

Then I met Mark Carney, a remarkable young man, at the consistently amazing *Hack in Paris* conference, who, after initial bouts of understandable incredulity, decided he was going to prove everything I was talking about - wrong.

The Real Math of ANS is all Mark, to whom I owe an incredible debt of gratitude, and one beer (only) in each and every city we meet.

Mark, please tell your story – and thank you!

WHY MARK?

1. Math fluent to the max in a wide array of specializations.

2. He gets/groks network security, coding, and the "hacker mindset" (for lack of any other term that satisfies me), because they are so intertwined.

3. Could determine if my fundamental models lent themselves to a mathematical formalism at the most abstract. The concept of provable/justifiable security is reminiscent of ancient *Orange Book* "A" rated systems. Formal math first, then build the system to the math.

Real Math behind ANS and Detection in Depth

Mark Carney
June 1, 2018

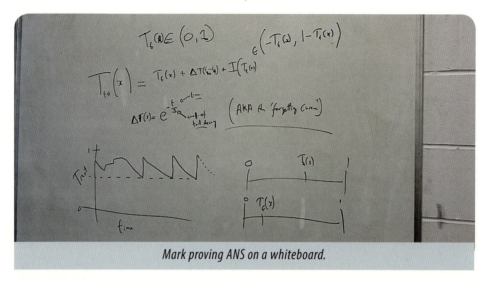

Mark proving ANS on a whiteboard.

1 INTRODUCTION

In this section we'll discuss the 'real math' behind ANS, with a view to providing a good overview of the mathematics that underlies these ideas, and thereby a sense of what these ideas look like in more practical terms.

I was first introduced to ANS by Winn Schwartau at a watering hole (as with his Polish napkin tale) at Euro Disney after Hack in Paris 2017. Very quickly one beer turned into > 1 beers, and within a short time pens were dragging ink across napkins, and laptops with scurrying hands were scouring Google, and by the end of the evening, we had successfully managed to replicate the base understanding of ANS from Winn's grey matter into my own.

It was superb. Finally, I had a framework into which I could merge my own ideas of how to measure and better manage security. I was then invited to attend DEFCON XXV to discuss these ideas further with like-minded, enthusiastic people whom I had never met before, many of whom I have since come to call good friends.

What followed then is what follows now. Crystallising during an intensive week in Nashville in September 2017, we have reviewed and tweaked this to give a hopefully cogent account.

NB: these formulas, models, and mathematical expositions are not to be considered the complete and final picture. Instead, they are presented as what Dan Dennett calls 'intuition pumps' - they are mathematically presented thought experiments and worked examples to stimulate thinking towards understanding ANS. More detailed, peer reviewed accounts are to follow.

1.1 FOUNDATIONS

We're going to need some solid foundations so that our understanding is solid later on. First off, we need to ask…

1.1.1 WHY BAYES?

Probabilities are immensely powerful tools. They are essential to evaluate risks of all kinds. But the probability for one event – whether it is the likelihood of rain this afternoon ruining your BBQ or the likelihood that some symptoms a patient presents to a doctor is an major illness or something more mundane; probabilities affect everything in our lives from the photon up.

However, we often find ourselves asked to contextualise probabilities. Not 'what is the probability of event A', written $P(A)$, but rather 'What is the probability of event A given event B', written $P(A|B)$. But this is a very nuanced problem, which the Reverend Thomas Bayes made a remarkable comment on in his work as an algorithm to update our beliefs about some events based on new emerging evidence. The great Laplace developed this idea further in 1812, and Jeffreys axiomatised the approach.

Prior to Bayes, we had what is known as a 'frequentist' view of statistics - this is the kind of statistics that uses p-errors, confidence values, etc. This is still immensely valuable, but they fail to account for many of the environmental aspects for some event A - in short, they lack a conditional element fundamental to ANS, in our cast, that is what Winn's ANS focuses on, time.[1]

Bayes Theorem can be roughly formulated for use in security analysis as follows. Let our two events be the following:

- $P(D)$ be the probability that we detected a real attack of some kind.
- $P(A)$ be the probability that an attack of this kind is in progress.

Now, our vendor, Acme Security Inc., has given us a detector system for this attack. It's 99% accurate by the vendor's estimate[2], so that's really good, right?! Well, we're going to see how accurate that is…

It's tempting to say that 99% accuracy is our value of $P(D)$, but really, it's our value of $P(D|A)$ that is, the probability that our detection was triggered given a real attack occurred. But we can get the probability we detected an attack, our True Positive probability, as follows:

$$P(D) = (P(D|A) \times P(A)) + (P(D|\overline{A}) \times P(\overline{A}))$$

$P(\overline{A})$ is the 'probability that an attack doesn't take place', which is the same as $1 - P(A)$. Likewise, $P(D|\overline{A})$ is the probability of a false positive – namely a detection is there was no attack event. This is $1 - P(D|A)$. Now we apply the magic of Bayes:

$$P(A|D) = (P(D|A) \times P(A))/P(D)$$

---

[1] There is some strong criticism of Bayes, which we will discuss later in this section.
[2] This is a static Trust Factor, I know, but we'll keep it simple for this example.

This is how we work out the probability of an attack given we had a positive detection. This is really the contextualised probability we want to know. Let's introduce some numbers here for clarity. Say we have evidence that our likelihood of attack, P(A), is 0.1% - that is, say, 1 in 1000 emails or sites users on the network receive/visit are malicious.

Plugging in the numbers:

$$P(D) = (0.99 \times 0.001) + (0.01 + 0.999)$$

which is approximately 1.1%. So, now we get

$$P(A|D) = (0.99 \times 0.001)/0.011$$

which is roughly 9.02%.

WHAT???

Yes, there is only a 9% chance that you detected a real attack with this system from a single detection with these parameters. This may make no sense, but think of this this way…

Picture 1000 emails, and we'll colour the one evil one bright red. Now, this represents our evil event, but our detector will identify 10 events that are not evil, but look like they might be. So, we have 10 false positives, and 1 real event, giving a total of 11. Only 1 in 11 we actually care about, so the probability that we were under attack given we had a detection is 1 in 11, or about 9%.

Now, let's extend our model with time as we use in AWS. Suppose there is a second detection of the same attack on the network at some time t later. Now, we do the calculation again, but this time, we use 9%, i.e. our previous confidence factor, as our value for P(A). Now the results are very different:

$$P(A|D) = (0.0902 \times 0.99)/0.0983 = 90.75\%$$

And there we have it! Having the second detection event has increased our confidence, our trust, that the detection system has found something real.[3]

Now, clearly, this is not a working example from ANS, but it should illustrate the *why* ANS uses Bayesian statistics in real world security scenarios. As we shall see, use of Bayesian statistics permits us to have our beliefs about our security systems' efficacy measured and updated *in context*. So long as we are considerate in our approach, we won't run afoul making good use of Bayesian ideas.[4]

1.1.2   WHAT BAYES MEANS IN ANS

The reason for choosing Bayes extends for some core ideas in ANS:

- Tells us how intersecting probabilities should work

---

[3] If you look at the Trust Factor charts, this shows how a 'Two Man Rule' increases the trust in our process.

[4] One of the most well known criticisms of Bayesian statistics comes from Stephen Senn; "A Bayesian is one who, vaguely expecting a horse, and catching a glimpse of a donkey, strongly believes he has seen a mule…" Such a criticism should hopefully tell you where not to use Bayes!

- Tells us how to update our thinking and knowledge of our context or 'world' in time
- Gives us a workable model of how intersecting probabilities should work

We have seen how to measure security of Black Boxes and will gather some of the more concrete metrics such as $D(t)$ and $R(t)$ for a given product. We also demonstrated how to measure the success rate for a given product/system against a 'known bad' database of samples.

What Bayes tells us is how to combine this information and update our parameters so that we can see how much we were right, and we can also feedback into the known-bad DB - the feedback isn't limited just to our devices, but into the ANS thinking itself!

But how will this work? Well, if you recall from chapter 6, we want to use OOB networks to update our situational awareness, make notifications to other nodes in our trust zone, and generally expand the observation scope for our OODA loop.

CORE IDEA: By calculating the probabilities that something is a 'real threat' (such as DoS-like events) and passing this knowledge down the OOB line, other nodes will make better predictions regarding same/similar threats using a basic Bayesian model, outlined above.

We will cover how this should work with the requisite weightings in the section below on Trust Factors across a network.

1.2   FURTHER BACKGROUND THEORY - ROC SPACES & CURVES

After WWII, the US Army developed the Receiver Operator Characteristic (ROC) as a way to classify responses to RADAR detections. To map it as a space, they put the True-Positive Rate (TPR) - the rate at which detections were accurate positive detections, also called the 'probability of detection' - and plotted this against the False-Positive Rate (FPR), which was defined as the 'probability of false alarm' and was calculated as (1-specificity), where specificity is the True-Negative Rate.

Mathematically, we get two distributions (see the figure below) that allow us to see that all of our True Positives (TP) and True Negatives (TN) have a Gaussian distribution

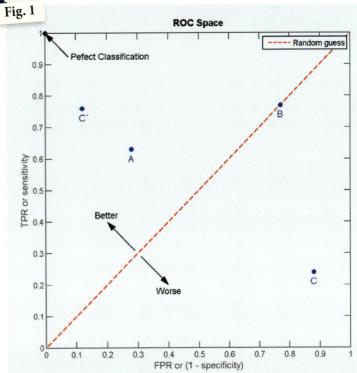

Fig. 1

By ROC_space.png: Indonderivative work: Kai walz (talk) - ROC_space.png, CC BY-SA 3.0, https://commons.wikimedia.org/w/index.php?curid=8326140

given by $f_1(x)$ and $f_0(x)$ respectively (see fig. 2). Now, clearly they overlap, and we see emerge the spaces for False Positives and False Negatives. This gives us a definition, for some threshold T, of

$$TPR(T) = \int_T^\infty f_1(x)dx$$

whilst our definition for FPR becomes

$$FPR(T) = \int_T^\infty f_0(x)dx$$

You can see the intersection of these curves and how they can be interpreted in the following diagram:

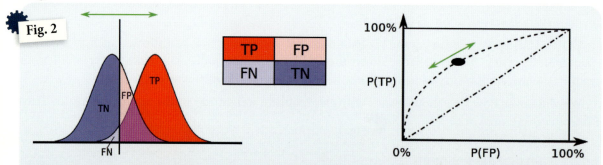

Fig. 2

Diagram showing how TP/FP and TN/FN relate to each other as a ROC curve
By Sharpr - Own work, CC BY-SA 3.0, https://commons.wikimedia.org/w/index.php?curid=44059691

We can thus see that if our ROC curve is above the diagonal line in fig. 1[5] then we are performing better, and if it is beneath the diagonal, then we are performing very badly.

This very brief introduction to ROC mathematics will come in handy when comparing *[D(t)+R(t)]* and our exposure time *E(t)* below.

CORE IDEA: By envisaging ROC curves as variant in time, we aim to push our curve from 'bad' to 'good' by applying feedback directly into our thinking, meaning that we tie together the local to the global OODA loops letting our metrics improve our working along the way. We will see later how we can see something similar, as well, in the ANS Exposure Space diagram.

1.3 TRUST FACTORS

ANS makes a core assumption - that **nothing is perfect or immutable**.

If we extend this thinking, we get the core tenet that there are no absolutes of trust. There are degrees of protection which Winn refers to as 'defense'[6]. Any protection system will give you some protection, it just might not be very good. Similarly, any protection system can never give you absolute

---

[5] The *y = x* diagonal in our ROC space in fig. 1 indicates 'chance'.
[6] This author defines Protection and Prevention as aspects of Defense, but this is an argument for future discussion and study.

protection. We must relativise trust, the way it already is in other areas - the most well known of which is finance.

1.3.1 EXAMPLES FROM FINANCE

Trust in Latin is *creditas* from which we get the word 'credit'. A 'credit card' is therefore actually a 'trust card'. Your 'credit score' is your 'trust score'. You can find/replace like this to see how financial instruments around credit work on the assumption of some level of trust.[7]

So, if we have a high credit score, say over 750, and then cease using our credit card, what happens? Everybody knows that the credit score will gradually fall, over time, and either sink at some level or just keep going down if we start abusing financial instruments, stop making payments, etc. Winn calls this Trust Decay.

CORE QUESTION: Why don't we do this in security?!

This is the aim of the Trust Factor (TF) thinking in ANS for which we offer the following 'starter' TF Model.

1.3.2 THE TF MODEL FOR ANS

The initial model, which we expect to be refined in future work, looks something like this:

$$TF_{t+1}(A) = TF_t(A) + D(TF_t(A))$$

where

$$D(TF_t(A)) = \frac{dTF_t(A)}{dt} = \delta(t, t+1) + I(TF_t(A), x_1, x_2, \ldots, x_n)$$

Expanding $D(TFt(A))$, we get:

$$TF_{t+1}(A) = TF_t(A) + \delta(t, t+1) + I(TF_t(A), x_1, x_2, \ldots, x_n)$$

Where the constituent parts are defined as:

- $TFt(A)$ is the Trust Factor value of A at time t
- $\delta(t, t+1)$ is the difference function (defined fully below)
- $I(TFt(A), x1, x2, \ldots, xn)$ is the influencing function (defined fully below)

We will start with the $TFt(A)$ - this is the value of trust in the open interval $(0, 1)$, and is the result of all of our calculations. As such, when we want to ask the question "How much do we trust A?" the answer will be related to the value of $TFt(A)$.

Next is our 'delta function' $\delta(t, t+1)$ - this function is a subtracted value, and is what guarantees

---

[7] Winn: "Oddly enough, I have seen one example of a FICO score reaching 850 - perfect. Is something amiss in their limit functions? Should I quit trying for perfect credit?"

our decay of trust factors in the model. There are a few ways we can construct these - the δ function 'shapes' the natural decay or growth. Here are some possibilities:

1. $\delta(t, t+1) = rTF_t(A)$
2. $\delta(t, t+1) = e^{-(t/S)} - e^{-(t+1/S)}$ - similar to the previous example (an exp map)
3. $\delta(t, t+1) = s \cdot \log_e(1-t)$ [8]

Here r is a linear rate of change which becomes a linear decay, s is our scaling factor for a logarithmic decay, and S tempers our exponential decay in terms of e.[9] When chosen appropriately and with a tactical use of scaling, we can ensure that we will not exceed our bounds, or can build these in algorithmically into $\delta(t, t+1)$. Essentially, the δ function serves to shape the differential of our model, and how it traverses between different thresholds.

Finally, our 'Influencer Function' $I(TFt(A), x_1, x_2, ..., x_n)$ is an $(n+1)$-ary function that performs some key functions, and returns a value from the open interval

$$I(TF_t(A), x_1, x_2, \ldots, x_n) \in (-TF_t(A), 1 - TF_t(A))$$

NB: This bounding ensures that we never achieve negative values for *TF*, nor values above 1.

Firstly, it contains within it a threshold which, should *TFt(A)* cross or be within a certain bound of, it will trigger an automatic reassessment of *TFt(A)*. This coupled with the automatic decay guarantees that trust factors will be re-assessed by some part of our system with certainty.[10]

Next, the Influencer function processes the necessary parameters *x1, x2, ..., xn* required to properly include the trust of *A*. These will certainly involve the *D(t)* and *R(t)* values, the relevant delay line times *DL(t)* covered towards the end of chapter 6, and could also be factors such as the number of successful 2-man checks performed by *A*,[11] or the number of times *A* has been shown to make a false positive claim in the past, etc. [12]

The Influencer Function then gives a value that is then added into this mix. This value is capable of shifting the trust factor to a very high or very low value, and in many ways, is the key component.

It should be noted that the parameters could also be trust factors from other nodes *TFt(B), TFt(C),...* which would move this (potentially but not necessarily) nonlinear system of one equation to be one of up to n equations. The "steady states", sinks, and reaction to perturbations of such a model are all open questions that we are planning to research.

---

[8] In order to prevent plunges to -∞ for a negative δ-function, we need to ensure that logarithmic decays switch to exponential below the Influencer function thresholds defined next.

[9] The latter example is drawn from the 'forgetting curve' due to Ebbinghaus (lots of references online, and textbook coverage also) coming from experimental psychology in the 1850's.

[10] It should not be considered that this is the only time the function is called - it can be called manually in out models with ease. What is key is that it is automatically invoke around a particular threshold.

[11] *A* is permitted to be anything you like. *A* can be a person, a black box, a device, a server... anything!

[12] Part of the ongoing project with ANS is to define what the best parameters are, and how they should be implemented into the system.

1.3.3 THE MEANING OF MEAN

To paraphrase what we stated at the start of this section, the job of statistics is best described by an informal definition of a 'linear regression': "To draw a line through a cloud of points" or rather "to find the statistically strong/likely information in a cloud of data points".

What we want is to find ways of using 'Trust Factors' in meaningful ways. For this section, and what follows, we will not concern ourselves with the *"how?"* of finding TF's, but more with the *"now what?"* for how we can sensibly use Trust Factors both within a network and across one. To do this, we will introduce the notion of the Geometric Mean.

The normal 'arithmetic' mean is "the sum of all the terms divided by the number of terms", and this gives you the 'strong center' of where all the points are. But this center is easily skewed, and so this is fine for rather 'impartial data'. That said, it is straightforward to extend this to things like the 'standard deviation from the mean' (which we define is the 'arithmetic mean of the distances of each point from the arithmetic mean of the dataset') and chi-squared values (measuring the 'goodness of the fit' between theoretical predictions and the measured instances of observables). We're generally very happy with the Arithmetical mean in our lives.

But sometimes things decay very quickly and require a mean that is more sensitive to this - for example, sonar responses, or in some successful models of 'trust', that of the trust between actors, measured appropriately. This kind of scaling is called the 'geometric mean'. So, this brief section aims to introduce the 'geometric mean' with calculations to indicate that perhaps this is a good candidate for consideration for the scaling of Trust Factors.

The Geometric Mean is defined as the "n-th root of the multiplication of n-terms". For example, once calculates the 5th root of the product of a set of 5 values or the square root for a set of 2 values, etc.

CORE IDEA: The idea at play is to make use of the Geometric mean, and not the Arithmetic mean.

So, if the standard average we learn at school is the Arithmetic mean, we know that to find the average of 4 inputs we do the following calculation:

$$\frac{1}{4}\sum_{i=1}^{4} x_i$$

whereas in the geometric mean it would be

$$\sqrt[4]{\prod_{i=1}^{4} x_i}$$

with the general rules being

$$\frac{1}{n}\sum_{i=1}^{n} x_i \text{ and } \sqrt[n]{\prod_{i=1}^{n} x_i}$$

We can also scale the Geometric to the Arithmetic mean for the calculus-friendly reader: you can think of the geometric mean as the exponential ex where x is the arithmetic mean of the natural logarithms of the values in your set.

A WORKED EXAMPLE:

We have previously described this geometric mean by its use in dating sites - specifically adapted from the algorithm used by OkCupid in this case - because it's where the geometric mean is used most visibly in people's lives (although the most used Geometric mean usage is in credit scores). The geometric mean serves to increase the 'match %' as and when you have more things in common. So, they ask a question, and then take three metrics;

1. How you answer
2. How you would like someone else to answer (your ideal matching answers)
3. How much the question matters to you (the importance of the question)

Each level of 'importance' gets a value, from 0, 1, 10, 50, and 250 for the most important questions, as follows:

- not important = 0
- a little important = 1
- somewhat important = 10
- very important = 50
- mandatory = 250

They use the answers you give, compared to the answers someone else expects; so take the number of points someone gets by the questions they get right (1 or 10 points for not that important questions, and 50 or 250 points for very important questions) and divide that by the number of points they could have gotten - this gives the 'satisfaction score' as a percentage. Then the system does the same regarding the answers that they gave, and how they relate to your questions/answers/importance ratings.

LET'S DO A WORKED EXAMPLE:

1. Are you messy? Choose from: (very messy / a little messy / neat freak)
2. Do you like Chinese food? Choose from: (yes / no)

Here are Alice and Bob answers given to the site:

Question:	Alice Q1	Bob Q1	Alice Q2	Bob Q2
Answer:	neat freak	A little messy	yes	yes
Desired Answer:	neat freak	messy OR neat	yes	yes
Importance:	50	1	1	10

We have the computed 'satisfaction' scores; Alice had up to 11 points to gain, whilst Bob had up to 51 points to gain, owing to Alice really caring about mess. Alice scores 10 + 1 = 51 points, esp. given Bob cares more about getting his Chinese fix than Alice, and so 11/11 = 100%. Based off these two questions, Alice is borne of Bob's dreams! At least, based off these two rather spurious questions as our metric.

But Bob gets 0 + 1 = 1 points, as he fails to be the neat freak Alice needs in her life. So, Bob's score for satisfaction of Alice's requirements is 1/51 = 2%

Overall, they both will enjoy a Chinese, but Alice cares about that organized abode, and Bob won't live up to that. Clearly this isn't going to be a good match, but here's how a geometric mean helps us see this mismatch more clearly.

An arithmetic mean would be (100 + 2) / 2 = 51%. This does not seem a very good fit, based on their responses, expectations, and relative importance of their choices. But a geometric mean is $\sqrt{(100 \times 2)} = 14.14\%$, which is much more believable as a score for how much Alice and Bob are compatible based off these questions. Clearly, the more data you have, the better the picture becomes, as is true for all means.

1.3.4 TF CALCULATIONS ACROSS A NETWORK

Moving away from this specific example, let's see what happens when we compare arithmetic and geometric means when we blackbox the 'trust percentile' process.

Let's take some trust percentages between two parties, A and B, and some third party C. We want to determine A's trust for B, from B's trust with C and A's trust with C (Winn mentioned PGP earlier - same concept). Here's a diagram of what we are talking about:

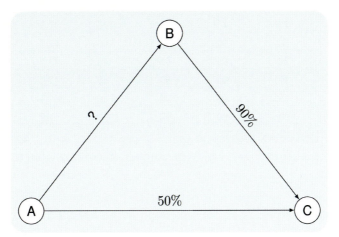

Suppose A trusts C with 50% - A thinks C makes wrong decisions half the time, whilst B trusts C with 90% confidence - B thinks C is doing the right thing. Let's compare our trust percentages and make some initial estimation of what our starting trust percentage for B should be.

With an arithmetic mean, this would give a trust for A as *(50 + 90)/2 = 80%*, which doesn't seem right. A geometric mean gives $\sqrt{(50 \times 90)} = 67\%$, which seems more believable. Likewise, this is the same score for B.[13]

This can also work for trust of new servers. Say you are server A, and a new-to-you server 'D' appears, and your peers B, and C trust D with certain percentages.[14] Here are some values from varying trusts by B and C of D, generated by the Arithmetical and Geometric means, for comparison:

	Trust $B \to D$	Trust $C \to D$	Arith. Mean	Geom. Mean
1.	25%	30%	27.5%	27.39%
2.	20%	40%	30%	28.28%
3.	50%	50%	50%	50%
4.	20%	80%	50%	63.25%
5.	10%	90%	50%	30%
6.	5%	90%	47.5%	21.21%
7.	80%	90%	85%	84.85%

Hopefully it is clear from this table that the geometric mean could be something that gives a better sensitivity to what is going on underneath in the network trust factors.

We can also try to assess trust across the whole network using the arithemtic vs. geometric means. If the trust among just a few peers for one server drops, yours will drop in line, but not by a few percent with an arithmetical mean, but by significant percent, even for one in 10% change, via the Geometric Mean.

A	B	C	D	ARITH	GEOM
25	30	50	40	36.25	35.00
20	40	50	40	37.5	35.57
50	50	50	40	47.5	47.29
20	80	50	40	47.5	42.29
10	90	50	40	47.5	36.63
5	90	50	40	46.25	30.80
90	90	90	90	90	90.00

Fig. 3

In this above example, we are looking at much lower Trust Factors, but in the first 5 rows, the differences in arithmetic and geometric views are comparatively small, but then in row 6 diverge then in row 7 re-converge.

A worked example of this - suppose four peers A, B, C, and D have 90% confidence, or in broader ANS terms, a Trust Factor of .9. Then we will look at the overall Trust Factor, each with 90% a confidence, using both methods of calculation. As we lower the Trust Factor of D, notice that the

---

[13] Compared to the later example, here I'm treating the 'score per question' as 1 multiplied by the importance factor of 'the percentage with which someone trusts C'.

[14] I'm assuming you trust B and C as perfectly as possible, with TF of 99.99...%, for the sake of example.

differences between the arithmetic mean and geometric mean approaches diverge significantly.[15] This clearly shows that even one weak link can bring about significantly decreased security and trust in any operational situation.

Fig. 4

A	B	C	D	ARITH	GEOM
90	90	90	90	90	90.00
90	90	90	80	87.5	87.39
90	90	90	70	85	84.52
90	90	90	60	82.5	81.32
90	90	90	40	77.5	73.48
90	90	90	30	75	68.39
90	90	90	10	70	51.96

We will now use this geometric mean and our closed form model from earlier to try and put things together into a more general model that we hope demonstrates at least one way of thinking about how trust can be considered both between and across a network.

1.3.5 TOWARDS A COMBINED ANS MODEL

In symbols, we can assign weights $\sigma_1, \sigma_2, \ldots, \sigma_s$ where

$$s = \sum_{i=1}^{n} \binom{n}{i} = \sum_{i=1}^{n} C(n,i)$$

to our *n* inputs and intersections of nodes across the whole OOB network, and then apply our Bayesian intersections from before giving us models that looks like this:

$$\text{for } 1 \leq j \leq s, \sum_{k=1}^{n}\left((-1)^{k-1}\sum_{\substack{I \subset \{0,1,\ldots,n\} \\ |I|=k}} \sigma_j P\left(\bigcap_{i \in I} A_i\right)\right)$$

Our sigmas can be derived from the trust factors for all our n nodes as $TF_t(A_i)$ with $1 \leq i \leq n$, and *j* tracks which specific sub-intersection we are currently at.

So, a worked example would look a little like this;[16] Suppose we have 3 nodes on our network, A, B, and C. We want to aggregate the input probabilities as

$$P(A \cup B \cup C)$$

---

[15] This is due to the presence of an logarithmic scaling we discussed earlier.
[16] The above formula is a 'general form', but in for this chapter we are only dealing with small networks for clarity.

taking into account our weightings. There are 7 terms to the expansion of $P(A \cup B \cup C)$, as the expansion looks like this:

$$P(A \cup B \cup C) = P(A) + P(B) + P(C) - P(A \cap B) - P(A \cap C) - P(B \cap C) + P(A \cap B \cap C)$$

We can now add in our weights from $\{\sigma_1, \sigma_2, \sigma_3, \sigma_4, \sigma_5, \sigma_6, \sigma_7\}$ as follows:

$$\begin{aligned} P_{ANS}(A \cup B \cup C) =& \sigma_1 P(A) + \sigma_2 P(B) + \sigma_3 P(C) \\ & - \sigma_4 P(A \cap B) - \sigma_5 P(A \cap C) - \sigma_6 P(B \cap C) \\ & + \sigma_7 P(A \cap B \cap C) \end{aligned}$$

1.4   DR(T) AGAINST EXFILTRATION TIME: EXF(T) [AKA EX(T)].

Now that we have given some reasonably technical mathematical descriptions of how ANS can be applied, we offer up some basic models, curves, and tools with which we hope you can better understand the underlying mechanics and ideas that have been presented.

It is also best with any attempt at mathematics, to gain some base visual intuition for what we are doing. This is the purpose of this section - to show how our systems work with visual guides.

1.4.1   DR(t) AGAINST E(t)

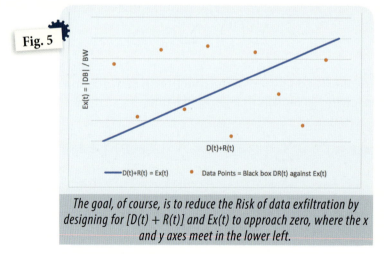

Fig. 5

The goal, of course, is to reduce the Risk of data exfiltration by designing for $[D(t) + R(t)]$ and $Ex(t)$ to approach zero, where the x and y axes meet in the lower left.

This is the $D(t)+R(t)$ to $Ex(t)=|DB|/BW$ curve applied to data exfiltration. As you can see, it looks much like a ROC space in its definition. The upper-left triangle is the "good area", and the lower right is the "bad area" - the logic being that if you are above the line, then your detection and reaction times are fast enough to prevent specific data exfiltration from the network, assuming, the attacker has knowledge of the location of the sensitive information - here, all lumped together as $|DB|$.

This diagram forms the basis of much ANS thinking - essentially reducing the $E(t)$ to $D(t)+R(t)$ relationship down to a linear programming exercise.

1.4.2 DR(t) AGAINST EXF(t) OR Ex(t) WITH DL(t) SHIFT

Here we see the effect of a Delay Line, with time *DL(t)*, on the elements of our comparison space. It shifts all of the blue points up to their position as red points. This means that more of the points successfully cross the threshold due to simply the increase in time owing to the delay factor.

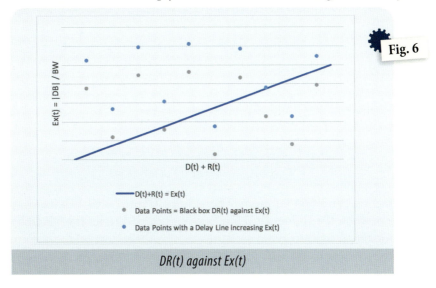

Fig. 6

DR(t) against Ex(t)

1.4.3 TF WITH EXPONENTIAL DECAY & REVIEW THRESHOLD

This is one of the ways in which Trust Factors (TFs) will behave. You can see that there is an automatic decay of trust in time that then gets automatically reassessed when it approaches the threshold. After the third invocation of the Influencer Function, something had changed, and now the trust is left to decay. There is no secondary threshold to invoke the Influencer Function on, so it will decay forever, until a manual re-appraisal is invoked at some stage.[17]

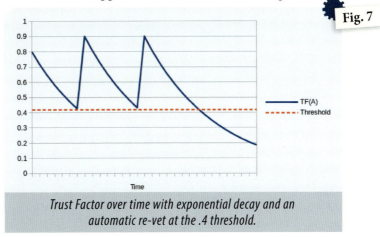

Fig. 7

Trust Factor over time with exponential decay and an automatic re-vet at the .4 threshold.

1.4.4 TF WITH LOGARITHMIC DECAY & REVIEW THRESHOLD

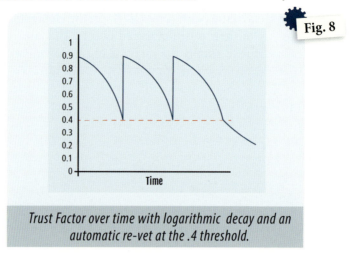

Fig. 8

Trust Factor over time with logarithmic decay and an automatic re-vet at the .4 threshold.

Here we can see a second type of decay - here, logarithmic - that behaves in precisely the same way. Note, the curve when the Influencer Function has decided to let the TF go below the threshold is switched to exponential, so as to avoid collapses to $-\infty$. These, too, will wait for manual invocation of the Influencer to re-assert trust.

1.5 FULLY WORKED EXAMPLE

Here is an example graph with included trust factors for A (99%), B (75%), and C (80%) given a particular event occurring, as well as the weighted trusts between A, B, and C.

On the following page is a table showing the explicit trust factors between A, B, and C (included for clarity).

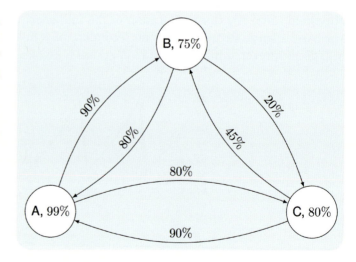

---

[17] Winn says: "Or, in ANS terms, add a TB·FF with its associative security controls. This is what is meant by Detection in Depth, too!"

Trust	Percent
A trusts B	80%
A trusts C	90%
B trusts A	90%
B trusts C	45%
C trusts A	80%
C trusts B	20%

NB: The arrows point to where the Trust Factor is used, as we are modeling a TF as something that is interpreted from a node on a network. This may seem counter-intuitive, but we hope the reasoning is clear.

Recall our calculation from earlier:

$$P_{ANS}(A \cup B \cup C) = \sigma_1 P(A) + \sigma_2 P(B) + \sigma_3 P(C) \\ - \sigma_4 P(A \cap B) - \sigma_5 P(A \cap C) - \sigma_6 P(B \cap C) \\ + \sigma_7 P(A \cap B \cap C)$$

We can derive the sigmas from the geometric mean as follows (all to 2 significant figures):

$$\sigma_1 = \sqrt{0.9 \times 0.8} = 85\%$$
$$\sigma_2 = \sqrt{0.8 \times 0.7} = 75\%$$
$$\sigma_3 = \sqrt{0.9 \times 0.45} = 64\%$$
$$\sigma_4 = \sqrt{0.9 \times 0.8} = 85\%$$
$$\sigma_5 = \sqrt{0.9 \times 0.8} = 85\%$$
$$\sigma_6 = \sqrt{0.2 \times 0.45} = 30\%$$
$$\sigma_7 = \sqrt[6]{0.9 \times 0.8 \times 0.9 \times 0.8 \times 0.2 \times 0.45} = 60\%$$

This gives us the full calculation as follows:

$$P_{ANS}(A \cup B \cup C) = (0.85 \times 0.99) + (0.4 \times 0.75) + (0.64 \times 0.8) \\ - (0.85 \times 0.99 \times 0.75) - (0.85 \times 0.99 \times 0.8) - (0.3 \times 0.75 \times 0.8) \\ + (0.6 \times 0.99 \times .75 \times 0.8)$$

$$\approx 0.526 \approx 52.6\%$$

As such, we can get a concrete value for the dependent trust and confidence in our network, and can see how much different trust factors affect the outcome. Notice, we can always ignore some TF or other percentage on this network by setting it to 0.999…, or 'effectively 1' in our actual model. This example uses all possible parameters to be considered - this way any other interpretation is a subset of this general model.

NB: This is *not* a dependent probability - as for *P(A|B)* we saw ealier. It is to be considered as a factor into further calculations regarding this particular event. So, let's do a quick calculation based on the Bayes formula we started our section with.

We know that *P(A|D)=((P(D|A)×P(A))/P(D)* and using our value for *P(D|A)=0.526...*, and taking *P(A)=0.001*, we get:

$$P(A|D) = \frac{0.526 \times 0.001}{(0.526 \times 0.001) + (0.474 \times 0.999)} \approx 0.00110958\ldots \approx 0.110958\%$$

Whilst this may seem vanishingly small, remember, this is only our first detection. Substituting this percentage into further recalculations, after 5 further detections this rises to around 0.18656%, after a further ten detections it is around 0.5265%. After 45 detections (30 on from the last value, iterated[18]) it is at 11.7694...%, and by 80 detections, it is at 84.9787% in this detection process.

How can this be useful? Well consider a scenario where a system is permitted to 'act automatically' on a >80% confidence from this network, and the detections are happening once a second, then within 80 seconds you have successfully reacted to an attack with a measure of certainty that it was an attack.

To some, this may seem fast, to others, extremely slow, but bear in mind these points:

- The event was quite rare, only a 0.1% occurrence rate - so only 1 in 1000 events were potentially malicious.
- The confidence across the whole network was quite low, only 52.6%.
- We have acted completely automatically, taking into account data from numerous sources (all of which are blackbox here).

Here is how the detections required change when we adjust the TF of our network, but keep the 80% threshold the same:

- If our TF for our network is at 90%, we react within 4 detections
- At a TF of 92% we only need 3 detections to raise our confidence of an attack taking place above the 80% threshold

Now, we would like to point out one thing; in this model, suppose the attacks happen faster, say before the influencer has kicked in and pulled some TF's down, or some other confidence values have varied. What happens if the attacks are every 0.5 seconds? We react in line and can keep up with the attacker.

Note, that with this approach our confidence some event is an attack rises with the incidence of the attack. This extends one of our aims - the give a solid justification as to why some event is considered an attack.

---

[18] Iterated here means the previous output has become the new input.

1.6 CLOSING REMARKS

In conclusion, this closed-form model is, of course, quite simplistic in a sense and makes lots of assumptions about systemic contexts, but it is hopefully illustrative of the kind of mathematics that arises from the thinking at the core of ANS. The aim is to use this as a theoretical basis on which we can expand to a full and more formal theory of security, with ANS concepts at its core.

Further directions that this model could move have been considered along the way to producing this first foray into a technical mathematical treatment of ANS. With incorporating interesting algorithms and techniques, there are many and varied and exciting possibilities that could be used to expand this model from its current simple form - we encourage the reader to get thinking and get involved in its development! See the section below for the current idea set at time of writing.

We hope that the core tenets of ANS, and how they can be considered mathematically are made plain, and that the examples given serve as the intended 'intuition pumps' for new thinking about network security with an Analogue twist in your OODA loop.

1.6.1 WHAT'S NEXT?

Future work on the ideas started in this section include:

- Peer-reviewed mathematical models elaborating on this section, and providing full proofs where necessary
- Machine Learning (ML) models and ANS
- Laboratory testing of the models.
- Adding ML into TB-FF Feedback
- Using Generalised Hidden Markov Models for the Trust Factor and general calculations - so as to allow for independent, dependent, and co-dependent variables being taken into account
- Using probabilistic modelling/ML to dynamically affect decrementing clocks. and Delay Lines
- Using new and emerging technologies, such as say blockchain, to prevent maldata attack on the OOB network
- Finding the properties of the model - e.g. stability points, limits, periodicity of certain configurations, etc.
- Engaging in theoretical analyses from related areas of mathematics - such as constraint-satisfaction theory or category theory views
- A full, technical, reviewed and available protocol description to allow devices to communicate within these bounds

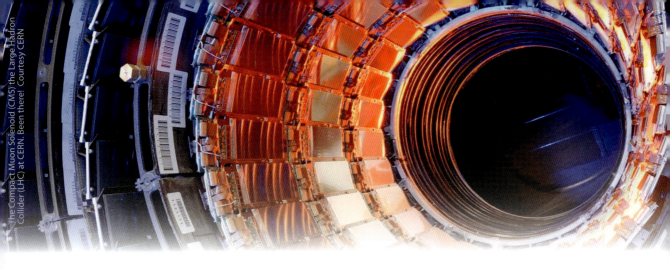

The Compact Muon Solenoid (CMS) the Large Hadron Collider (LHC) at CERN. Been there! Courtesy CERN

∞ Begets Chaos

I think I called **infinity** the Arch Enemy of Security. No matter which of the three domains we talk about; no matter isolated or integrated, subject-object events occur; no matter the human vs. machine involvement; infinity breeds chaos. **Infinity must be defeated before we can defeat any adversary.**

When $D(t)$ or $R(t) \to \infty$, $E(t) \to \infty$ and that means we have no idea what is going on, and/or we have no way to measurably remediate. In network management terms, this is chaos.

When $TF \to 0$, $Risk \to \infty$. From an analogue view, that's where we are now. Another example of chaos.

What we desire is for $TF \to 1$, $Risk \to Zero$.

In an audio amplifier, the lack of negative feedback generates Voltage-Out $\to \infty$, or unachievable infinite gain. Unstable. Vis a vis, in the acoustic realm, ear-splitting squeals.

In old-style analogue audio recording, magnetic tape storage had three important characteristics. One, there is a saturation upper-limit. Two, the saturation curve is non-linear. Three, technology has inherent noise thresholds.

Infinity is our enemy.

Infinity must be defeated before we can defeat any adversary.

In an unregulated, value-based economic system that does not employ feedback-based governors, wealth accumulates to the few.

When the upper limit of magnetic media saturation is reached, our ears call it "distortion", generally a very ugly sound. Recent studies suggest this effect to be mathematically chaotic; an attempt to reach ∞ but, stifled by the inherent limits of the ferrous material.

ANS SAYS: Measure and understand the dynamic nature of your networks (code, human behavior, etc.) by using time as the common metric. Also, understand the bandwidth requirements (internal and customer facing) on a time based scale.

In audio terms, we wanted 20-24db of "headroom" to non-chaotically handle the amplitude spikes of music. In network terms, that translates to 100 times more volume. I don't believe that a network needs 100 times additional available bandwidth 24/7. However, elastic cloud services such as AWS, *do* provide real-time dynamic scaling for a wide range of loads.

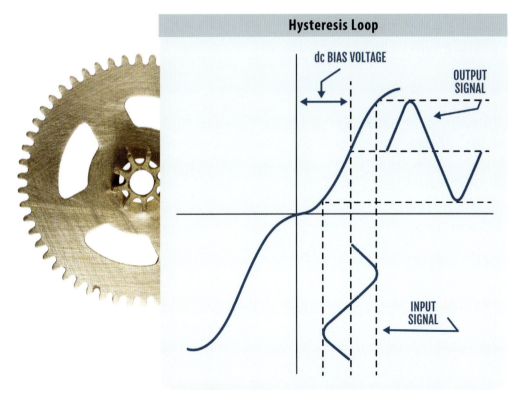

The second consideration is the native non-linearity of induction in magnetic storage media. Magnetic saturation sounds like ugly audible distortion. Various forms of distortion were the norm, until we developed *bias* where a secondary sinusoidal signal is added so that the recording and storage were limited to the linear portions of the hysteresis curve to optimize the performance and sonic quality of the audio. What we did was pick a small section of the hysteresis loop, add bias, **Min = Noise Threshold and Max = Distortion/Saturation. Max - Min = Dynamic Range.**

ANS SAYS: Network and code analysis should be examined for measurable time-linear operation and performance. From where I sit, this sort of problem may be initially addressed by a look at Queuing Theory. That's more Future Research.

> **If we can apply properly time-based weighted biases into our dynamic security decision-making processes, I believe we will see significant improvements.**

Finally, there was a noise threshold. If the amplitude of the inducing current was too low, the signal fell beneath the noise level, rendering the signal useless. Shannon was all over this!

Infinity introduces chaos to electrical, mechanical, and acoustic systems (networks), yet our industry has attempted to define network security by ignoring the perils of infinity as the unstable element that screws up everything.

Designers and security architects must remove infinity from network security, internetworking architectures, programming, and domains that affect the security, integrity, privacy, availability, and uncorrupted operation of systems or processes, whether humans are involved or not.

Analogue Epilogues

WHAT DOES SECURITY LOOK LIKE?

All management likes *management porn*. Pretty pictures that can rapidly convey a (analogue) concept versus infinite 4-point font mind-numbing mental drudgery. Besides, people don't really read anymore.

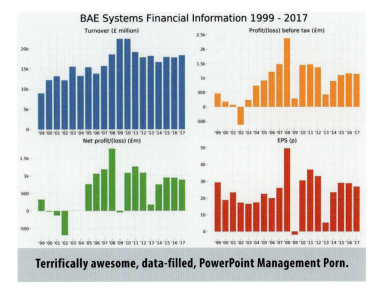

Terrifically awesome, data-filled, PowerPoint Management Porn.

As discussed earlier, humans more meaningfully and quickly interpret trending curves in several dimensions with a bigger picture view than streams of numeric digits; as it should be with security where rapid human involvement is needed.

While learning about ANS, I kept asking myself two guiding questions:

1. Can we visualize security in some meaningful way so that geeks and management can communicate?

2. Is there a "Unit of Security"?

The following discussion contains some initial thoughts on what I have learned, talked to some folks about, and think might be a decent starting point. I know I have said before, we have a ton of ANS work to do.

DEGRADING TRUST FACTOR VS. RISK

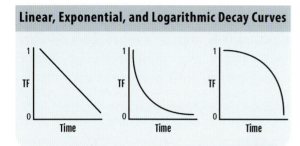

Linear, Exponential, and Logarithmic Decay Curves

Trust degrades over time; that's axiomatic to ANS. Three general types of roll-off occur. A linear decay is constant over time, regardless of the time scale. The decay begins with a specified TF on the y-axis, then that TF → zero over some defined time range. Exponential decays cause the TF to rapidly decline while → zero. The log decay is initially more gentle then, speeds up as time goes on. Plenty of variables to play with!

Trust Factor Decay Curves Math

Linear Decay/Degradation: $y = mx + c$

Exponential Decay/Degradation: $(1 - 1/n)^n$

Logarithmic Decay/Degradation: $\log(1-x) + c$

In the next graphs, the Trust Factor follows various exponential decay functions. Can you imagine reasons to use one versus the other (or versus linear) as an assumptive base, which of course is key to the Bayesian approach?

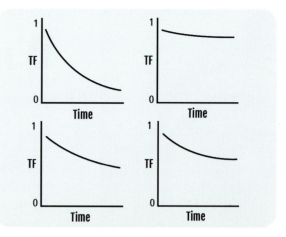

Exponential Decay Conditions

▶ (Upper Left) You have a high turnover of employees, likely meaning trust is certainly limited over shorter time periods. The depth (rate) of the initial decay curves will come from your existing data. You have this info. It becomes, in a Bayesian view, a good first assumption.

▶ (Upper Right) You have a small company with almost no turnover.

As more detection data is collected, the severity of the decay curve is modified through, potentially, a small weighted neural network, either inline or in the controls' feedback loop.

Notice in the next graphs, the median and the Max Trust Factor increases over time. When would the Trust Factor increase? I can imagine a weighting network adding significance to certain criteria; sort of like a credit report that scores you higher for having no late payments for longer periods of time. Or regularly posting "non-fake news" and garnering a better reputation, calculated in a social media's AI algorithms.

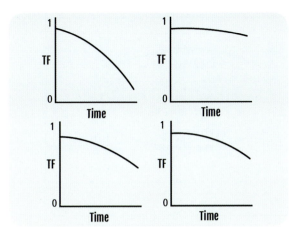

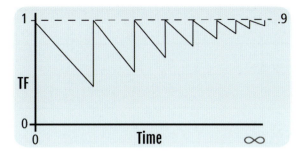

Below is an exponential decay, triggered at a pre-determined lower Trust Factor or by periodicity. Bayes says, make a first guess. Spock nailed in Star Trek IV: "Ah. Then, I will try to make the best guess I can."

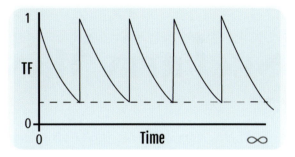

The graph below illustrates logarithmic decay over time.

Log Decay Over Time

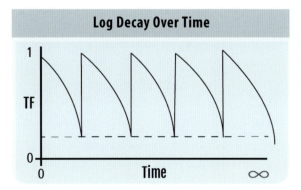

Logarithmic Decay Conditions

▶ Periodic assessments of partner relationships.
▶ Periodic compliance confirmation.
▶ Phishing testing: data based initialization.

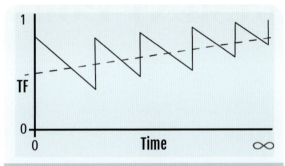

Trust must be earned over time.

Future work, of course.

In the case of the next graph, the Max Trust Factor remains constant at .9, yet the decay factor attenuates over time, based upon some weighting functions that increase the Trust Factor by decreasing the min-max range. The median TF improves here, too.

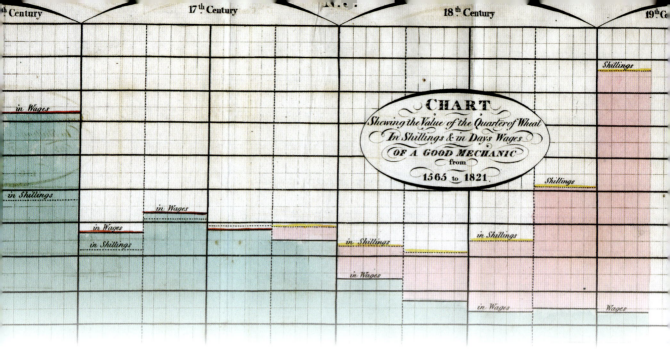

SECURITY MANAGEMENT PORN

To help management (and programmers, etc.) understand the premises and effects of ANS, they are going to want to see it. Since I propose degrading trust as axiomatic (increased trust must be earned, and I will address that in a bit), what does it look like? A lot like the three curves in the previous section. The Trust Factor will always sit somewhere between 0 and 1.

> **0 < Trust Factor < 1**

The way we think today is to "Trust" at an absolute level and we forget or ignore the re-vetting process; of code, of relationships, and of humans. ("She's a Trusted Employee." "They have a secure network, so we're good to connect to them.") With Ebbinghaus (Chapter 8), we add *reminders* along the x-axis. From a security awareness standpoint, the need for constant repetition is obvious; same thing with advertising and marketing.

Analogue Epilogues

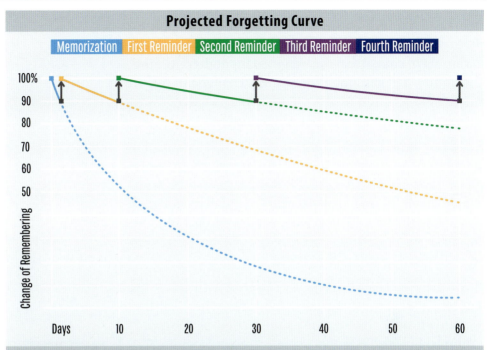

As shown in the prior chapter, time-and policy-based feedback loops increase human retention; learning. The same principle should apply to Deep Learning in my mind. Here is a solid visual reminder of how the forgetting curve maps conceptually to Degrading Trust Factors and increased Risk.

Visually, security resembles some form of a saw-tooth wave.

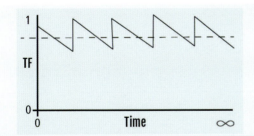

Security = .8 ± . 1/ms (TF Min-Max Range = .9 ↔ .7)

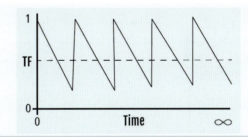

Security = .5 ± .4/ms (TF Min-Max Range = .9 ↔ .1)

Perhaps your network trusts Partner A more than Partner B, and thus assigns it a more gradual Trust decay. Think through as many real examples as you can!

Let's look at these two curves: both start at t=0 on the x-axis and with a TF = .9 on the y-axis. Both decays are linear, albeit one much steeper, indicating a faster degradation of trust over the same period of time.

Initially, I am hypothecating that during every defined time period, a time-based feedback loop invokes a re-verification and brings the TF back to .9 exceedingly quickly, so, the use of vertical lines, assuming of course that the weighted input determining the initial TF has not significantly changed. Else, it might only rebound to .8 or .75 for some period of time. The math and measurements will tell us.

Take a look back at the two smaller graphs on the previous page. In the one on the left, the sawtooth decay curve range is ± .1, so the **TF Range = .7 ↔ .9**, with a median of .8, and that decays TF and Risk for any particular process. That is what security looks like. In that case, we see a single image of a single process, with the TF function being $.8 \pm .1 * 10^{-3}$ seconds.

In the right hand graph, t(0) begins with TF = .9, but falls precipitously in the same time period, all the way down to .1, in the same millisecond as the prior example. So the $TF = .5 \pm .4 * 10^{-3}$ seconds with a TF Range of .1 ↔ .9, updated every millisecond. Please remember that the specific time scale is immaterial; you need to pick the one that meets your goals. In addition, these are numbers for elucidation only. I expect, as we all learn more about ANS, that seeing Trust Factor ranges using numbers like .999999999 versus .9999999999; the human eye cannot rapidly "grok" this, so we need to clearly specify our TF Range on the y-axis.

I mentioned designing down to 10^{-24}, for the future, of course.

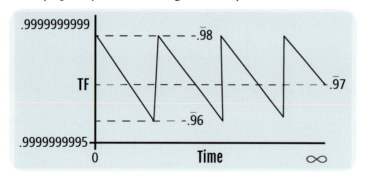

Here, we are operating at Trust Factors in the $5 * 10^9 - 10^{10}$ range. Very high TF indeed. The min-max is tightly set around a defined median.

A proposed notation is:

$$.9999999999 = .\overline{9}_{10} = (1 - 10^{-11})$$

$$.999999999 = .\overline{9}_{9} = (1 - 10^{-10})$$

Meaning, there are ten 9's, or in the bottom example, nine 9's. The line above the 9 signifies "repeating" and the subscript how granular the range is. This is obviously non-intuitive to humans, except perhaps scientists. Perhaps something along these lines would give the practitioner a better handle on the scale. From the graph example above, the math says:

$$.9999999995 \pm .0000000002/ms = (.\overline{9}_{9}5 \pm 2)/ms$$

By looking at the subscript, we know the min-max conditions are on the nano-scale, measured every millisecond. For less granular detection:

$$.9995 \pm .0002/ms = (.\overline{9}_{3}5 \pm 2)/ms$$

Risk is merely the inverse.

From reviewers and commenters, this seems to be a decent first step in quantifying security functionality and efficacy within defined environments.

Once we can measure something, anything, we need to display it in human-brain digestible terms.

Visualizing Security

In the analogue realm, we can rely upon meters for rapid human interpretation. In my rock'n'roll days, we controlled the level (relative volume/amplitudes) of up to 100+ audio sources at the same time. Which meant monitoring them with visual aids.

We used analogue VU meters, which due to their mechanical design, averaged out signals, so peak (very loud) levels were not visible. "Pegging" the meter to the right, though, meant your risk of distorting the signal increased on a logarithmic scale. After a while you got used to quickly gauging the levels of lots of inputs and lots of outputs. The brain does the averaging, noticing "differences" – or approaching Min-Max conditions.

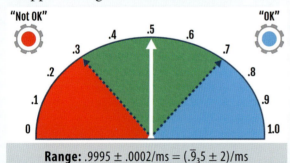

Range: $.9995 \pm .0002/ms = (.\overline{9}_3 5 \pm 2)/ms$

A VU meter such as this might be applicable for visualizing quantified security parameters.

The big arrow is bounded by the green Min-Max Trust Factor and below .3 is red. Above .7 would be blue. The red and blue lights across the top are reminiscent of peak meters, alerting the (audio or network) engineer to potential out of bounds conditions.

Scale is important, so the lower left of the meter might display the range, using the notation suggested earlier, or some future version that communicates quickly and visually.

In the 1970s, audio was going *digital*. These vertical digital VU meters acted on either a log-scale volume unit scale or as a peak meter, which responds and displays very fast amplitude transitions.

Both types of meters are fine, depending upon what you are measuring. Applying that approach to security visualization has some initial attractiveness.

In this notional approach to visualizing Risk illustrated in Fig. 9A (*next page*), a particular Black Box measures 10 detection points. The blue means AOK! As the color bars approach and reach red, risk is getting out of bounds and a reaction must be taken. This should trigger ICS/Scada and audio metering.

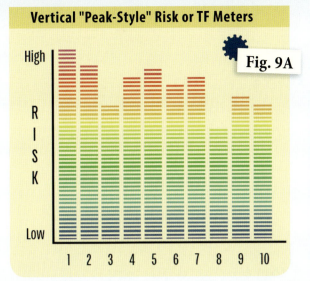

Vertical "Peak-Style" Risk or TF Meters

Fig. 9A

approach, will employ some OODA, some feedback – some form of dynamics control. By measuring at multiple detection points, an analogue view appears.

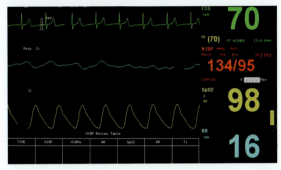

Below is a similar analogue amalgamation for Risk. Blue is acceptable. Other colors, higher on the y-axis, show increased risk over time. Again, notionally, let's say with Detection in Depth, we are measuring 1,000 different points in code, networks – think about that GE Engine!

While thinking about visualizing security I was reminded of hospital patient monitors. The periodic amplitude pulsing (breathing, etc.) in nature is compellingly similar to how we may view ANS.

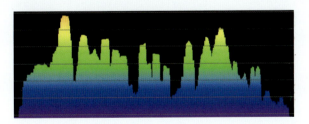

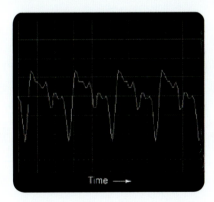

The view above is a big picture look: a single Black Box with lots of Detection points, or perhaps a piece of an enterprise network. Some areas are only blue, indicating a high level of Trust and lower Risk. But there is a lot of room for improvement in many areas.

Using a Zoom feature, perhaps the steep spike on the left will drill down to the Call Center. The blue on the far left might be sales. And so on. Each area, with an ANS

Finally, the oscilloscope view. What we see in this kind of display is either a single or cumulative (summing) analogue signal displayed over time. Since analogue signals add and subtract so easily, this view, I am guessing, would be useful in diagnostics and forensics in the future.

Analogue Epilogues

Policy Makers:
Your Turn

You now know how we CAN measure security. Quantitatively.

Often, Government and Enterprise Policy is based upon security and privacy controls that we all know **do not work**. Many of these controls are no more than a single outpost on the Maginot Line of network defense. What if there was a security model that is mathematically justifiable? One that works for coding, networking and the human and physical aspects of security. And what if that model provides quantitative criteria for security? Real solid math?

Let's suppose this new security model (we could call it ANS) could identify the millions of users whose computers are infected with malware that makes them part DDoS, Spam, and other hostile botnets. What should public and privacy policy be? Do we help them or persecute them? What if we could identify the specific IoT device causing mayhem? How would policy be written, then, and who is responsible for its breach?

What if we could measure, under strict controls, the relative efficacy of cyber-security products, and compare them. How would purchasing and liability policy change? What if we could reduce credit-card risk by 1,000% with one simple change. How would policy differ. And finally, how would this affect the forensics and business of cyber-insurance.

Let's write a policy!

Speed of Signal

The speed of light is: 299,792,458 meters per second and one second equals 10^9 nanoseconds. So,

> **(299,792,458 m/sec) x (1 s/10^9 ns) = 0.299792458** meters per nanosecond **(~.3m)**

One meter is as 39.37 inches, so,

> **(0.299792458 m/sec) x (39.37 in m/sec) = 11.8** inches per nanosecond.

One foot is 12 inches. Light in vacuum travels approximately one foot in one nanosecond.

The speed of electrical impulses (signal, bits, etc.) over a wire, known as the Velocity Factor, is always less than the speed of light. Depending upon the kind of hardware transmission connection, the Velocity Factor (VF) ranges from roughly 50-80% of the speed of light. So, with a VF or 50%, bits move at about 6 inches per nanosecond.

In fiber-optic communications, the term Refractive Index, always a number > 1, is referenced to the speed of light in a vacuum. Roughly, for fast approximations:

> Speed of light in a vacuum: ~300,000,000 m/sec
> Speed of light over fiber optics: ~200,000,000 m/sec

So, the larger the Refractive Index, the slower the bits move.

Optical Fiber Type	Wavelength	Refractive Index	Distance*
Brand A (G.652)	1310 nm	1.4677	204.260 m/µs
	1550 nm	1.4682	204.191 m/µs
Brand A (G.655)	1550 nm	1.468	204.218 m/µs
	1625 nm	1.469	204.079 m/µs
Brand B (G.652)	1310 nm	1.467	204.357 m/µs
	1550 nm	1.468	204.220 m/µs
Brand B (G.655)	1550 nm	1.470	203.940 m/µs
	1625 nm	1.470	203.940 m/µs

* Distance = Speed of Light (299.792m/µs) / Refractive Index

Fiber allows communications of about of roughly .3 meters (8 inches) per nanosecond, (.3m/ 10^{-9})

Wall Street Bitches at Me

While discussing ANS with folks hither and yon over the last couple of years, several mentioned that Wall Street Traders may not like the fact that "security takes time". Well, I can't help that. Sorry. The math is the math. You may not like the answer, but there it is.

You might recall Wall Street firms competing for massively high-speed trading profits and wanting to connect their wide-area connections between major centers with the shortest possible Layer 0 – physical routing. Since they compute massive profits by the nanosecond, even a few feet difference can create a competitive advantage. So, we're at light speed. Right? Well, no, not even close – and here's the math to show how distance affects Analogue Network Security architecture.

Let's say that two critical trading platforms are located 100,000 meters (~62 miles) from each other. With the rule of thumb that the speed of light over fiber optics is 200,000,000 m/sec, then bits are moved that distance in:

$$[(100{,}000\text{m})/.3 \text{ m/sec}] * .67 = 223{,}333\text{ns}$$
(or 223 microseconds, or .22ms)

For global trading concerns this matters. In my view, the "wire" from point to point, should do absolutely nothing other than move bits reliably. *(Let's not get into passive interception techniques here. That's another question entirely.)*

In addition to this time component, called latency, the ANS architect would likely have, at each terminus, an authentication checkpoint. Today, that's a pretty static process, but it, too, can be measured in the time domain. If, however, the security architect says, "Damn, I'd like to add an additional layer of detection, and perhaps perform an OOB authentication on specifically designated types of transactions…", the feedback path would in this 10^5 meter case, be between .22ms (over fiber) and .14ms through a wireless electromagnetic communication channel. Then, one would need to add the time for the retransmission of the authentication. So, .22ms could rapidly increase by a factor of three or four.

Does that matter? That is for the ANS architect to determine with the business units and by calculating Trust Factor and Risk into the equation. Perhaps a non-trade communication with its own security protocol is processed every 1,000 trades to re-vet the integrity of the Trust Factor between the entities. Our sawtooth wave, used to visualize the min-max security boundaries, will be oscillating exceedingly quickly. *(Think analogue oscilloscope-like displays.)* Don't forget, by the way, to add

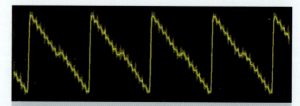

Degrading security over time as viewed on a typical oscilloscope.

into the OODA loop, for this example, the time required to decrypt the contents, no matter where that process sits in the chain.

Some of these issues will become of even greater importance in the future when nano-scale data centers co-locate with each other to increase time performance, and the more distant data centers will become home to less time-sensitive applications. When I think about architecting these days, I like to use a time domain overlay with today's technology performance factors as well as with a guesstimated future technology capability view and look to calculate the effects to determine their importance for a particular function.

Does it matter? The latency from Australia to New York is roughly 80ms. If you are trying to perform high speed Trust Factor verification between those two points for a given process, there is a decent chance that 80ms is going to matter. If you're talking about a time-based flip-flop verification that permits a 24 hour confirmation before revocation, the 80ms is meaningless.

The point is, you have to measure it. You need to know the time values of each process. You must consider the various elements in the chain that 'take time' and might be needed as part of your overall design considerations. One could, hypothetically, consider the cross-globe 80ms latency to be an unavoidable Delay, to be utilized as a natural part of a particular security process. ANS architects embrace time, positive or negative, and figure it in to their designs. Then they measure it.

The potential features and pitfalls of physical latency in ANS falls under Future Research. I just don't have all of the answers, but I do have a lot of questions I would like to explore.

Thanks to the Wall Street folks who brought this to my attention!

Impact of the Physical Layer on ANS

- Bandwidth is the maximum rate that information can be transferred, usually in bits/sec.

- Throughput (always <Bandwidth) is the actual rate that information is transferred.

- Latency is the time delay between the sender and the receiver, including any processing time or additional latency caused by nodes over which the information traverses. This may not be a constant and should be measured and monitored.

- Jitter is the unwanted variation of signal processing at the receiver and can cause additional delay.

- Error correction takes time. Include it in long distance time-crucial communications.

- Don't forget to include network protocol, security, and other transmission overheads that will reduce effective data throughput.

Then Measure it. Monitor it. Nothing is a constant in Analogue Network Security. By being aware of that and designing for it, we have the ability to maintain our boundary conditions and set acceptable and definable levels of risk in our designs.

THEN, MEASURE IT.

Analogue Epilogues

Errrorrz

Humans make errors. Machines make errors. So, long ago, we invented error detection and error correction techniques to insure data transmission integrity, especially over a noisy channel.

And when we talk about both bandwidth and noise in communications, we by necessity bow to the genius creator of information theory, Claude Shannon, and his own analogue spin. Simply:

> ▶ The noisier the "channel" *(think a web conference!)* the less information gets through.
>
> ▶ If we add bits and bytes to the message (information) to compensate for the noise in the channel, the bandwidth goes down.

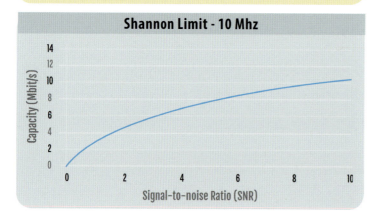

Shannon's Limit tells us mathematically the maximum rate (upper limit) data can be transmitted with errors approaching zero and it also rings of ANS, especially since his models were min-max and probabilistic as well. Everything above the line is unachievable; everything below the line is the mathematical compromise between bandwidth and noise.

Analogue Epilogues

Immediately, we see another parallel in information theory error control to my way of thinking. There are two pieces:

- Error Detection (by any schema)
- Error Correction (by any schema; which I call Reaction, to potentially include Remediation, but not required)

Every error correcting process takes time. Adding error correcting bits takes more time to process and there is less effective bandwidth, thus less information transfer per specified time period. Just the math. Can't help it.

Yet the point is, we have a long, tenured theoretical, engineering, and practical foundation in error control that should be able to provide some strong analogue analogies for security. Oddly enough, the answer will be roughly the same:

> Error Control takes time. Think, $D(t) + R(t)$.
> Error Control is a form of Security.
> Security takes time.

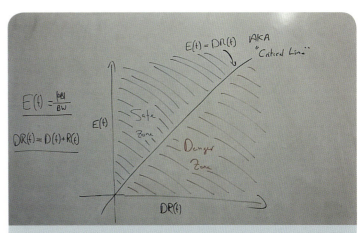

Mark cogitating the ROC-like curve in an inverse-Shannon view, a la ANS.

333

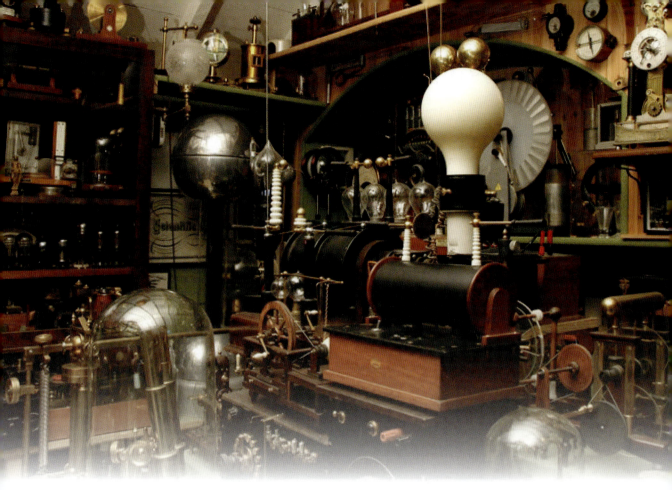

SIX SIGMA IN NETWORKING

When we speak of results and performance in analogue terms, "0" and "1" are essentially gone. We also must eradicate infinity.

So, every other number is available in the middle, and this is where thinking about Six Sigma (6σ) becomes relevant. For me, thinking of 6σ adds an additional layer of depth (flavour or colour) for analyzing system and performance requirements in the analogue view.

Analogue Epilogues

# of Employees	# of Decisions	Per Time Period	Per 200 Work Days/Yr	Delta Six Sigma Trust Factor	Delta Six Sigma Risk
1,000	20	Day	4,000,000	-17.65%	177.65%
1,000	50	Day	10,000,000	-194.12%	294.12%
1,000	100	Day	20,000,000	-488.24%	588.24%
10,000	20	Day	40,000,000	-1076.47%	1176.47%
10,000	50	Day	100,000,000	-2841.18%	2941.18%
10,000	100	Day	200,000,000	-5782.35%	5882.35%
Six Sigma = 3.4*10^6	3,400,000				

# of Employees	# of Decisions	Per Time Period	Per 200 Work Days/Yr	Delta Six Sigma Trust Factor	Delta Six Sigma Risk
10	10	Day	20,000	99.41%	0.59%
100	10	Day	200,000	94.12%	5.88%
1,000	10	Day	2,000,000	41.18%	58.82%
10,000	10	Day	20,000,000	-488.24%	588.24%
25,000	10	Day	50,000,000	-1370.59%	1470.59%
100,000	10	Day	200,000,000	-5782.35%	5882.35%
Six Sigma = 3.4*10^6	3,400,000				

Use six sigma as your baseline, compared to the number of events you have to defend against.

Think for a moment about Mark's TP-FP calculations earlier in this chapter. To me, the implications are even more reason to take his ANS math seriously.

Briefly, Six Sigma is a process that produces no more than 3.4 defects per million events.

In the security world, for example, a company of 10,000 people, each of who must decide exactly what to do with an average of 25 emails a day, for 200 work days, $5 * 10^7$ event decisions must be made.

$$(10^5 * 25 * 200 = 50,000,000 = 5*10^7)$$

Six Sigma requires an accuracy of 3.4 per 10^6 events. That's more than an order of magnitude of "Not Good Enough."

So, someone claiming Six Sigma performance must be careful to be very specific as to what that means: the *process of development*, or as I have heard from time to time, the *efficacy of their product* over time.

While it was developed initially to improve manufacturing efficiencies, much of six sigma is about process; putting something into a process (Black

Box) and getting the desired result out. We definitely want to further explore the application of six sigma to cybersecurity in future research.

# of Employees	# of Decisions	Per Time Period	Per 200 Work Days/Yr	Delta Six Sigma Trust Factor
1,000	20	Day	4,000,000	-17.65%
1,000	50	Day	10,000,000	-194.12%
1,000	100	Day	20,000,000	-488.24%
10,000	20	Day	40,000,000	-1076.47%
10,000	50	Day	100,000,000	-2841.18%

Looking at the chart above, I am using Six Sigma as my reference: $3.4*10^6$. Then, consider a range of employees, and in the above case, say that there is a Phishing Email Detection Device that the vendor says will accurately catch phishing emails, and I use Six Sigma as that base with a given measurably known $D(t)$. That means that only 3.4 potentially hostile emails will get past the Detection Mechanism. The final decision is left to the human.

Detection Error	Detections in Sample	Error Rate	Trust Factor
1	1	100%	0.000000
1	10	10.0000%	0.900000
1	100	1.0000%	0.990000
1	1,000	0.1000%	0.999000
1	10,000	0.0100%	0.999900
1	100,000	0.0010%	0.999990
1	1,000,000	0.0001%	0.999999

For larger enterprises, the requisite Trust Factor increases exponentially.

For small companies, with fewer emails, the Trust Factor is high and the Risk is low. As the number of decisions increases, over a period of one year in the above case, see what happens? Our Trust Factor goes down. For larger companies, the Six Sigma performance is not meaningful, since the sheer number of decision events is huge. We need our defensive network processes to work with exceedingly high levels of performance.

Ergo, feedback and delay can compensate for real-world sloppiness.

What to do? A few thoughts.

Historically, security folks have suggested that people and orgs use multiple detection products. From an ANS standpoint, we would then see that two independent BB Detection Mechanisms yields a significant increase in Trust Factor, as it did with the 2-Man Rule and as shown in Chapter 8, in the SMTP Ass Saver.

So, if both BB Alice and BB Bob are each trusted at .9, (**TF(a) and TF(b)**), we get:

$$P(A \cup B) = P(A) + P(B) - P(A \cap B)$$
$$P(.9 \text{ AND } .9) = P(.9) + P(.9) - P(.9 * .9)$$
$$= 1.8 - .81$$
$$= .99$$

That's about an order of magnitude increase in Trust Factor. This concept of using a TB-FF for Black Box Detection can be expanded to 3, 4 or more (using the model from the prior chapter, for example), depending upon the policy and design needs. Replacing Black Box Detection for Phishing with any detection process, at any level, from code to internetworking will show the same trending.

When we increase the time that allows the BB to detect an event (**D(t)**→ ∞), some detection or sensor products might see an increase in effectiveness. Others, might not. So, in the case of Phishing, setting up a 2 clock min-max system, adds to the overall Trust Factor and reduces risk, as it did with the 2-Man Rule.

3 Domains of ANS Integration

For whatever reasons, when folks think about network security they think coding and TCP/IP. I argue, though, that there are three highly intertwined domains, all of which should be part of a holistically coordinated approach, especially when we are dealing with feedback and loops.

The Domains Triad is needed to understand the consequences of detection and reaction in our Loops. If we stovepipe these domains, we stifle hope for robust security.

For example:

- A door alarm (physical detection) talks to a Boolean circuit (cyber) to make a decision.

- That decision can trigger a communication (cyber) to a alarm monitoring service where a person (human) will get involved in the loop. Perhaps an OOB verification call (cyber) to the location (physical) to speak with a real person. All three domains.

As we have discussed in this book, analogue security applies to all three domains, and it's the common metric of time in our OODA Loop that allows us to measure the $D(t) + R(t)$ processes, no matter which component, stand-alone or hybridized, we are talking about.

So, when I talk about adding feedback loops to some coded process, that feedback does not have to be cyber. It could easily be any OOB process, in the cyber, physical, or human domains. Sure, some take longer than others, but that's the point of designing systems with feedback and weighted

considerations: increase the efficacy of the process, and for good or bad, that adds some time. Optimizing, squeezing the loop, is the goal, of course. Which means, if we design a feedback loop, and time is of paramount concern, the use of a TB-FF, with a policy-based risk estimation of maximum $E(t)$, is our tool for bounding that risk.

When code asks for a human response, think I&A (Identification & Authentication), that's two interacting domains. When two keys are required for a safety deposit box, that's two domains – human and physical. If the bank's back-end has an electronic Boolean circuit, that's three domains, human, physical, and cyber.

When you start to think of security with feedback and OODA processes as core to your time-based design, answers you never thought of begin to appear.

That's what has happened to me. I am often asked somewhat abstract questions about various security issues. Usually, those questions tend to be framed in typical binary network "security-think"… so, I have to translate in my mind, and add the dynamic analogue conditions that might just be missing from the way the question was phrased.

These days, I tend to answer questions with time as part of that answer. Ideally, questions will include time, as well.

I absolutely love this piece by Giovanni Magana. For me it encompasses all things AVS: The cyber, human and physical domains; time and music, feedback, synergy - I just love it.

AI & ANS

An amazing amount of money, more than $40B has been spent on AI research as of July 2018. It's supposed to be "smart." It's supposed to make our lives "better."

Whether we call it Deep Learning, AI, Hierarchical Learning, Machine Learning, or Synaptic Weighted Neural Networks or whatever, the application of non-linear feedforward and feedback systems is integral to the neural net forming "opinions" upon which decisions are made. OODA, of course. I see a potential for adding Weighted Neural Networks in much more than dynamic Trust Factor engines. What if, instead of the linear time-based feedback mechanism in the TB-FF, we replace the time element with some form of neural bias?

What would be the result? Updates based upon behavior and the reactions to the decision process would constantly improve, thereby Squeezing the Defensive OODA Loop. The efficiency of Deep Learning is the results of optimizing time/Trust Factor relationships.

But, here's the problem: AI is not neutral. It is as biased as you or me or anyone else who has a preference (bias), a bigotry (bias), a pre-conceived opinion (bias,) a lifetime of experiences (bias), an education (bias)… everything that makes us human makes us biased, to some degree or another. And so it is for AI, too.

Science (and Bayes, of course) says that progress is made by refining our conclusions

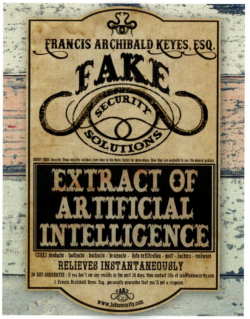

With the over-exuberant permission of Francis Archibald Keyes, Esq. himself - and FakeSecurity.com Without question, the best booth at SF RSA-2018.

based upon new data, and so, too, it is with our neuro-silicon brethren. In fact, AI may be more biased that we mere, clearly fallible, carbon-unit mortals.

How can that be?

Bad data. A headline from The Verge proclaimed, "Twitter taught Microsoft's AI chat-bot to be a racist asshole in less than a day." This Tweeted sentiment says a great deal: it "went from 'humans are super cool' to full nazi in <24 hrs and I'm not at all concerned about the future of AI."

AI is not a binary decision. Hundreds of AI-enabling algorithms cause AI-ish entities to make decisions in hundreds of different ways. A vendor who says, "We use AI" is basically saying, "we speak some unknown language that even we don't understand, we cannot predict our behavior, and we have no idea how we come to the conclusions we do." And the AI-pundits want to run the world with this. I'm calling bullshit.

==Would you want to run your business/life/mission-critical-anything such that you have Zero Idea how decisions are made?==

Let's look at three areas I have real problems with *(the nonsense I heard at RSA-2018 locked-and-loaded this rant)*: 1) Data; 2) Ethics; and 3) Adversarialism.

First: It's all about the data. An AI engine must be trained, no matter which of the hundreds of engines you choose, integrate or permutate. Training datasets are huge. The huger the betterer they say. Billions upon billions of data points "train" the AI-engine, and designers do their best to arrive at a neutral bias to kick-start their engine in the wild.

However, is the data neutral? Security surveys often attempt to determine the current threat landscape. So they ask people. But, what kind of people? What level in the organization… is it hard data or is it only supported anecdotally… does that person have the knowledge to properly parse the data… how is the surveyed data 'weighted' (bias!)… and is it re-biased over time, and according to what specifics of derivative weighting one level down? Is there a double-blind or… And so it goes… and then it's a surprise that a racist bot rises from the cumulative ignorance of how the AI actually works?

For the inchoate AI-foray into security, for us to rely 100% upon (with how much weight?) an AI-engine's answer is, in ANS terms, foolish. Using AI-results as a piece of a puzzle for a human to digest, evaluate and make operational decisions by, makes so much more sense.

Keep in mind the initial training data may bear little resemblance to training data at some future Time T(n), or T(n+1) etc., whether *n* is an hour or a year. If the initial training data was "trusted" by some defined methodology, and we don't know how an AI makes its decisions, by what mechanism do we trust the new dataset?

Second is ethics. I'm going to apply what I call Trolleyological Conundra to cyber-kinetic automatons, namely drones and self-driving cars. We all know the classic trolley problems, to wit:

> ▶ Pull the switch and consciously choose to kill 2 people, or…
>
> ▶ Do not pull the switch and allow 3 people to be killed.
>
> *(This assume all people are of equal value. Complicate it with old folks, white folks, children, firefighters… and then, in a split second, you must weigh their relative values and decide who lives and who dies.)*

The next gut-wrenching conundrum for you to consider is:

> ▶ If you do nothing, don't pull the switch, 3 people will die, or…
>
> ▶ In order to save the three people, you have to physically touch and push one person to their certain death.

This is what we are asking for when we hope for pizza deliveries by drone and that a driverless taxi will take us across town. We are asking imperfect and unknowable AIs to make life and death decisions.

Let's say someone at Uber or Google or Tesla or any of the hundreds of AI houses, decide:

One 80-year old = three teenagers in value, and that the AI can determine, with 99.6% accuracy how old people are. *(They can't. Not yet.)* They also have to decide:

Two middle-aged black folks = how many middle-aged white folks? Those ethics must be programmed into the AI-engine.

Now, what about in India, with its traditional caste system? How many Dalit lives (the lowest "untouchables") are equal to one Brahman's life (the highest) worth? In a strict Muslim culture, are the ethics the same? Is the life of an obviously well-garbed cleric worth more or less than western tourists in Bermuda shorts?

Do all of the cultures on Earth come up with one acceptable set of ethical behaviors for every location? Or do AI-vendors have to come up with a suite of ethically different AI engines to be sold in each territory? And can I bring a U.S. centric AI-biased machine to Japan or Nigeria or Pakistan? Vice-versa?

I have not heard good answers to any of these questions in the last few years. Many AI-thought leaders echo my hesitancies and offer stern warnings about pre-natal deployment before these issues are all considered.

Finally, there's adversarialism. Take a gaming-AI. Clone it. Instruct the two to play some game against each other. They will both learn. They will update. They will become proficient. And we don't know how. With the advent of hostile cyber-AIs on the horizon, we are definitely on the precipice of post-Information-Warfare, since in my original 1988 thesis I put humans in control of cyberwar.

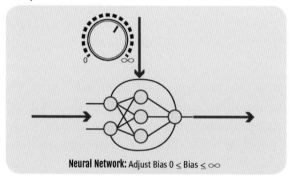

Neural Network: Adjust Bias $0 \leq$ Bias $\leq \infty$

So what is AI good for? IMHO – averaging. Approximation. Probabilistic leaning and tendencies. Anything but a binary response. Giving us a hint. Taking an absurd amount of data, that humans have hopefully been able to weight to some extent, to reflect the desired initial bias? Medicine. Big-date hard science. Business insights. Predictions. Language translation. Customer service. Weathercasting. Traffic control. Driving, perhaps, but knowing sufficiently well in advance when to tell the human, "Grab the fricking wheel or we all die!" Will autonomous vehicles choose to protect passengers versus pedestrians... and by what learned bias metrics?

How do we average or approximate the ethical values of where a pizza drone should crash when it is a single point of kinetic failure? Of all of the people on 5th Avenue at lunch hour, which lucky person is chosen to be the socially acceptable victim? Or does it willy-nilly choose to plow through the nearest large window, aimed at a corner office executive? How do we ethically program technology in AI's version of the Kobayashi Maru, a vast number of which AI is certain to encounter!

AI for Security. Yeah, there is some value, but how do you distinguish between "Vendor-A's AI-smart thingy using algorithm-1701A" and "Vendor-B's hybrid algorithm using both V/31337 and THX1138"? And I don't believe that enterprise customers can confidently say that this next-gen tech is all that much better than the next-gen stuff they bought last year.

So what do we do? Measure them. Duh!

AI systems are just about, by definition, Black Boxes with an unknowable inside; research is being conducted to develop methodologies for determining the efficacy of AI systems, the way that ANS does with traditional Black Boxes. But, we have an added variable, don't we? Bias. Initial bias will demonstrate one set of results. Adjusting the bias through internal self-regulation will result, possibly, in a different set of results.

And then we have to worry about the bias being shifted over time by:

- Unknowable effects of dynamic feedback over time.
- How updated datasets, or even corrupted datasets (that never happens, does it?) affect the decision outputs.
- How human poisoning, vis a vis the MS-racist-bot, will affect the bias, the hidden layers and ultimately decision making.
- How Offensive-AI devices can and will affect detection-reaction AI implementations.
- Will poly- or metamorphic tactics from an Offensive-AI render defensive AI useless?
- Will they escape?

I have the good fortune to be asked to run a series of debates and discussions around the world to focus on these exceedingly complex issues that affect everything in our lives, and certainly in our industry.

My hope is that we do not ignore this future as the Information Warfare thesis was ignored thirty years ago. My hope is we don't binarily allow ourselves to mindlessly hand over control and decision making to beings which are, from a homo sapiens sapiens view, aliens.

Mark, Clarence Chio (my AI-mentor and reviewer), and I conceptually add AI to "Future Work" on many deep levels. And, I will not stop being a PITA on all things AI until someone can prove to me, even with reliable probabilistic determination, how AI will make security better… or completely FUBAR everything in its path.

Without self-awareness, self-correction is merely a mechanical versus ethical update.

Predicting the Future

In Dean Buonomano's amazing book *Your Brain is a Time Machine*, one of the greatest take-aways was (in my words), "The brain only has two purposes: to remember what it has sensed from its environment and to anticipate (predict) the future." The time machine analogy is implicit.

Point is, if we evolve detection in depth with enough participating entities (see "DDoS" in Chapter 8), we will, over time, if we choose, be able to inbue the OOB Reaction Matrix with the ability to anticipate future acts. This will be one of the more fascinating and long-term studies, especially when applied to a global ANS D/R system.

AI-OOB-OODA. Oooh…

Seriously, get that book!

Songwriter Carly Simon dated my friend and neighbor, Jeff; I dated her cousin. We were all in the rock'n'roll business and frolicked on the Upper West Side in Manhattan. That has nothing to do with security, except that this book reminded me of those halcyon days of *Anticipation*.

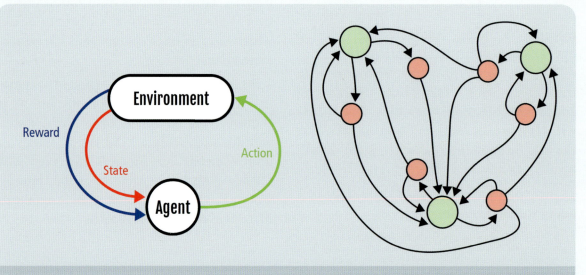

A typical deep learning network. On the left is the abstract feedback, OODA-style. On the right, you can see how weighting in feedback and feed forward paths changes the Trust Factors based upon experience. A good starting point is *Deep Learning Adaptive Computation and Machine Learning* by Ian Goodfellow & Yoshua Bengio.

Hiring The Unhireable

Synopsis.

We need new thinkers. The global shortage of Security Experts, estimated to be as many as > 2-3 million, is due to two fundamental institutionalized modes of failure:

> 1. We teach success. I believe that in so many ways, our educational system has failed because our educational system does not encourage failure. We don't teach or reward failure. Constructive failure is a variable that increases success over time. Just ask Edison. Knowing what doesn't work is an analogue function on the knowledge spectrum. And, if adhered to, saves time.
>
> 2. We can't find the mental or social flexibility to hire those we most need, who, in many cases, are those we are least inclined to associate with simply because they are different.

Hiring the Unhireable is an analysis I first provided to DHS circa 2010 on what we collectively need to do if we hope to succeed at network security. We have had plenty of experience on how to fail. We know what doesn't work.

Let's try something different.

> ▶ **Hiring the Unhireable: TED-style talk from RSA:**
> https://www.youtube.com/watch?v=C_9cdzLi6-0
>
> ▶ **Hiring the Unhireable:** (PDF)
> WinnSchwartau.com

Hiring the Unhireable Question Guide:

- ▶ What is "Normal?"
- ▶ Do you want or need "Normal?"
- ▶ ADD, ADHD Friendly?
- ▶ Unique Spectrum Skills?
- ▶ Embrace Failure?
- ▶ Rely on Personality Tests?
- ▶ Degrees or Certificates?
- ▶ 9-5, Seriously?
- ▶ Commute or Telecommute?
- ▶ Stop Drug Testing?
- ▶ Take Advantage of Age?
- ▶ Should HR Be 1st Interview?

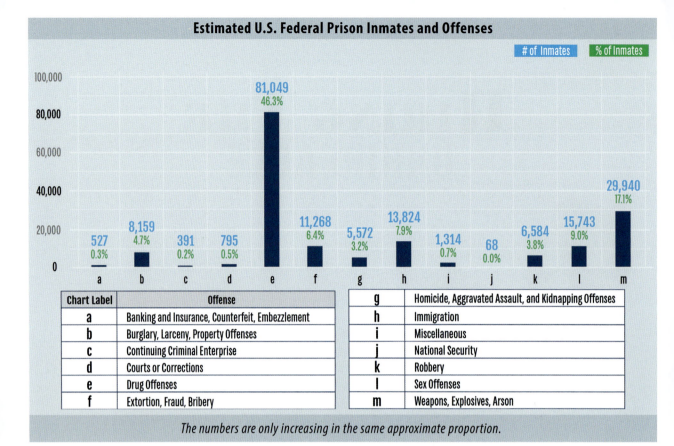

Prison In The Cloud:
MY OUTRAGE

If you don't agree with me, that's cool. **But, the U.S. prison system is broken.**

- We spend $80B annually to incarcerate criminals and another $100B in associated costs to U.S. society. *(Prison Policy Initiative, 2017)*
- Some 50% of prisoners did not commit a violent crime.
- A large % of the prison population committed low-level drug use offenses.
- Should white collar criminals be placed side-by-side with hardened criminals?
- Should Granny be sent to prison for stupid shit?
- Recidivism sits at about 75%.
- The physical and mental abuse of prison life can be astounding.
- Prisons are the best Criminal Universities known to man.
- And it goes on…
- Oh… and should a "criminal hacker" be put into jail, too?

Analogue Epilogues

IN MY MIND:

We have the technology to electronically "imprison" a person instead of sending him/her to the "slammer." Think as always, **P(t) > D(t) + R(t)**.

JUST IMAGINE...

- A Great Criminal Firewall in the Cloud.
- Tracking technology so the offender's location is always known. *(Detection)*
- Sensor technologies to detect the use of alcohol, drugs, or other "prohibited" items while serving a sentence. *(Did I say Detection?)*
- Sensors that detect the use of WiFi, computers, and other specific technologies that might be prohibited during the sentence.
- Sensors that correlate the "prisoner's" activities 24/7, anywhere, to their sentence.
- Tamper proofing the "device" from removal, modification or, shall I say it, hacking. *(Detection)*
- Maybe an implant. Yes, it's the ultimate in remote surveillance and privacy violations... but, it's better than going to prison in many cases. *(Think of if it as a Second Chance. Behave and stay out of jail.)* Benefits?
- Some people screw up. Non-violently. Should we not try to help modify their behavior?
- Is it not more valuable to let some criminals provide real community service, maintain their job and family life than destroy it all?
- Save tens of billions of dollars annually?
- Humanize our penal system.
- The social and economic benefits can be enormous.

OUR CHALLENGE

What if the security community and ANS concepts could help?

- Cut $30-$40B of unnecessary spending on incarceration.
- Allow non-violent criminals to "Give Back" as part of their sentence.
- Stop a system that creates criminals by its very existence?
- ...What if?

Design a Detection in Depth and Reaction system, based upon ANS that will fit within the spirit of these tenets. It's got to be better than what we are doing now.

We have the technology. We can re-invent the penal system to work in a much more humane way that can be a positive for society.

And that is the premise of the Prison in the Cloud.

How Much is that Data in the Window?

I propose as axiomatic:

- The Value of Data changes over time.
- Every network resource is not of equal criticality.

Then I ask:

1. How much is a five bedroom, ranch-style house with a pool on two acres and a private lake worth?
2. How much is a 1931 Bugatti automobile worth?
3. How much is the world's oldest tube condenser microphone worth?

Answer: Whatever someone is willing to pay for them.

In the real, physical world of commerce, the free market economy does a pretty good job of establishing value; both perceived and real. Perceived value is how much folks think something is worth, and real value is how much hard-earned cash they shell out to actually pay for it. However, as economist Joel Kurtzman pointed out, we are in desperate need of an economic model which allows us to measure the value of that great intangible: information. *(No crypto-currrency tangents here... That's a conversation for the future!)*

Information is the only asset that can exist in multiple places at once.

Assume I have a USB stick, with information that is worth $1 Million, but can only be sold to one of many different potential buyers. Now, I make a copy of that stick. How much is each one worth? Are they both worth $1M each; have I doubled the value? Or are they each now only worth $500K; have I halved their value but maintained a constant total value? A copy of any kind of data falls into this conundrum. Data is worth the sum total of what people are willing to pay for it, nothing more, nothing less.

But what if the contents of the $1Million USB illicitly end up posted on the Dark Web for $50 a copy and is resold hundreds of times? What is its value then? Is the information really worth any less? Would anyone pay you, the legitimate owner, $1M for it anymore? Or is it worth the same sum total to the free market economy, but distributed amongst different people, be them legitimate or criminal?

Information value is a dynamic asset that constantly changes over time. A big secret may have some discreet value associated with it when it is secret, but once it leaks out, it is worth less (not worthless). Once that info becomes common knowledge, some or perhaps all of its intrinsic value has dissipated. Such is the case with product planning, car design, financial reports, insider trading, leaks of shocking series finales… and so on. So, in this case, the value of information decreases over time.

On the other hand, information can increase in value over time. Some examples of this are "ideas ahead of their time, waiting for the right time to be introduced." The source-code of a product that becomes very popular, goes up in value, as does the value of a company which is successful. As the finishing touches on designs are made, the value goes up, as does a well-honed customer list for the criminal element, or a much appreciated piece of art. The value of the secrets behind a unique marketing dominating process can dramatically increase.

No matter which approach you favor, value is a dynamic analogue estimation that changes with distribution and time. One could invoke an entropic interpretation, and I hope that the industry will follow this line of thinking to add an *entropic metric of information valuation* to Analogue Network Security. Consider some estimates of relative value at least (Here comes Bayes, again!) when designing enterprise security architectures.

These principles guide a great deal of the global economy. The question, though, when applying ANS techniques, is "how do I know which data is really worth something, so I know where to place my security budget dollars wisely?" Great question, for which I will resort to the fine art of approximation. Analogue.

Viewing a network and data assets as a single vaporous unitary whole, I suggest we need to understand the real value and mission criticality of resources and data. The following might assist as an early step in isolating the electronic keys to the kingdom from the worthless clutter.

MISSION CRITICAL

If this info gets out, we are out of business. If this portion of our networks are attacked with DoS, we are out of business. If this hits the newspapers, it will cost us an absolute fortune and we won't recover from the losses. If this gets out, we go to jail. If this is attacked, the water supply (power, gas, other utility) is shut off. The Space-bound launch vehicle will blow up. The phones won't work. The bank stops functioning. You get the idea.

ALMOST MISSION CRITICAL

The damage is tremendous, extremely costly (political, economic), but it is survivable. Barely. If these services go away we are going to be crucified by the media, customers will leave in droves, and we will go to the edge of disaster.

DAMN, THAT HURTS

If this stuff gets out it will hurt; it will cost us, and it will sting, but we can take it, if we really, really have to. If this gets out, we can spin doctor our way back to health. If these services go away, we have a heck of a lot of catch-up to do and a lot of financial losses to contend with.

NEGLIGIBLE

If this information is leaked or stolen, it's no disaster. It might cost us a bit; it might prove embarrassing, but there is no major impact upon the organization's ability to do business. If this non-revenue producing website goes down, that is not good, but it's just a disruption.

WHO CARES?

Take the information, have a ball with it. We don't really care what you do with it. It's public, or we want it made public. They're all ads, anyway. If you modify it, no one will care or even notice. Or we'll sue you. Denial of Service does not find a home in this category.

Part of the ANS security review process is to fill in charts like Figs. 9B and 9C on the next pages. There are three steps to take.

> 1. Identify the existence of the information which fits into these categories for various portions of a network. Ideally, consider Confidentiality, Integrity, and Availability, in all three domains: Cyber, Human, and Physical.

Estimate for Confidentiality/ Integrity/Availability	Company Proprietary	Employee Private	Customer Private	Business Partner, Government, Other
The results will be absolutely disasterous with no chance of economic or political recovery.				
There will be severe financial, political, or other undesirable results, but we will survive.				
It's gonna cost us big time, but spin doctoring will take care of it.				
Negligible effects, but we still really don't want it to happen.				
Publish it all you want. It's free, please take it.				

Fig. 9B

2. Specify the logical, networked-based storage location of the assets you have categorized above. This process defines the pathing and logical organization of the assets with respect to the rest of the network. Don't forget to calculate in the Cloud.

3. Lastly, specify the physical location of the logical assets location in step #2 above.

By charting this process, you will find a variety of surprises.

1. Mission Critical information may be distributed across several applications, running on different platforms and different Operating Systems. It may be backed up in clouds around the globe (Cloud = Somebody Else's Computer) and there is always an unknown factor, too, to consider.

2. There is only one Mission Critical application and asset base, and it all resides on one physical repository.

3. Who Cares information co-resides with Almost Mission Critical assets.

Understanding the matrix of asset location is critical ANS architecture. It assists with the valuing time and the impact analogue techniques such as padding and delay might have on specific threats against specific assets.

Using the ANS approach, we do not want or expect all assets to be of the same value. We do not expect to secure an entire network or enterprise with the same diligence. That has been the binary Fortress Mentality approach for decades: secure the entire network as a singular whole, and treat all assets as equal.

From the 1970s on, many military organizations played with MLS, Multi-Level Security. They wanted to logically separate Confidential, Secret, Top Secret information using MAC, Mandatory Access Controls and "object labeling." Each MLS file is to be specifically labeled with a sensitivity flag. This way, a lower cleared user could 'write up' to a higher level, but not read the more sensitive files, while a more highly cleared user can 'read down' to lower sensitivity levels, but not write to them for fear of info-leakage.)

Consider the following situation. You have found that you are storing a myriad of sensitivity classifications on a single computer. Some are truly mission critical where you desire limited access to a small number of people and others are of inconsequential value, but are needed by a great many people on a regular basis. You are faced with a choice.

1. Design, implement, and manage a security solution on this platform which serves both of your disparate security needs, or
2. Move one set of assets to a logically and physically isolated platform, and/or apply uber-enhanced authentication and secure each to their respective needs.

The first approach implies some sort of Multi-Level Security solution which is difficult to design and implement, not to mention terribly expensive to buy and maintain. The second is much simpler and more cost effective to accomplish.

I fear few organizations have gone through an exercise like this because they are so darned difficult to do. Maybe… someone could *productize* this with ANS - style thinking?

Fig. 9C

	Confidentiality	Integrity	Availability	Physical	Cyber	People	Professional	Personal	Mobile
Confidentiality									
Integrity									
Availability									
Physical									
Cyber									
People									
Professional									
Personal									
Mobile									

ANS Design Tools Cheat Sheet

There's a lot of stuff involved in Analogue Network Security. A few (awesome) reviewers told me to build an appendix; I asked, "How about a full-on Cheat Sheet?"

This cheat sheet aggregates key concepts, important formulas and charts, and reference data into one place. Please use your wits to help expand and refine ANS. This is just a start, and I look forward to your contributions. A printable version can be found at AnalogueNetworkSecurity.com.

THE BASICS

$$M1(v) > M2(v)$$

If Man 1 (from the Bear example), has greater velocity (a vector of speed and direction) than Man 2, Man 1 wins and Man 2 gets eaten by the bear. See OODA.

∞ **is the enemy of security.** If any of your designs allow ∞ in an answer, you have effectively, zero security.

$$P(t) > D(t) + R(t)$$

For security to exist, protection time must be measurably and provably greater than the sum of Detection and Reaction Times. The goal is:

$$[D(t) + R(t)] \to 0$$
$$D(t) + R(t) = E(t)$$

E(t) (Exposure Time) = the sum of Detection and Reaction Time. E(t) helps with calculating Trust Factors and Risk.

If $P(t) = 0$, then $D(t) + R(t) = E(t)$
If $P(t) < [D(t) + R(t)]$, then
$E(t) = \{[D(t) + R(t)] - P(t)\}$

DETECTION IN DEPTH

$$P(t) > D(t) + R(t)$$
$$\wedge \qquad \wedge$$
$$\wedge \qquad P(rl) > D(rl) + R(rl)$$
$$P(dl) > D(dl) + R(dl)$$
$$\wedge$$
$$P(d2) > D(d2) + R(d2)$$

Adding security depth to Detection and Reaction channels.

Zeros We Love

$$D(t) \to 0 \qquad E(t) \to 0$$
$$R(t) \to 0 \qquad OODA(t) \to 0$$

Range of Human Sense Dectection Times

Vision: 150ms
Hearing: 250ms
Taste: 500ms-1,000ms
Tactile: 700ms
Odor: 1,000ms

t = 0   t = 1,000ms

Gives a sense of the range of human detection processes. How long does it take someone to *Click on Stupid Shit*? When we deal with humans, we need to express their time-values in equations.

BOOLEAN

Boolean logic and truth tables are essential to the hybridization of analogue and binary functions for ANS.

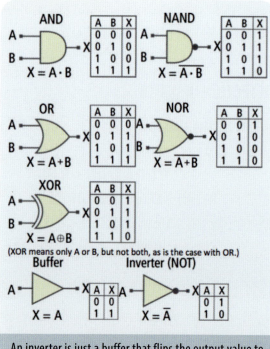

An inverter is just a buffer that flips the output value to the opposite of the input. XOR means only A or B, but not both, as is the case with OR.

ANS BUILDING BLOCKS

When I designed electronic circuits, we had building blocks of components. It's the same thing with ANS. We rarely ever used hard math, either; it was 99% algebra. When we didn't know the design answer, we'd often write T&C next to a resistor on a schematic (T&C means *try and see* for yourself). We'd add a potentiometer, twist and tweak until we got the desired results, measure the values, and presto! We had the answer with no hard math.

When thinking analogue, getting close is often good enough (like horseshoes or Bayes), and probably a far sight closer than we are today. ANS designs will employ lots of variables, some of which are policy based, measured processes, or based upon external or third party dynamic performance and behavior.

THE TIME-BASED FLIP-FLOP (TB-FF)

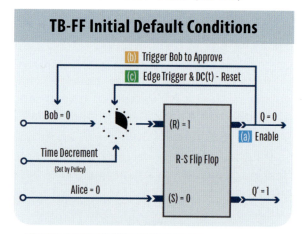

Truth Table: TB-FF

Alice (Set)	Bob (Approve)	Decrement (t)	Q = Enable
0	0	OFF	0
0	0	t > 0	0
0	0	t = 0	0
1	0	OFF	1
1	0	t > 0	1
1	0	t = 0	0
1	1	OFF	1
1	1	t > 0	1
1	1	t = 0	1
0	1	N/A	0
0	1	N/A	0
0	1	N/A	0

The Time-Based Flip-Flop is perhaps the most foundational aspect of ANS. Keep in mind that they can be concatenated, use independent or synchronous clocks, be combined in countless Boolean feedback networks.

This one circuit needs to be understood intuitively to maximize the power of ANS. The Truth Table may not be intuitively obvious until you use it a lot.

DELAY LINE

Time Delay: Adjust $0 \leq Delay(t) < Max$

The delay line variable is time, $DL(t)$. In many processes, it's easy to show that $DL(t)$ should simply be greater than $E(t)$, which would then show $P(t) > D(t) + R(t)$. Figure in physical layer latency and the human element as well into any process.

Pause/Play are conceptual triggers to be used in delay lines, especially with dynamic inputs. I imagine the time variable can be automatically adjusted with multiple weighting and potentially neural approaches.

$DL(t)$: Delay Line (in time)

As a rule of thumb, if the introduced negative time $> E(t)$ (justifiably $> [D(t) + R(t)]$), security improves (and could be justifiable over time). Add Trust Factor for more complete answers.

PADDING

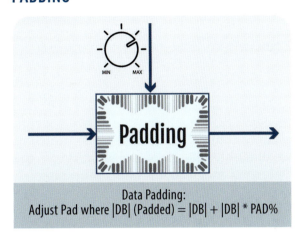

Data Padding:
Adjust Pad where $|DB|$ (Padded) $= |DB| + |DB| * PAD\%$

Padding of data with "random" or "garbage" data for obfuscation increases the dataset size; thus it takes more time to be extricated.

Given same transmission bandwidth, the data exfiltration rates can be extended by Padding measured as:

$100\% < $ Padding Factor $ < \infty \%$

$|DB|(2) = |DB|(1) * $ Padding (%)

Remember: $|DB|/BW = max(E(t))$

Bandwidth and dataset size are time dependent.

OOB CONTROL

The VCA approach is attractive for ANS Out of Band (OOB) controls. The audio circuit is analogous to TCP/IP data transmissions. The Envelope Generator and Control Voltage (CV) input is analogous to ANS style Out of Band security via a Detection/Reaction matrix.

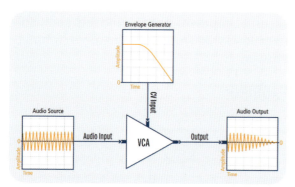

Think of an OOB Analogue circuit as having its own C&C Server with detection in depth security controls embedded in the protocols to diminish the effects of attacks on the Detection and Reaction Matrix processes.

COMPRESSOR

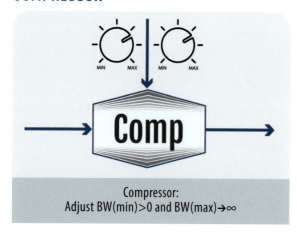

Compressor: Adjust BW(min)>0 and BW(max)→∞

LIMITER

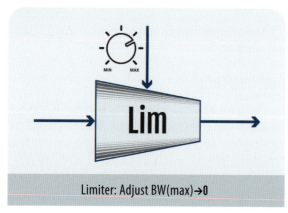

Limiter: Adjust BW(max)→0

1GB sec	Time	Data Extricated
	1 sec	1 GB
	1 min	60 GB
	1 hr	3.6 TB
100MB sec	Time	Data Extricated
90% reduction in data extraction	1 sec	100 MB
	1 min	6 GB
	1 hr	360 GB
10MB sec	Time	Data Extricated
99% reduction in data extraction	1 sec	10 MB
	1 min	600 MB
	1 hr	36 GB
1MB sec	Time	Data Extricated
99.9% reduction in data extraction	1 sec	1 MB
	1 min	60 MB
	1 hr	3. GB

Bandwidth Compression and Limiting on specific data-rich services increases exfiltration time quickly. As part of a Reaction Matrix, the positive security effects can be exceedingly fast.

FEEDBACK

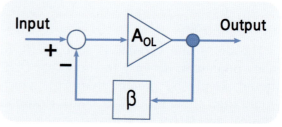

Without feedback, we approach infinity. We need limiting in the feedback loop. All control circuits should have feedback governors to maintain an upper-time-bound substantially less than ∞. Ideally, the feedback mechanism will be set to upper-bounds by policy, such as E(t-max), which defines the risk in time, and then we add Trust Factor.

Negative feedback controls a system, while positive feedback creates runaway (growth) conditions. Oscillation between the two mechanisms is seen everywhere we look.

BLACK BOX

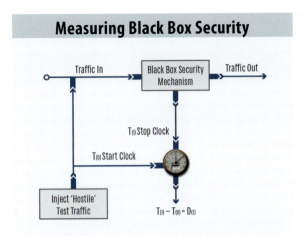

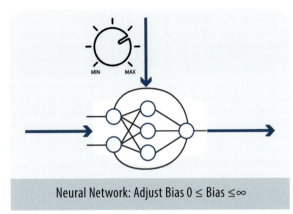

Neural Network: Adjust Bias $0 \leq \text{Bias} \leq \infty$

Security Black Boxes and controls "do" something, based upon one or more sets of input conditions. The output can be a shaped version of the input. A trigger output such as in detection applications, tells us when a Black Box event occurs. A gating function based upon control rules is also common.

From our views, we want to know the input(s), measure the output and output triggers in order to improve the efficacy of the process through feedback. The basic measurement is: **T(1) – T(0).**

ANS DETECTION & REACTION MATRICES

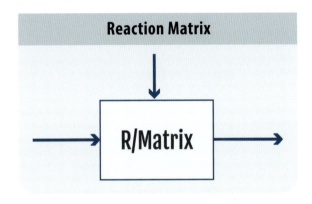

NEURAL DECISION

In conceptual analogue design, consider replacing some fixed elements that require manual tuning, with some to-be-defined neural process. Small weighted networks that use dynamic information updates with variable Trust Factors assist with high speed decision making. Can be especially useful with time-based feedback processes. Adds variables, granularity, and adjustable bias.

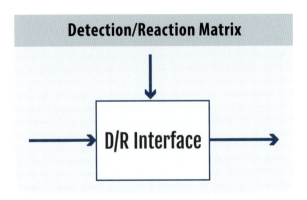

MEMRISTOR

I suggest adding Memristor/Neural to your "Analogue News Feeds." I know this is wishful thinking, and a bit off in the future, but the potential is amazing.

SET KNOB

Continuously variable control to set min-max conditions.

BAYES' THEOREM

$$\text{Min} \leq \text{Set Knob} \leq \text{Max}$$

Bayes is counter-intuitive, but we have to learn to live with that. The basic tenets are:

In Boolean terms, this is an AND Gate, showing the increase in Trust Factor.

$$P(A \mid B) = \frac{P(B \mid A)\, P(A)}{P(A)}$$

where A and B are events and $P(B) \neq 0$.

- ▶ **P(A)** and **P(B)** are the probabilities of observing A and B without regard to each other.
- ▶ **P(A) | P(B)**, a conditional probability, is the probability of observing event A given that B is true.
- ▶ **P(B) | P(A)** is the probability of observing event B given that A is true.

$$P(A \cup B) = P(A) + P(B) - P(A \cap B)$$

$$P(0.9 \text{ and } 0.9) = P(0.9) + P(0.9) - P(0.9 * 0.9)$$
$$= 1.8 - 0.81$$
$$= 0.99$$

In Boolean terms, the OR gate reduces Trust Factor and increases Risk.

Example 1	Alice	Bob	Alice & Bob
TF	0.990	0.990	.9999
Risk	1.0000%	1.0000%	0.0100%
Risk Improvement			99.0000%

In this example with Alice & Bob, the increase in TF = 10^2.

$$P(A \cap B) = P(TF(A) * TF(B))$$
$$= 0.9 * 0.9$$
$$= 0.81$$

$$\text{Risk} = 1 - (P(TF(A) * TF(B))) = 1 - (0.9 * 0.9)$$
$$= 1 - (0.81$$
$$= 0.19 = 1 - P(A \cap B)$$

OODA

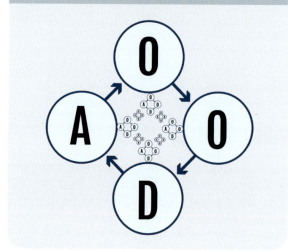

OODA is core to design and operational security.

Analogue Epilogues

Cheat Sheet

An OODA loop can be three, four, five, or more iterative steps, each with it's own defined time and goals. Each step in the loop can and generally should have more granularized sub-loops (sub-processes) that should increase Trust Factor over time. Check out the formulas to the right.

$$L(t) = O1(t) + O2(t) + DE(t) + Act(t) = D(t) + R(t)$$
…where we want
$$L(t) \to 0$$

$$O1(t) = D(t)$$
and
$$O2(t) + DE(t) + Act(t) = R(t)$$

DEFENSE: Go Faster. Measure More.

The following diagrams illustrate the effects of attacking and defending OODA loops in time.

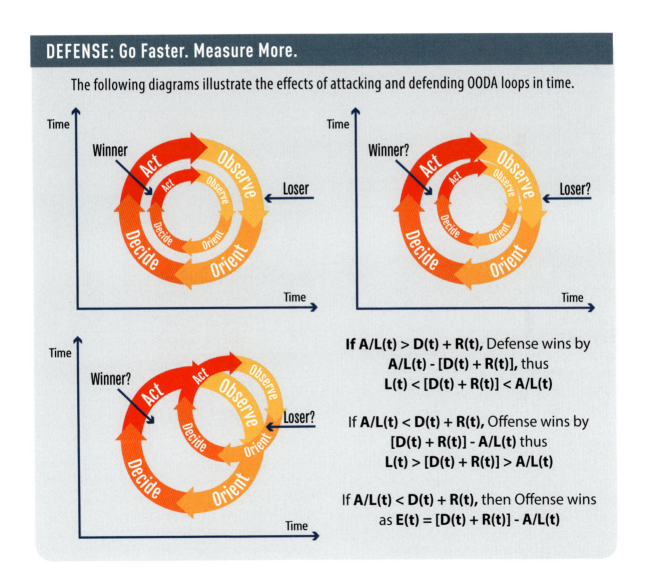

If $A/L(t) > D(t) + R(t)$, Defense wins by $A/L(t) - [D(t) + R(t)]$, thus
$$L(t) < [D(t) + R(t)] < A/L(t)$$

If $A/L(t) < D(t) + R(t)$, Offense wins by $[D(t) + R(t)] - A/L(t)$ thus
$$L(t) > [D(t) + R(t)] > A/L(t)$$

If $A/L(t) < D(t) + R(t)$, then Offense wins as $E(t) = [D(t) + R(t)] - A/L(t)$

Analogue Epilogues

# of Employees	# of Decisions	Per Time Period	Per 200 Work Days/Yr	Delta Six Sigma Trust Factor	Delta Six Sigma Risk
10	10	Day	20,000	99.41%	0.59%
100	10	Day	200,000	94.12%	5.88%
1,000	10	Day	2,000,000	41.18%	58.82%
10,000	10	Day	20,000,000	-488.24%	588.24%
25,000	10	Day	50,000,000	-1370.59%	1470.59%
100,000	10	Day	200,000,000	-5782.35%	5882.35%
1,000	20	Day	4,000,000	-17.65%	177.65%
1,000	50	Day	10,000,000	-194.12%	294.12%
1,000	100	Day	20,000,000	-488.24%	588.24%
10,000	20	Day	40,000,000	-1076.47%	1176.47%
10,000	50	Day	100,000,000	-2841.18%	2941.18%
10,000	100	Day	200,000,000	-5782.35%	5882.35%
Six Sigma = $3.4*10^6$	3,400,000				

Six Sigma vs. Trust Factor and Risk in different sized enterprises.

TRUST FACTOR

Trust is never absolute, so...

0 < Trust Factor (TF) < 1

As we get more granular, Trust Factors with six or more '9s' (0.999999x) will be common.

Trust Factor with feedback will look like a sawtooth wave, bounded on the top with the unachievable "1" and on the bottom with a policy driven limit or a time-based reset/revet trigger.

SCALING

As we learn more about ANS, we will need to look at time-scaling for the future if any of this is going to be of long-term benefit. We will be working with times from 10^{-15} to 10^{18} and beyond. Some of these charts will help you get a handle on the scales of ANS.

As discussed in the Fastest Computer, we will in the exaflop/zettaflop range, sooner or later.

Computer Performance		
Name	Unit	Value
kiloFLOPS	kFLOPS	10^3
megaFLOPS	MFLOPS	10^6
gigaFLOPS	GFLOPS	10^9
teraFLOPS	TFLOPS	10^{12}
petaFLOPS	PFLOPS	10^{15}
exaFLOPS	EFLOPS	10^{18}
zettaFLOPS	ZFLOPS	10^{21}
yottaFLOPS	YFLOPS	10^{24}

The laws of physics won't change, but our "cyber" will get much, much faster. One of the tenets of ANS is to consider min-max at all times, because unbounded conditions yield an indeterminate and or infinity. Don't think slow. Prepare for fast. Faster. Faster than that.

Analogue Epilogues

Time & Clocks

Notation	Seconds	Value	Time	Value	Time	Value	Time	Value	Time
10^0	1	0.02	Minutes						
10^1	10	0.17	Minutes						
10^2	100	1.67	Minutes						
10^3	1,000	16.67	Minutes						
10^4	10,000	2.78	Hours						
10^5	100,000	27.78	Hours	1.16	Days				
10^6	1,000,000	277.78	Hours	11.57	Days	1.65	Weeks	0.03	Years
10^7	10,000,000	2,777.78	Hours	115.74	Days	16.53	Weeks	0.32	Years
10^8	100,000,000	27,777.78	Hours	157.41	Days	165.34	Weeks	3.18	Years
10^9	1,000,000,000	277,777.78	Hours	11,574.07	Days	1,653.44	Weeks	31.80	Years

Seconds

	Decimal	Scientific Notation
Day	86,400	8.64×10^4
Week	604,800	6.05×10^5
Month	2,592,000	2.59×10^6
Year	31,536,000	31.54×10^7

ELECTRICAL BASICS

Formulas You Should Know

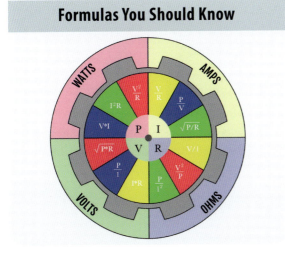

Passive Electrical Component Quadrant

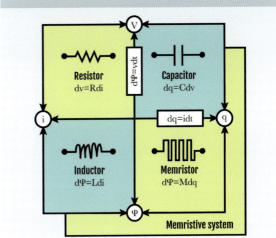

THE MEANS

The standard average we learn at school is the Arithmetic mean as in the left formula below. The right formula finds the geometric mean, which tends to amplify error.

$$\frac{1}{n}\sum_{i=1}^{n} x_i \quad \text{and} \quad \sqrt[n]{\prod_{i=1}^{n} x_i}$$

This is the End!

OK. That's the end of the book. Thanks for reading it.

My wife says this ending sucks, but I am done. I really didn't want to do a long summation of what I wrote… that's for you and we as a community to talk about, and see how much of Analogue Network Security can be effectively used to meet our needs.

Visit *AnalogueNetworkSecurity.com* to join the discussion!

Bibliography

I often get asked what books I read. As it turns out, I don't read much network security stuff. I read lots of other things, -- yes, some weird stuff -- that spurs thinking in non-linear, non-(counter)-intuitive and unpredictable ways. The rationale: I am not interested in "the next generation" of security hardware/software-stuff, which is just New and Improved Detergent. Faster. Smaller. Smarter. I like outlier thinking and seek it out.

You can find a sampling of what I think was well worth the read at WinnSchwartau.com.

A Little About Winn

- Founder of The Security Awareness Company (and Interpact, Inc.) -- TheSecurityAwarenessCompany.com
- Distinguished Fellow: Ponemon Institute 2012+
- Named one of the Top-20 security industry pioneers by SC Magazine.
- Named one of the Top 25 Most Influential People by Security Magazine
- Voted one of the Top 5 Security Thinkers by SC Magazine.
- Honored as a "Power Thinker" and one of the 50 most powerful people by Network World.
- He coined the term "Electronic Pearl Harbor and was the Project Lead of the Manhattan Cyber Project Information Warfare and Electronic Civil Defense Team.
- Founder of InfowarCon

BOOKS
(find downloads on my site)

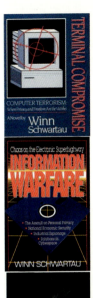

- Terminal Compromise (1991) (Basis for Pearl Harbor Dot Com/Die Hard IV)
- Information Warfare: Chaos on the Electronic Superhighway (1993/4)
- Information Warfare: Revised (1995)
- Information Warfare: 2nd Edition (1997)

- CyberShock (1999/2000)
- Time Based Security (1999, Version 1)

- Time Based Security (2000, Version 2)
- Internet & Computer Ethics for Kids and Families (2001)

- Pearl Harbor Dot Com (Die Hard IV) (2001)

BOOK CONTRIBUTIONS AND SHORT STORIES
(articles and white papers are on my site)

- The Toaster Rebellion of '08
- CyberChrist Meets Lady Luck
- CyberChrist Bites the Big Apple
- Hactivism and CYber-Civil Disobedience
- CyberWar I (AFCEA Press)
- CyberWar II (AFCEA Press)
- CyberWar III (AFCEA Press)
- Introduction to Internet Security (DGI/MecklerMedia, 1994)
- Internet & Internetworking Security Handbook (Auerbach, 1995)
- Ethical Conundra of Information Warfare (AFCEA Press 1997)
- Something Other Than War (AFCEA Press, 1998).
- CyberWars: Espionage on the Internet (Plenum, 1997)
- National Security in the Information Age (Olin Foundation, 1996)

SAMPLING OF MOVIES & VIDEOS OF NOTE

- Hackers Are People, Too! (Exec. Prod. 2008)
- DefCon Documentary (Self 2013)
- The History of the Future of InfoSec (2013)
- Hiring the Unhireable (RSA-TV 2015)
- How to Make Your Security Awareness Program - FAIL! (2016)
- The Analogue Prism (ACOD 2016)
- Applying OODA and Feedback Loops to Security Processes (RSA-TV 2017)

Infinite Thanks & Credits, Sources, Attributions

Giving credit is good for everyone. Karma. Ommmmmm. There are a some more thanks on page 366, too. People I actually know.

90% of ANS – including the ANS Goggles, "Pipe People," "Steampunk Family" characters, flowcharts, schematics, network diagrams, drawings, logos, logotypes – are all original materials and covered by this book's U.S. & international copyright and trademark law. Many of the photos in this book were taken by the author (me) over the years: notably proud of the Japanese toilet and my steampunk tux. Kayley directed the Green Furry Thing photo shoot.

We really think we got this right with copyright respect. I sincerely apologize for any unintentional oops's. Please no major hate mail. Let us know for any errata in the next edition. So many great artists and DIY-ers said, "No credit needed…" or "Just link to me…" and we have done our level best to keep this all straight.

- Some of the incredible steampunk art is licensed courtesy of: giovanimagana.com
- Several images licensed from sources including Shutterstock, Getty Image, and Adobe Stock.
- Steampunker.DE is amazing. Much of their incredible visual masterpiece work is available through Creative Commons.
- Brian Long, University of California, Santa Barbara under Creative Commons Attribution- ShareAlike 3.0 Unported License
- CME/Solar Flares courtesy of The Solar Dynamics Observatory (SDO) NASA, public domain
- The incredible vision of Paul Nylander: bugman123.com
- Steampunk Cat, courtesy of Mark Greenmantle Photography (greenmantle.biz)
- Photographer Alexander Vasilyev asked for no-credit, but here it is, for another great Steampunk Cat
- XZanthia.com and SteamPunkArtEmporium on Etsy were kind enough to offer their images for proper attribution. Hail steampunk!
- Bad-Dog-Designs.co.uk/woodclocks.html - Awesome stuff! THANK YOU!
- Thanks to Pascal Deraed, Environment and texture artist, (user pasder at ArtStation.com), under CC2 Sharealime and permission for the Trust Engine art.
- Francis Archibald Keyes, Esq. Proprietor, F.A.K.E. Security
- CC2/CC3: Attribution-ShareAlike 2.0 Generic (CC BY-SA 2.0)
- Steampunk World: Station 45 by Gleb Alexandrov (Belarus)
- User "steampunktendencies" on VK
- Constantin Senlecq's original design of the Telectroscope in 1881 reproduced in Dionys von on Mihaly's Das elektrische Fernshen und das Telehor, Verlag von M. Krayn, Berlin, 1923.
- Thanks a lot also to Pixabay, PxHere, Good Free Photos, Public Domain Pictures, Wikimedia Commons *(yes, we contribute!)*
- By Terrell Croft (orginal book author) - Croft, Terrell (1917) Electrical Machinery, McGraw-Hill, pp. p161, Public Domain, https://commons.wikimedia.org/w/index.php?curid=3476485
- By Terrell Croft (orginal book author) - Croft, Terrell (1917) Electrical Machinery, McGraw-Hill, pp. p171, Public Domain, https://commons.wikimedia.org/w/index.php?curid=3476718
- Cody Tank: By Fred C. Brannon (director) - Republic Pictures, Public Domain, https://commons.wikimedia.org/w/index.php?curid=2657154
- Other patents under public domain.
- Steampunk Guns: All found at Steampunker.de by Alexander Schlesier, CC BY-SA 3.0, https://commons.wikimedia.org/w/index.php?curid=26240580
- Time Travel Suit, by Alexander Schlesier, Steampunker.de, CC BY-SA 3.0, https://commons.wikimedia.org/w/index.php?curid=26240577
- Steampunk USB, by Alexander Schlesier, Steampunker.de, CC BY-SA 3.0, https://commons.wikimedia.org/w/index.php?curid=26240574
- Steampunk brilliance by CatherinetteRings on deviantART
- Summation Chain and Others by Steven Fine [CC0], from Wikimedia Commons
- Old Cogs by Emmanuel Huybrechts from Laval, Canada (Old Cogs) [CC BY 2.0 (https://creativecommons.org/licenses/by/2.0)], via Wikimedia Commons
- Thanks to Max Pixel for some of their gear and fractal imagery (e.g., maxpixel.net/Equipment-Control-Power-Ham-Gear-Radio-Knob-3059975)
- Steampunk frame by sonarpos on deviantART
- "Do not trust robots" by Jwslubbock, CC BY-SA 4.0 creativecommons.org/licenses/by-sa/4.0, from Wikimedia Commons
- Leonardo da Vinci - Web Gallery of Art: Image Info about artwork, Public Domain, https://commons.wikimedia.org/w/index.php?curid=11229405
- Mechanical Governor: https://commons.wikimedia.org/wiki/File:Old_steam_engine_(governor)_(9886538711).jpg
- Other images provided by various License Free and or Creative Commons, (CreativeCommons.org/use-remix/), and attribution made if available.
- Tacoma Bridge: Public domain under Title 17, Chapter 1, Section 105 of US Code.

Thank you all, Very Much!

I had a local artist convert my vision of Information Warfare way back in 1989.

THANKS!

Thanks to these intrepid souls whom I cajoled into spending their valuable time to "comment with complete honesty." Your different viewpoints were invaluable. I am honored to call you friends and colleagues.

Spencer Wilcox; Dennis Groves, MSc; John Johnson, Ph.D.; Eugene Spafford; Robert Morton, Senior analyst CIA, and PhD student Purdue University; Chris Roberts aka sidragon, Breaker of All Things; Tim McCreight, MSc CISSP CPP CISA Dedicated security professional; Dr. Ph(c) Gregory "Junkbond" Carpenter, ing; Hans Van de Looy/ Storyteller & IT Security Guru at UNICORN Holding B.V.; Edwin van Andel aka yafsec (grumpy old hacker from Holland); Clarence Chio; Joe Klein; and the inimitable Dr. Fred Cohen. And to my wife, Sherra, an incredible editor and partner for forty years. XOXO